DAVID ANSELL

· B.T. BATSFORD LTD LONDON ·

ACKNOWLEDGMENT

© David Ansell 1985
First published 1985

All rights reserved. No part of this publication may be reproduced, in any form or by any means, without permission from the Publisher

ISBN 0 7134 3837 1 (cased)

Typeset by Tek-Art Ltd, Kent
and printed in Great Britain by
R J Acford Ltd
Chichester, Sussex
for the publishers
B. T. Batsford Ltd.
4 Fitzhardinge Street
London W1H 0AH

The author would like to thank the numerous individuals, manufacturers, government agencies, and other organisations that kindly provided the reference material to prepare this book. Particular thanks are given to the following: Major Apajakari, John Bjerkestrand, Graeme Brown, David Bullivant, Frank Dolman, Frank Dougan, John East, Dennis Howard, Douglas Jackson, Barry Jones, David Lewis, Hannu Lindell, Herve Le Manach, Rob van Meel, Marie-Anne Paridaens, Sven-Olof Persson, Phil Saunders, Gunnar Schroder, Miroslav Sochor, Bart Vanderveen, Stig Widerberg, and Finn Yding.

The motorcycle factories which assisted were: Azienda Gilera SpA, Benelli SpA, BMW Motorrad GmbH, BSA Company Ltd, Bultaco SA, Condor SA, Cycles Peugeot, Fabrique Nationale Herstal, Hagglund & Soner, Harley-Davidson International, Hercules-Werke GmbH, Heron Suzuki GB Ltd, Husqvarna Motorcyklarn AB, Jonas Øglaend As, Maico GmbH, SEIMM Moto Guzzi SpA, Oy Polar Metal Plast Ab, Steyr-Daimler-Puch GmbH, and Zundapp-Werke GmbH.

Further information was provided by the following: Australian Army GHQ at Brisbane, Austrian Embassy at London, Belgian Embassy at London, British Embassy at Rome, British Embassy at Stockholm, Canadian Defence GHQ at Ottawa, Danish Embassy at London, Danish Army Material Command at Hjorring, Finnish Army GHQ at Helsinki, French Embassy at London, High Commission of India at London, Italian Embassy at London, Musée Royal d l'Armée et d'Histoire Militaire at Bruxelles, Norwegian Embassy at London, Royal Netherlands Embassy at London, South African Embassy at London, Swedish Embassy at London, Swiss Defence GHQ at Bern, The Center of Military History at Washington, The Royal College of Military Science at Swindon, and the US Army Military History Institute at Pennyslvania.

LIST OF MODELS ILLUSTRATED

1: 1908 FN MODEL 3.5HP	B	
2: 1912 FN MODEL 2.75HP	B	
3: 1912 SCOTT MODEL 3.75HP	GB	
4: 1913 BSA MODEL H	GB	
5: 1914 ARIEL MODEL 3.5HP	GB	
6: 1914 DOUGLAS MODEL V	GB	
7: 1914 NSU MODEL 1.5HP	D	
8: 1914 P & M MODEL 3.5HP	GB	
9: 1914 PUCH TYPE R-I	A	
10: 1914 RUDGE 3.5HP MULTI	GB	
11: 1915 CLYNO MODEL 5-6HP	GB	
12: 1915 MILITAIRE MODEL 1300	USA	
13: 1915 TRIUMPH MODEL H	GB	
14: 1916 HUSQVARNA 145-A	S	
15: 1917 EXCELSIOR 7-10HP	USA	
16: 1917 HARLEY-DAVIDSON 7-9HP	USA	
17: 1923 WALTER MODEL 750	CS	
18: 1924 RENÉ GILLET MODEL G	F	
19: 1926 HUSQVARNA 180A	S	
20: 1926 TRIUMPH MODEL P	GB	
21: 1928 BMW MODEL R-62	D	
22: 1929 DOUGLAS MILITARY 350	GB	
23: 1930 HARLEY-DAVIDSON VL	USA	
24: 1932 MOTO GUZZI GT-17	I	
25: 1933 VICTORIA MODEL KR-6	D	
26: 1934 BMW MODEL R-4	D	
27: 1934 JAWA MODEL 350-SV	CS	
28: 1934 ZÜNDAPP K-500-W	D	
29: 1934 ZÜNDAPP K-800-W	D	
30: 1935 CZ MODEL 175	CS	
31: 1935 MOTO GUZZI GTV	I	
32: 1936 MILITARY MODEL 86	B	
33: 1936 PUCH TYPE 800	A	
34: 1937 FN MILITARY MODEL 12	B	
35: 1937 JAWA MODEL 175	CS	
36: 1937 NIMBUS MODEL 750	DK	
37: 1937 SUECIA MILITARY 500	S	
38: 1938 BMW MODEL R-61	D	
39: 1938 BSA MODEL M20	GB	
40: 1938 NSU MODEL 251-OSL	D	
41: 1938 NSU MODEL 601-OSL	D	
42: 1938 ZÜNDAPP KS-600-W	D	
43: 1939 BENELLI MODEL 500	I	
44: 1939 MOTO GUZZI ALCE	I	
45: 1939 NORTON MODEL 16-H	GB	
46: 1939 SERTUM MODEL 500	I	
47: 1939 TERROT TYPE HDA	F	
48: 1939 TRIUMPH MODEL 3SW	GB	
49: 1939 ZÜNDAPP DB-200-W	D	
50: 1940 ARIEL MODEL W-NG	GB	
51: 1940 VELOCETTE MDD-WD	GB	
52: 1940 ZÜNDAPP KS-750-W	D	
53: 1941 BMW MODEL R-75	D	
54: 1941 GILERA MILITARY MODEL	I	
55: 1941 MATCHLESS MODEL G3L	GB	
56: 1942 HARLEY-DAVIDSON WLA	USA	
57: 1942 HARLEY-DAVIDSON XA	USA	
58: 1942 MONARK MC-42	S	
59: 1942 ROYAL ENFIELD WD-RE	GB	
60: 1944 INDIAN MODEL 148	USA	
61: 1947 JAWA 250 PERAK	CS	
62: 1948 CONDOR MODEL A-580	CH	
63: 1949 TRIUMPH MODEL TRW	GB	
64: 1950 GILERA MILITARY	I	
65: 1950 MOTO GUZZI FALCONE	I	
66: 1950 TERROT TYPE HCT	F	
67: 1950 TERROT TYPE RGST	F	
68: 1951 FN MILITARY MODEL 13	B	
69: 1952 MOTO GUZZI AIRONE	I	
70: 1955 BMW MODEL R-50	D	
71: 1955 DKW RT-175-VS	D	
72: 1955 MONARK MC-252	S	
73: 1956 AJS MODEL 18CS	GB	
74: 1956 GILERA MILITARY G-175	I	
75: 1956 HARLEY-DAVIDSON FL	USA	
76: 1957 JAWA 350 KYVACKA	CS	
77: 1959 PUCH TYPE 175-MCH	A	
78: 1960 BMW MODEL R-27	D	
79: 1960 MOTO GUZZI 125	I	
80: 1965 BSA MODEL B-40	GB	
81: 1965 TEMPO MILITARY 175	N	
82: 1967 HUSQVARNA 256-A	S	
83: 1967 MOTO GUZZI V-7	I	
84: 1968 CONDOR MODEL A-250	CH	
85: 1968 DNIEPER K-650	SU	
86: 1969 BMW MODEL R-60/6	D	
87: 1969 MZ MODEL ES-250-2	DDR	
88: 1969 PUCH TYPE 250-MCH	A	
89: 1970 HERCULES K-125-B	D	
90: 1970 MOTO GUZZI FALCONE	I	
91: 1973 CONDOR MODEL A-350	CH	
92: 1974 HÄGGLUND XM-74	S	
93: 1974 JAWA 350 TYPE 634	CS	
94: 1975 MAICO M250-M	D	
95: 1976 HONDA CB-250	J	
96: 1977 WINHA AUTOMATIC 340	SF	
97: 1978 SUZUKI MILITARY GS400	J	
98: 1979 BOMBARDIER MODEL	CDN	
99: 1979 BULTACO COMMANDER	E	
100: 1979 DNIEPER MT-12	SU	
101: 1980 HUSQVARNA 258-A	S	
102: 1980 YAMAHA MILITARY 250	J	

ABBREVIATIONS

A	:	Austria	**DP**	:	Double-piston	**NSU**	:	Neckarsulmer Radwerke
AKD	:	Abingdon King Dick	**ES**	:	Spain	**NV**	:	Nymans Verkstader
AJS	:	Albert John Stevens	**EMW**	:	Eisenach Moterne Werke	**OHC**	:	Overhead cam
AUS	:	Australia	**F**	:	France	**OHV**	:	Overhead valve
AUTO	:	Automatic	**FN**	:	Fabrique Nationale	**POL**	:	Poland
B	:	Belgium	**GB**	:	Great Britain	**P & M**	:	Phelon & Moore
BD	:	Breitfeld-Danek	**HO**	:	Horizontally-opposed	**R**	:	Reverse
BHP	:	Brake horse power	**HP**	:	Horse-power	**RSA**	:	South Africa
BMW	:	Bayerische Moterne Werke	**Hz**	:	Horizontal	**S**	:	Sweden
BSA	:	Birmingham Small Arms	**I**	:	Italy	**SC**	:	Side-car
CCM	:	Cubic centimeters	**IND**	:	India	**SF**	:	Finland
CDN	:	Canada	**IOE**	:	Inlet-over-exhaust	**SU**	:	Soviet Union
CH	:	Switzerland	**J**	:	Japan	**SV**	:	Side-valve
CS	:	Czechoslovakia	**JAP**	:	John Alfred Prestwich	**TS**	:	Two-stroke
CWS	:	Centraline Warsztaty Samochodowe	**K**	:	Kardan/Shaft	**TWN**	:	Triumph-Werke-Nurnberg
CYL	:	Cylinder	**MAG**	:	Motosacoche	**USA**	:	United States of America
D	:	West Germany	**MV**	:	Meccania Verghera	**V**	:	Vee-twin
DDR	:	East Germany	**MZ**	:	Motorradwerk Zschopau	**Vt**	:	Vertical
DK	:	Denmark	**N**	:	Norway	**W**	:	Wehrmacht
DKW	:	Das Kleine Wunder	**NL**	:	Netherlands	**WD**	:	War Department

FOREWORD

As powered vehicles were developed and became more reliable, so various individuals began to realize the military potential of the motor cycle. These people were in the minority, however, and the early machines were strongly opposed from within the ranks of the professional soldier. The cavalry, in particular, objected, as the motor cycle was considered as a possible replacement for its horses. Even so, the advantages of the motor cycle were clearly demonstrated at military manoeuvres, and had been adopted by armed forces throughout the world by 1910. The use of motor cycles continued to expand during the First World War and, although none of these machines was particularly well-equipped for front-line duties, interest expanded in this form of transport for military service.

During the immediate post-war period a large number of military motor cycles were sold as surplus to requirement, but, although various new designs were introduced during the intermediate years, it was not until the threat of a second war approached that further machines were adopted in any number. While the majority of earlier adopted machines had originally been intended for civilian use, from the mid 1930's a number of manufacturing countries developed motorcycles specially designed for military service. The cross-country type combination was the most common purpose-built military machine of this period. The military combination was largely replaced during the Second World War with the introduction of the four-wheel drive Jeep with its greater carrying ability and personnel protection. It was then decided that the motorcycle was better used as a solo despatch rider machine, or as a collapsible lightweight within a parachute regiment.

A vast number of motorcycles were again sold as war-surplus after 1945, and a number of countries began to disregard the military motorcycles during the following decade. With the return of interest in private motorcycles during the late 1960's, and the further techincal development this brought about a number of the armed forces regained an interest in two-wheeled transport. The new models adopted were mainly for cross-country type use, and, while the majority had originally been designed for riding in civilian trials, a number had also been prepared from military specifications, the major difference in military requirements being long periods between maintenance and an easy-to-use machine. This resulted in a number of automatic models with a shaft final drive, but as a number of these machines developed various difficulties, the converted civilian machine remained the more often adopted.

This book is not a definitive study of the subject; it presents 102 machines to trace the development of motor cycles within military service. The examples have been chosen to give a comparison of the various manufacturing countries, and to keep a balance throughout the past eight decades; a number of similar machines from the same country have not been included in the main text. To complete the presentation further, a specification table of machines from more than 20 countries and 80 factories has also been included. With the difficulty of obtaining information on all things military this cannot be complete, but certainly includes the principal models that have been adopted to date.

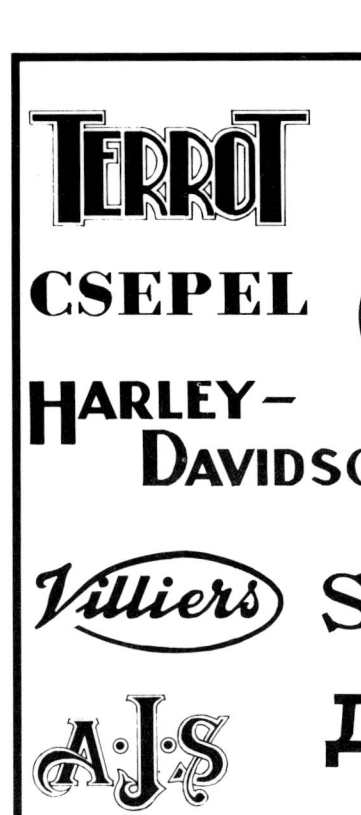

© DAVID ANSELL

· 1908 ·
FN MODEL 3.5HP
(Belgium)

The factory of La Fabrique Nationale d'Armes de Guerre was founded in Herstal, in 1889, for the manufacture of small arms and ammunition. By the turn of the century this factory was producing bicycles, and, in 1902, the first FN motorcycle had been assembled. This machine had a single cylinder 133cc engine mounted within a standard bicycle frame. The FN company continued to develop motor cycles, and after a much publicised tour of Europe, a quite different FN model arrived in Paris in late 1904. This 3hp machine had an in-line four-cylinder engine, employing an enclosed shaft and bevel gear drive to the rear wheel, and remained in production in various stages of development until 1923. It was designed by Paul Kelecom, who had manufactured various proprietory engines under his own name, and had been fitted to the London based Ormonde models, forerunner of the Vellocette.

The engine capacity started at 363cc, but, with the bores increased from 45 to 48mm, it grew to 412cc by 1906. It was further increased to 491cc by 1911, and by 1914 had reached 748cc; the general layout had also changed considerably. While this quite advanced machine was not accepted by everyone immediately, a number were adopted by the Belgian military six years before the First World War. That year the FN four-cylinder model was fitted with a clutch and two-speed gearbox, a cradle frame with hydraulic damped girder-type front fork suspension, and an internal expanding rear wheel brake operated by a back-pedalling mechanism. This was also supplemented by a hand-operated external contracting band upon the same drum.

Brief specification

ENGINE TYPE	: FN – Vertical in-line 4 cylinder
DISPLACEMENT	: 412cc (48×57mm)
VALVE DESIGN	: Automatic inlet valves
COMPRESSION	: –
POWER OUTPUT	: 3.5HP
ELECTRICS	: 6 volt
CARBURETTOR	: One – FN spray type
GEARBOX	: Hand change, 2 speed, unit construction
TRANSMISSION	: Enclosed shaft final drive
FRAME	: Tubular construction
SUSPENSION	: Hydraulic damped parallelogram front forks
	: No rear suspension
TIRE SIZE	: 26×2.5″
BRAKES	: No front-wheel brake
	: Internal expanding/external contracting rear-wheel drum
DRY WEIGHT	: Solo 75kg
DIMENSIONS	: Wheel base 1541mm
MAX SPEED	: Solo 40mph

1908 FN MODEL 3.5HP & BELGIAN SOLDIER

· 1912 ·
FN MODEL 2.75HP
(Belgium)

While the FN factory of Herstal continued to develop its in-line four-cylinder machine, a further single cylinder model was introduced in 1909. This 2.25HP machine adopted the established FN enclosed shaft final drive, with the engine held low within the distinctive cradle-type cycle frame. On one end of the longitudinally mounted crankshaft an external flywheel with a leather-lined cone clutch was connected to a two speed gearbox. The gear and clutch handlebar levers interconnected to control the gear-changing procedure. As on the four-cylinder machine, a suction operated automatic inlet valve design was adopted, and lubrication was by means of a hand pump. Though sometimes discarded, auxiliary cycle pedals were also fitted.

The first shaft drive FN single-cylinder model had an engine capacity of 249cc, but with the stroke increased from 75 to 86mm, this grew to 285cc during 1912. This larger machine was adopted by the Belgian and various allied armed forces during the two years before the First World War, and, while the FN factory returned to armament production, many of these machines were used for solo despatch rider service during the war. There was little military conversion during this period, but the machines were equipped with acetylene lighting, and an overall coat of the appropriate service livery.

Brief specification

ENGINE TYPE	: FN – Vertical single cylinder
DISPLACEMENT	: 285cc (65×86mm)
VALVE DESIGN	: Automatic inlet valve
COMPRESSION	: –
POWER OUTPUT	: 2.75HP
ELECTRICS	: 6 volt
CARBURETTOR	: One – FN spray type
GEARBOX	: Hand change, 2 speed, unit construction
TRANSMISSION	: Enclosed shaft final drive
FRAME	: Tubular construction
SUSPENSION	: Hydraulic damped parallelogram front forks
	: No rear suspension
TIRE SIZE	: 26×2.00″
BRAKES	: No front-wheel brake
	: Internal expanding rear wheel drum
DRY WEIGHT	: Solo 54.5kg
DIMENSIONS	: Wheel base 1321mm
MAX SPEED	: Solo 35mph

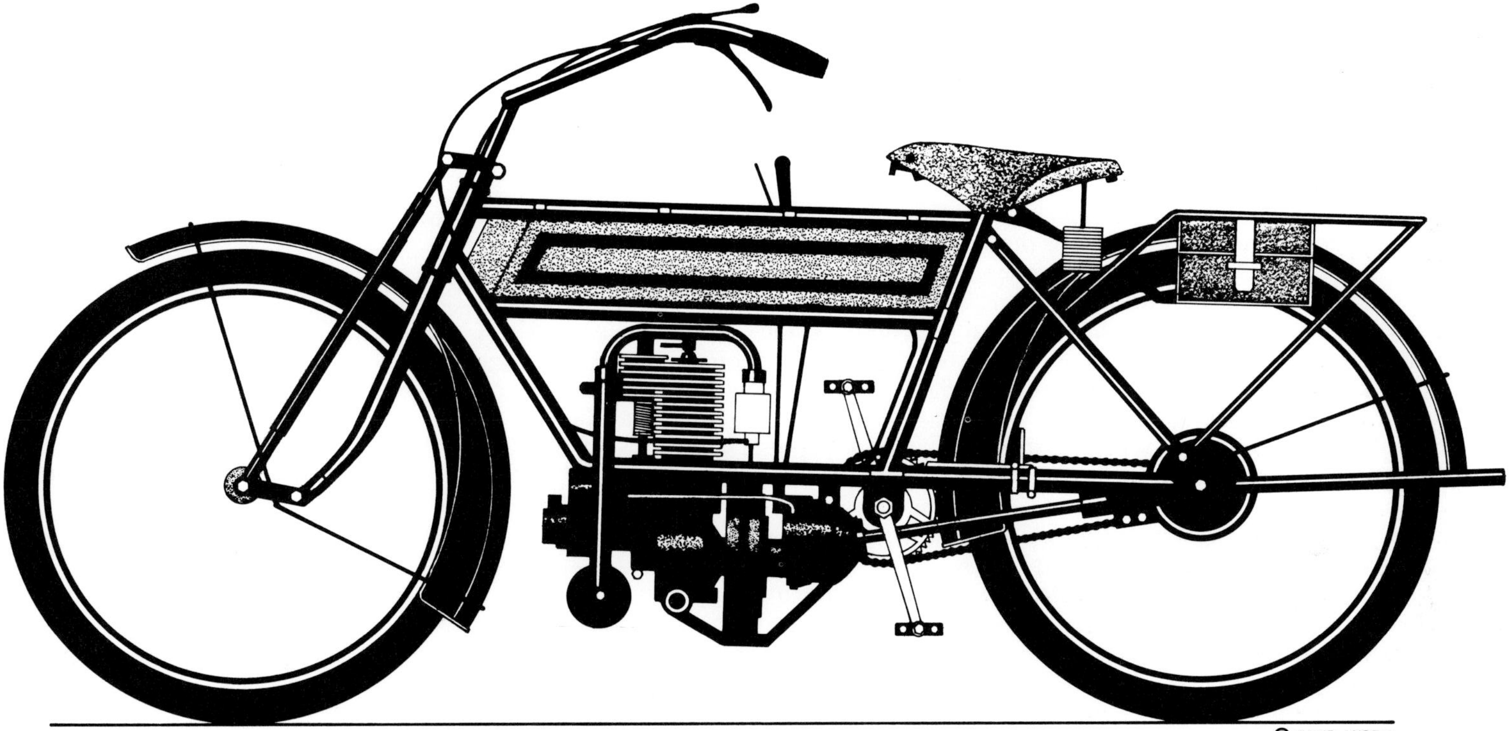

1912 FN MODEL 2.75HP BELGIUM

· 1912 ·
SCOTT MODEL 3.75HP
(Great Britain)

Alfred Scott assembled his first motor cycle in 1897, with a 2HP twin-cylinder two-stroke engine mounted above the front wheel of a Premier bicycle. With this design, Scott is regarded to be the originator of the twin-cylinder two-stroke engine. The first Scott machines produced commercially were assembled by William and Benjamin Jowett in Bradford, then, with the financial help of his brother Charles, the Scott Engineering Company was founded in Bradford in 1909.

By this time Scott had established the open triangular cycle frame design that remained characteristic of Scott machines for many years. The Cammell Laird Ordnance factory selected the Scott 2.75HP model as the most suitable carrier of their Laird-Menteynè machine gun which had a long magazine projecting downward: only a motor cycle with an open frame would permit the full turning movement of the front wheel. After undergoing a series of tests, an example of the machine was exhibited at the Olympia Show of 1912, but, although the British armed forces were interested in the possible use of motorcycles in military service, it was not adopted.

With the declaration of the First World War, the Vickers Ordnance factory approached the Scott Company with the proposal to produce a machine gun carrying sidecar outfit, and within a very short time the Scott 3.75HP model became the basis of such a vehicle. The Scott/Vickers machine was designed for operation in unites of three: one with an armour plated shield and Vickers machine gune, a second with the shield but without the machine gun, and a thired without armour and carrying spare ammunition. At the time of the armistice in 1918, the British armed forces had a total of 411 of these machines in their possesion.

Brief specification

ENGINE TYPE	: Scott – Forward-sloping twin cylinder
DISPLACEMENT	: 486cc (69.8×63.5mm)
VALVE DESIGN	: Two stroke
COMPRESSION	: 5:1
POWER OUTPUT	: 3.75HP
ELECTRICS	: 6 volt
CARBURETTOR	: One – Scott
GEARBOX	: Foot change, 2 speed, separate unit
TRANSMISSION	: Exposed chain primary drive
	: Exposed chain final drive
FRAME	: Tubular construction
SUSPENSION	: Hydraulic damped parallelogram front forks
	: No rear suspension
TIRE SIZE	: 26×2.5″
BRAKES	: Mechanical caliper on front wheel rim
	: Mechanical caliper on rear wheel rim
DRY WEIGHT	: Solo 100kg
DIMENSIONS	: Wheel base 1295mm
MAX SPEED	: Solo 50mph

Scott

1912 SCOTT MODEL 3.75HP
GREAT BRITAIN

· 1913 ·
BSA MODEL H
(Great Britain)

The Birmingham Small Arms Company was founded in 1861, for the manufacture of armaments, at Small Heath in Birmingham. In 1878 production also began on components for the bicycle trade, and in 1880 the piled arms trademark was applied for the first time to a powered vehicle, the Otto Dicycle. After experimenting with engines from various manufactures, the first completely BSA engineered motorcycle was assembled in 1910. This machine had a single cylinder 3.5HP side-valve engine, with a single-speed belt drive and auxiliary cycle pedals. With the success of this machine the BSA factory introduced the model H three years later.

The first BSA model H had a single cylinder 4.25HP engine, with a pedal-operated two-speed rear wheel hub gear. Although the BSA factory returned to arms manufacture during the First World War, a large number of BSA 3.5HP and 4.25HP models were also supplied to the British and Allied armed forces. The majority of these were used for solo despatch rider service, a number also with various sidecars attached. At the time of the armistice in 1918, the British armed forces had a total of 1088 BSA models produced between 1912 and 1917. The military conversion consisted of an overall coat of khaki paint, the fitting of acetylene lighting, a rear carrier and pair of leather tool boxes, and a bulb horn mounted on the handlebars.

Brief specification

ENGINE TYPE	: BSA – Vertical single cylinder
DISPLACEMENT	: 556cc (85×98mm)
VALVE DESIGN	: Side valves
COMPRESSION	: 5:1
POWER OUTPUT	: 4.25HP
ELECTRICS	: 6 volt
CARBURETTOR	: One – BSA
GEARBOX	: Foot change, 2 speed, rear wheel hub
TRANSMISSION	: Enclosed chain primary drive
	: Enclosed chain final drive
FRAME	: Tubular construction
SUSPENSION	: Friction damped parallelogram front forks
	: No rear suspension
TIRE SIZE	: 26×2.5″
BRAKES	: Mechanical caliper on front wheel rim
	: Mechanical caliper on rear wheel rim
DRY WEIGHT	: Solo 118kg
DIMENSIONS	: Wheel base 1397mm
MAX SPEED	: Solo 50mph

BSA 1913 BSA MODEL H
GREAT BRITAIN

· 1914 ·
ARIEL MODEL 3.5HP
(Great Britain)

After successfully manufacturing bicycles for 24 years, the Ariel factory of Coventry introduced its first powered vehicle in 1898. This was a tricycle with a single cylinder 1.75HP De Dion type engine mounted ahead of the rear axle, with an exposed chain final drive and auxilliary cycle pedals. As demand for motorised vehicles increased at the turn of the century, the Ariel company became involved with two-, three-, and four-wheeled machines, with differing degrees of success and failure.

In 1910, all previous Ariel motor cycle designs were replaced by a 3.5HP model that was to remain in almost unchanged production for the following 15 years. This machine had a single-cylinder 500cc engine with its side valves set 4.5 inches apart, and as a result became known as the 'Ariel with valves a mile apart.'

Although the factory produced a variety of armaments thoughout the First World War, a large number of these Ariel 3.5HP models were also supplied to the British and Allied armed forces. While the majority were used for solo despatch rider service within units operating in Russia and Mesopotamia (Iraq), at the time of the armistice in 1918, the British armed forces had a total of 52 of these machines in their possession. The military conversion mainly consisted of an overall coat of khaki paint.

Brief specification

ENGINE TYPE	: Ariel – Vertical single cylinder
DISPLACEMENT	: 490cc (85×86.4mm)
VALVE DESIGN	: Side valves
COMPRESSION	: 5:1
POWER OUTPUT	: 3.5HP
ELECTRICS	: 6 volt
CARBURETTOR	: One – Brown & Barlow
GEARBOX	: Hand change, 3 speed, separate unit
TRANSMISSION	: Enclosed chain primary drive
	: Enclosed belt final drive
FRAME	: Tubular construction
SUSPENSION	: Friction damped parallelogram front forks
	: No rear suspension
TIRE SIZE	: 26×2.5"
BRAKES	: Mechanical caliper on front wheel rim
	: Block brake on belt wheel rim
DRY WEIGHT	: Solo 106.6kg
DIMENSIONS	: Wheel base 1422mm
MAX SPEED	: Solo 45mph

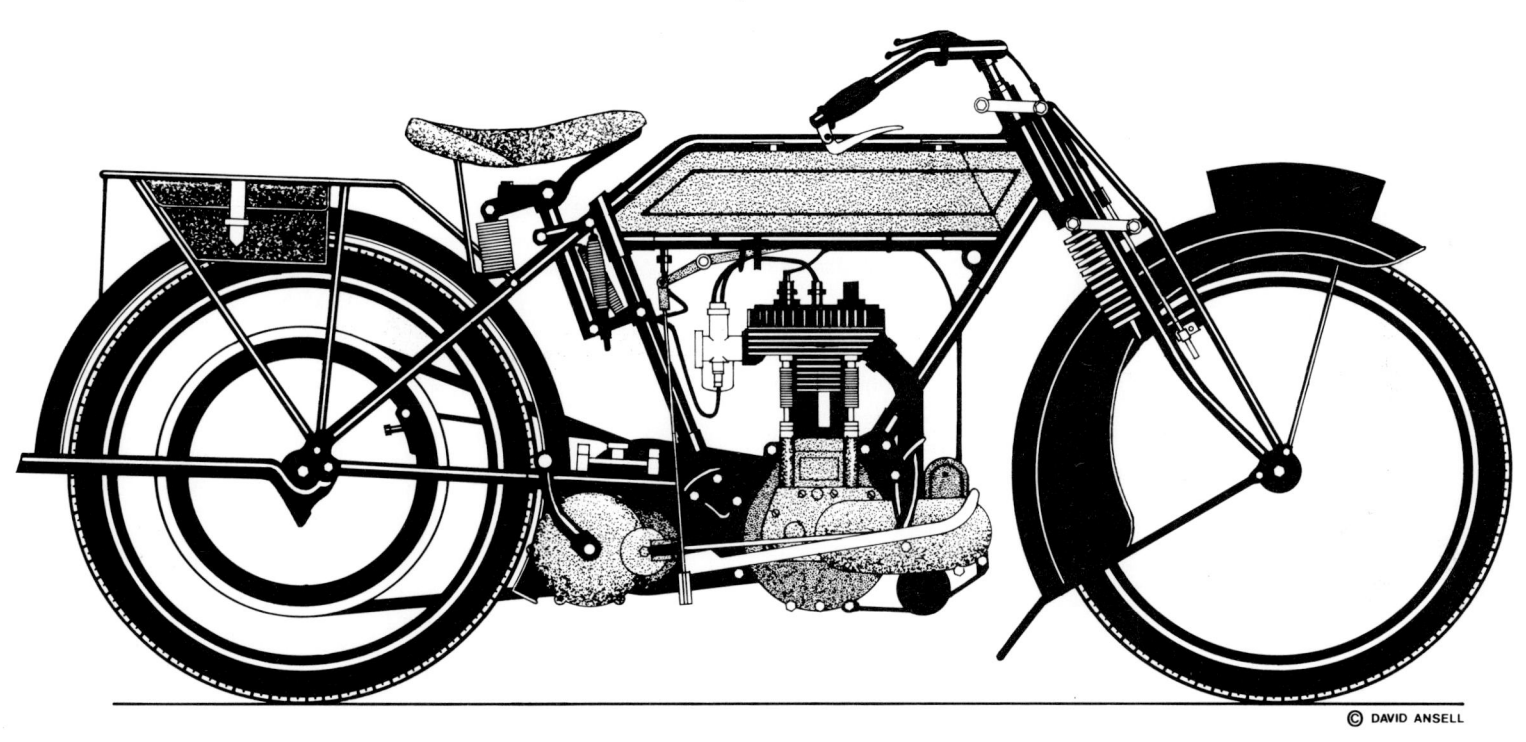

ARIEL

**1914 ARIEL MODEL 3.5HP
GREAT BRITAIN**

· 1914 ·
DOUGLAS MODEL V
(Great Britain)

At the turn of the century the brothers William and Edward Douglas supplied pistons and cylinders to the motorcycle designer Joseph Barter. These machines had a single-cylinder engine at first, but were replaced by an opposed twin design mounted in line with the frame. The Barter machines were produced under the name of Fairy until 1906, when William Douglas obtained the manufacturing rights. The flat twin-engine design was continually improved and the new Douglas motor cycle company soon became interested in competitive riding. In 1912, Douglas machines finished first and second in the Junior TT and first in the 350cc Spanish Grand Prix. With such success and the general ease of handling, the Douglas factory gained the contract to supply their model V to the British armed forces for solo despatch rider service.

The Ministry of Munitions banned the manufacture of civilian motor cycles in November 1916, and the Douglas factory began total military production until the end of the war. From 1916, the larger capacity Douglas model B was also adopted by the armed forces to be used with a sidecar. Although not the most technically advanced models of the period, the Douglas factory supplied approximately 25,000 machines to the British and Allied armed forces, and they became some of the widest and most popular used during the First World War. At the time of armistice in 1918, the British miliary had 13,477 of the model V and 4,816 of the model B in their possession.

Brief specification

ENGINE TYPE	: Douglas – Longitudinal opposed twin cylinder
DISPLACEMENT	: 348cc (60.8×60mm)
VALVE DESIGN	: Side valves
COMPRESSION	: 5:1
POWER OUTPUT	: 2.75HP
ELECTRICS	: 6 volt
CARBURETTOR	: One – Amac
GEARBOX	: Hand change, 2 speed, separate unit
TRANSMISSION	: Exposed chain primary drive
	: Exposed belt final drive
FRAME	: Tubular construction
SUSPENSION	: Friction damped parallelogram front forks
	: No rear suspension
TIRE SIZE	: 26×2.25"
BRAKES	: Mechanical caliper on front wheel rim
	: Block brake on belt wheel rim
DRY WEIGHT	: Solo 90.7kg
DIMENSIONS	: Wheel base 1346mm
MAX SPEED	: Solo 35mph

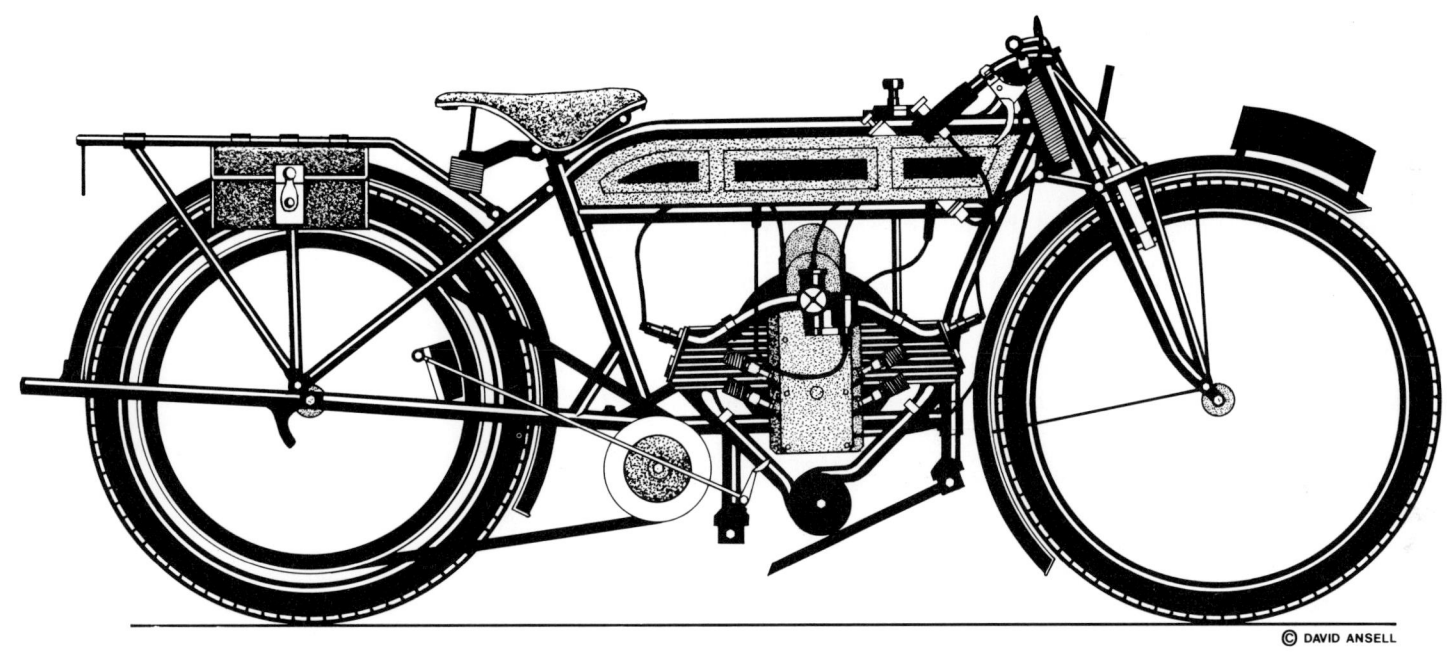

Douglas   1914 DOUGLAS MODEL V
GREAT BRITAIN

· 1914 ·
NSU MODEL 1.5HP
(Germany)

After 14 years of successfully manufacturing bicycles, the Neckarsulmer Radwerke factory assembled its first motor cycle in 1900. While this machine was little more than a powered bicycle, it was sufficiently developed for a 4HP version to be tested by the German armed forces withing the following 4 years. During this period the business also began to use the initials NSU as a trade name.

In the following 10 years the Neckarsulmer factory developed and introduced various NSU models with single and V-twin cylinder engines. These machines had such advance specifications as girder front fork, and sprung rear sub-frame suspension, two-speed final drive, and an internal expanding rear hub brake. A number of NSU models were adopted by the German military during this period, and, by 1918 the majority of German military motor cycles were NSU machines.

Although the Neckarsulmer factory was converted to manufacture munitions during the First World War, the business also produced a 1.5HP model with a single-cylinder engine, a 3.5HP model with V-twin-cylinder engine for solo military service, and a 7–9Hp model with a V-twin cyclinder engine and sidecar for military service. This larger machine was used with a removable mounted machine gun on a platform-type sidecar. When solo, this machine weighed 136kg and could maintain 60mph.

Brief specification

ENGINE TYPE	: NSU – Vertical single cylinder
DISPLACEMENT	: 190cc (58×72mm)
VALVE DESIGN	: Inlet over exhaust
COMPRESSION	: 5:1
POWER OUTPUT	: 1.5HP
ELECTRICS	: 6 volt
CARBURETTOR	: One – NSU
GEARBOX	: Hand change, 2 speed, separate unit
TRANSMISSION	: Exposed chain primary drive
FRAME	: Tubular construction
SUSPENSION	: Friction damped parallelogram front forks
	: No rear suspension
TIRE SIZE	: 26×1.25″
BRAKES	: No front brake
	: Block brake on belt wheel rim
DRY WEIGHT	: Solo 48kg
DIMENSIONS	: Wheel base 1321mm
MAX SPEED	: Solo 37mph

1914 NSU MODEL 1.5HP GERMANY

· 1914 ·

P & M MILITARY MODEL 3.5HP
(Great Britain)

Joah Phelon assembled his first motor cycle in 1900, with a single cylinder De Dion type engine mounted as the front downtube of the cycle frame. With this design began the recognisable trademark that was to remain characteristic of the later P & M models. The first commercially produced Phelon machines were assembled at the Humber-Beeston factory of Coventry, but after the death of his partner Harry Rayner in 1903, Phelon went into partnership with Richard Moore the following year and these machines were produced under the P & M name as Cleckheaton.

The first Phelon machine had a chain-drive transmission, and one of the first developments of the P & M partnership included the introduction of a two-speed gear system, involving two primary chains and a selective clutch. Within a few years the auxiliary cycle pedals were discarded and the transmission was fully enclosed. Further early developments included a leading link front fork suspension, a contracting band rear brake, and magneto ignition. By the early 1910's, the P & M factory was manufacturing one of the most advanced motor cycles available.

As a result of the British War Office manoeuvres of 1913, the P & M factory received a contract to supply the Royal Flying Corps during the First World War with their 3.5HP model for solo and sidecar service. The military conversion included the use of redesigned front forks, the fitting of acetylene lighting, and an overall coat of khaki paint. The factory became entirely devoted to the production of these machines for the British and Allied armed forces during the war, and by the armistice the British military had a total of 3,383 in their possession.

Brief specification

ENGINE TYPE	: P & M – Forward-sloping single cylinder
DISPLACEMENT	: 475cc (82.55×88.9mm)
VALVE DESIGN	: Side valves
COMPRESSION	: 5:1
POWER OUTPUT	: 3.5HP
ELECTRICS	: 6 volt
CARBURETTOR	: One – Brown & Barlow
GEARBOX	: Hand change, 2 speed, separate unit
TRANSMISSION	: Enclosed chain primary drive
	: Enclosed chain final drive
FRAME	: Tubular construction
SUSPENSION	: Friction damped leading link front forks
	: No rear suspension
TIRE SIZE	: 26×2.25″
BRAKES	: Mechanical caliper on front wheel rim
	: External contracting rear wheel drum
DRY WEIGHT	: Solo 86kg
DIMENSIONS	: Wheel base 1372mm, Ground clearance 140mm
MAX SPEED	: Solo 50mph

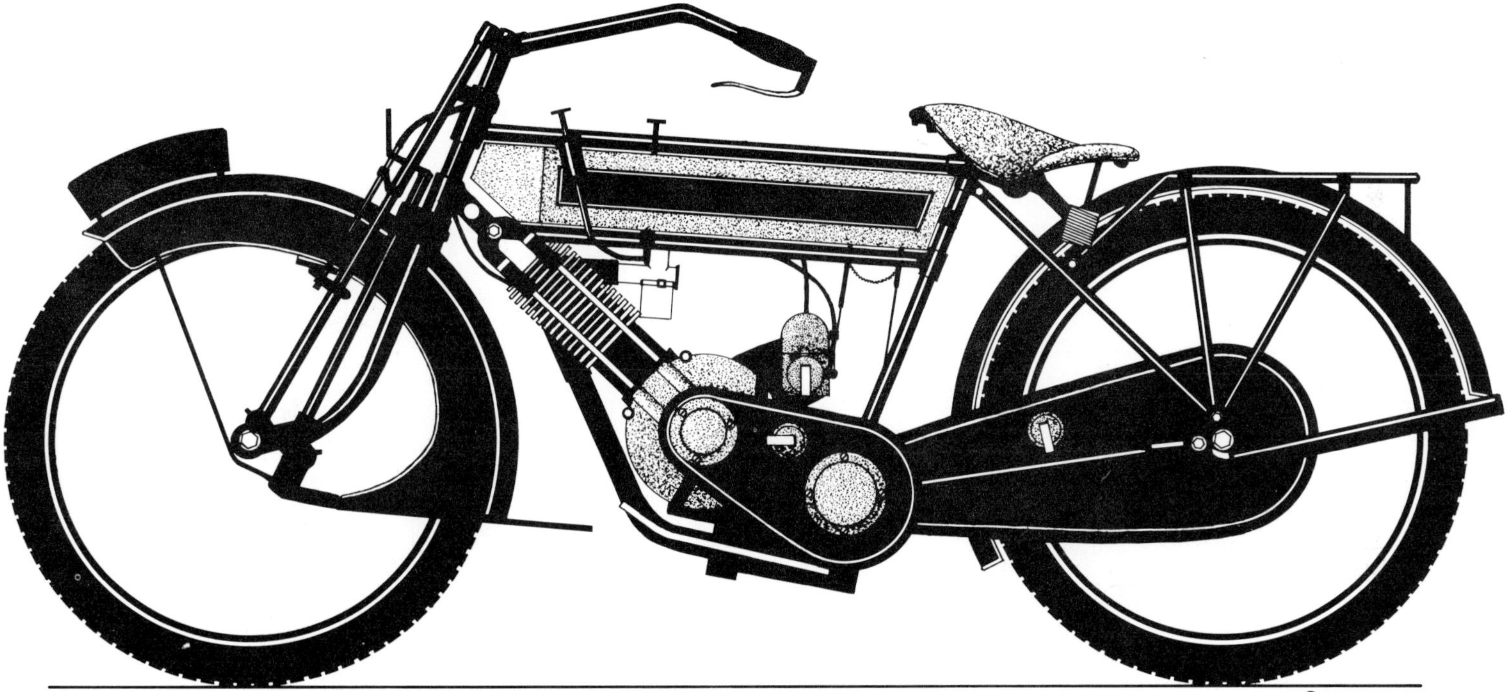

 1914 P & M MODEL 3.5HP
GREAT BRITAIN

· 1914 ·
PUCH TYPE R–1
(Austria)

Johann Puch was sent to Graz for his compulsory national service in the Austro-Hungarian armed forces. During this time he completed an apprenticeship as a bicycle mechanic, and, in 1889, set up his own repair business. After some success, he founded the Johann Puch & Comp- Fabriksmassige Erzeugung von Fahrradern in 1891, and began to manufacture his own bicycles. This company was bought out in 1897 by the forerunner of the German Durkopp business.

Two years later, Puch founded the Johann Puch – Erste Steirmarkische Fahrrad Fabriks AG, and began experimenting with motorised transport. A prototype car was built in 1901, soon followed by a number of three-wheeled cycles. The first Puch motor cycle was assembled in 1903, with a single-cylinder 2.75HP inlet over exhaust valve engine mounted centrally in a cycle type frame. After further developments, larger 3.25HP and 3.5HP Puch engines were also available.

But Puch had driven himself too hard and died in July 1914. The business had been renamed Johann Puch AG in May 1914, and with a reliable team of engineers and workforce of 1,200 the new company remained in production. When the First World War was declared the Puch factory began to supply the 2HP type R–1 and 2.5HP type R–2 models to the Austro-Hungarian military. These machines were very similar, but the R–2 was used for various experiments with gear change designs and front fork suspension.

Brief specification

ENGINE TYPE	: Puch – Vertical single cylinder
DISPLACEMENT	: 254cc (68×70mm)
VALVE DESIGN	: Side valves
COMPRESSION	: 5:1
POWER OUTPUT	: 2HP
ELECTRICS	: 6 volt
CARBURETTOR	: One – Spritvergaser
GEARBOX	: Single speed, no gearbox
TRANSMISSION	: Exposed belt final drive
FRAME	: Tubular construction
SUSPENSION	: No front suspension
	: No rear suspension
TIRE SIZE	: 26×1.75″
BRAKES	: No front wheel brake
	: External contracting rear wheel drum
DRY WEIGHT	: Solo 52kg
DIMENSIONS	: Wheel base 1300mm
MAX SPEED	: Solo 30mph

**1914 PUCH TYPE R-1
AUSTRIA**

· 1914 ·
RUDGE 3.5HP MULTI
(Great Britain)

By 1914, the Rudge-Whitworth factory of Coventry exported at least half of its production, and, although some of these sales were lost with the declaration of the First World War, the good name of the company also gained it a number of military contracts. A Russian order for 400 of the civilian 3.5HP model was completed in late 1914, and a Belgian order for the same by early the following year. Any possible contract for replacement machines was lost with the revolution in Russia and the fall of Belgium to the German army.

Although no order was received from the British army, the company was able to publish photographs of their models in British military service, as despatch riders recruited in 1914 were able to use their own machines and, also, the Admiralty had placed a small contract. At the time of the armistice, the British armed forces had a total of 395 Rudge-Whitworth machines in their possession.

During the early years of the war the British War Office had considered the possibility of producing a standard military motor cycle from the best British parts, and in 1916 Rudge-Whitworth contributed a number of wheels and frames for experimental use. This idea was not undertaken and when the Ministry of Supply banned the production of civilian machines in November 1916, the Rudge-Whitworth factory had virtually ceased to manufacture motor cycles. Although the factory continued to assemble wheels for Crossley ambulances and various aircraft, it mainly produced ammunition.

Brief specification

ENGINE TYPE	: Rudge-Whitworth – Vertical single cylinder
DISPLACEMENT	: 499cc (85×88mm)
VALVE DESIGN	: Inlet over exhaust
COMPRESSION	: 4:1
POWER OUTPUT	: 3.5HP
ELECTRICS	: 6 volt
CARBURETTOR	: One – Senspray
GEARBOX	: Hand change, multi ratio, separate unit
TRANSMISSION	: Exposed belt final drive
FRAME	: Tubular construction
SUSPENSION	: Friction damped parallelogram front forks
	: No rear suspension
TIRE SIZE	: 26×2.25″
BRAKES	: Mechanical caliper on front wheel rim
	: Block brake on belt wheel rim
DRY WEIGHT	: Solo 97kg
DIMENSIONS	: Wheel base 1397mm
MAX SPEED	: Solo 55mph

Rudge

**1914 RUDGE 3.5HP MULTI
GREAT BRITAIN**

· 1915 ·
CLYNO MODEL 5–6HP
(Great Britain)

The Clyno Engineering Company of Wolverhampton first displayed its model 5–6HP at the Stanley Show of Islington in 1909. This belt-driven machine had a proprietory V-twin engine built by the Stevens brothers of the later A.J.S. motor cycle factory. While the Stevens brothers were proprietory manufacturers, the Clyno company also acted as their agents, but by 1911 Clyno had obtained the manufacturing rights of this engine and displayed a further six machines at the Olympia Show that year. The model 5–6HP now had enclosed engine valves, a fully enclosed chain transmission, and the option of two or four speeds.

The Motor Machine Gun Corps was formed with the outbreak of the First World War and by 1915 the Clyno sidecar outfit had been converted for this service. These machines were designed for operation in units of three: one with an armour plated sidecar and a Vickers machine gun mounted on a detachable tripod, a second with armour plate but without the machine gun, and a third without armour and carrying spare ammunition. At the time of the armistice the British armed forces had a total of 1,792 of these machines in their possession. A number of Clyno 5–6Hp machines were also supplied to the Russian armed forces, and in 1917 a further 1,500 Clyno machines with a larger 8HP J.A.P. engine assembled for the Russian military.

Brief specification

ENGINE TYPE	: Clyno – V-twin cylinder
DISPLACEMENT	: 744cc (76×82mm)
VALVE DESIGN	: Side valves
COMPRESSION	: 5:1
POWER OUTPUT	: 5–6HP
ELECTRICS	: 6 volt
CARBURETTOR	: One
GEARBOX	: Hand change, 3 speed, separate unit
TRANSMISSION	: Enclosed chain primary drive
	: Enclosed chain final drive
FRAME	: Tubular construction
SUSPENSION	: Friction damped horizontally sprung front forks
	: No rear suspension
TIRE SIZE	: 26×3.5″
BRAKES	: Mechanical caliper on front wheel rim
	: Internal expanding rear wheel drum
DRY WEIGHT	: Solo 136kg
DIMENSIONS	: Wheel base 1499mm
MAX SPEED	: W/SC 50mph

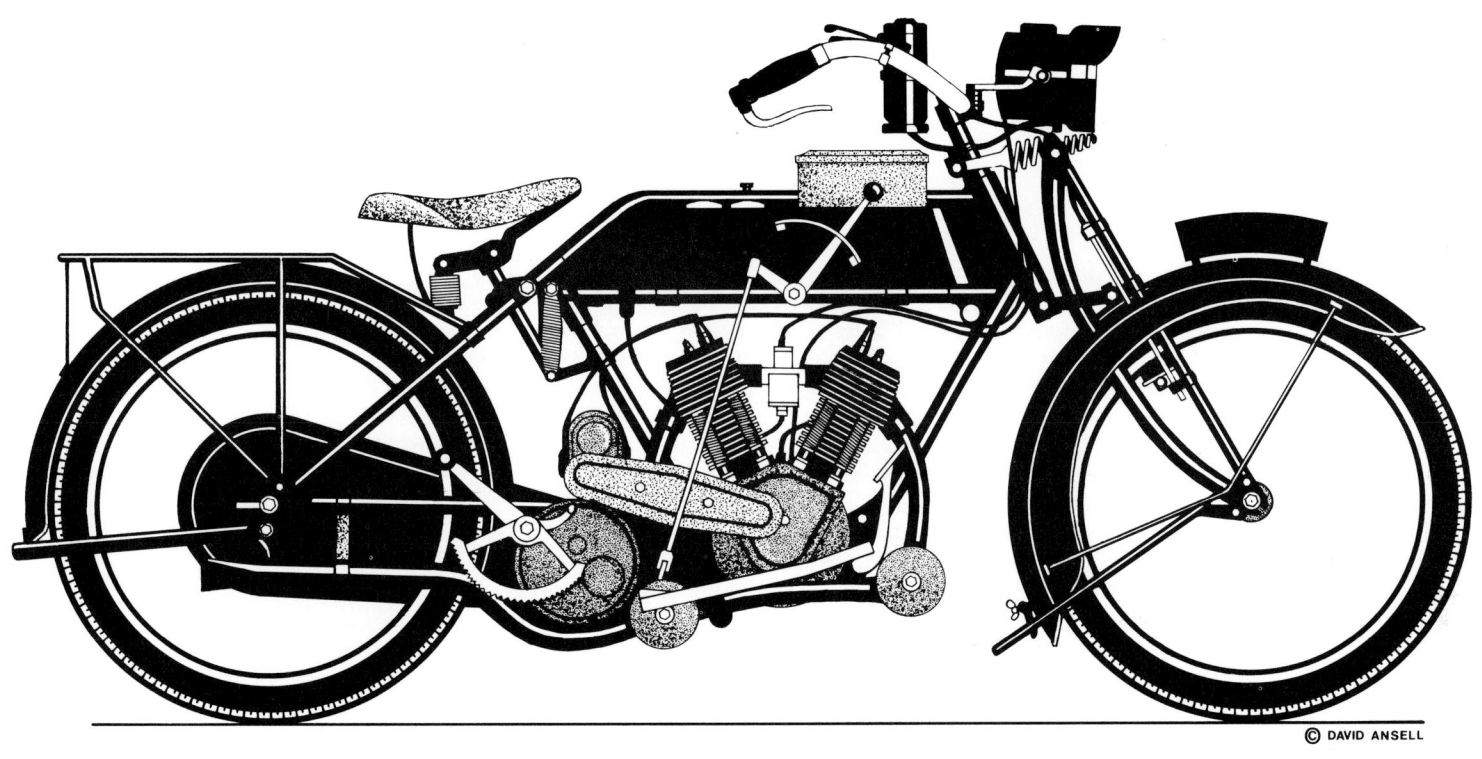

ⒸLYNO

1915 CLYNO MODEL 5-6HP
GREAT BRITAIN

· 1915 ·

MILITAIRE MODEL 1300
(America)

The Militaire Auto Company of Cleveland introduced its first motor cycle designed for military service in 1912. This machine had a vertical single-cylinder 480cc engine mounted on a pressed steel car-type chassis with wooden artillery-type wheels. This construction was supported at slow speeds with small outrigger wheels which also enabled the use of a reverse gear while solo. The steering was controlled with a car-type wheel and a bucket seat was held vertical on a sprung pillar. Very few of these machines were produced and the following year a further design was introduced.

The single-cylinder engine of the first model was replaced by an in-line four-cylinder design with a shaft final drive. While the engine was more car-like, the steering wheel was replaced by more conventional handlebars; there were few other changes. After a number of mechanical and financial problems, the business became Militor of Jersey City in 1917, before eventually gaining its first order from the American armed forces. A small number of these machines were taken to France in 1918, but, with a weight of over 363kg with a sidecar, they sank badly into the battlefield mud and were totally disliked by their riders. The Company was reorganised again after the First World War and became the Sinclair Militor Corporation, but with continued mechanical difficulties the factory finally closed in 1922.

Brief specification

ENGINE TYPE	: Militaire – Vertical in line four cylinders
DISPLACEMENT	: 1306cc
VALVE DESIGN	: Inlet over exhaust valves
COMPRESSION	: 5:1
POWER OUTPUT	: 11HP
ELECTRICS	: 6 volt
CARBURETTOR	: One
GEARBOX	: Hand change, 3/R speed, unit construction
TRANSMISSION	: Exposed shaft final drive
FRAME	: Pressed steel construction
SUSPENSION	: No front wheel suspension
	: No rear wheel suspension
TIRE SIZE	: 28×2.75″
BRAKES	: No front wheel brake
	: Internal expanding/External contracting rear wheel drum
DRY WEIGHT	: W/SC 363kg
DIMENSIONS	: Wheel base 1651mm
MAX SPEED	: W/SC 35mph

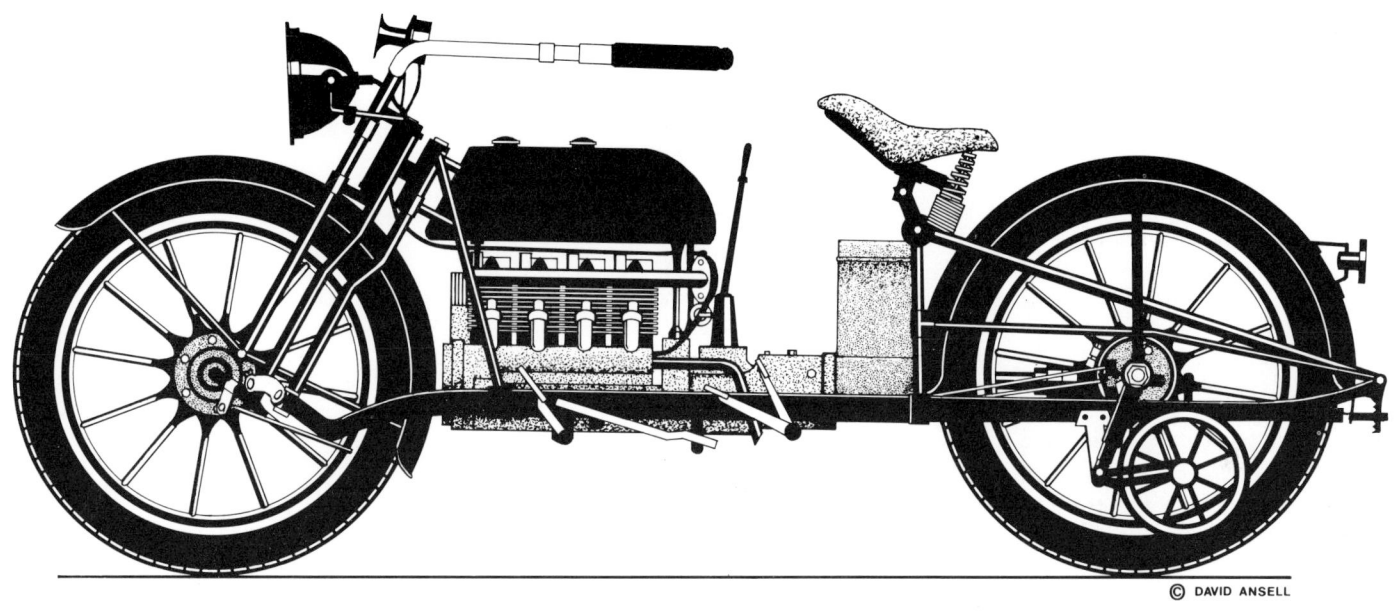

MILITAIRE

1915 MILITAIRE MODEL 1300 AMERICA

· 1915 ·
TRIUMPH MODEL H
(Great Britain)

The Triumph factory was founded in London by Siegfried Bettmann, to manufacture bicycles. Two years later, in 1887, a fellow German named Mauritz Schulte joined the company and began to experiment with the use of engines. The first Triumph motor cycle was introduced from a new factory in Coventry in 1902, with a Belgian 1.75HP Minerva engine mounted in a standard Triumph bicycle frame. The first all-British engineered motor cycle to be assembled at the Triumph factory was in 1904 with a 2.5HP J.A. Prestwich engine.

The factory introduced the first completely Triumph engineered motor cycle in 1905 with a 3HP engine. The following year this machine was introduced with a new cycle frame and horizontally sprung front forks and in 1908 the engine was increased to give 3.5HP. By 1913, a three-speed Sturmey-Archer rear wheel hub gear was available, and in 1915 the auxiliary cycle pedals were discarded and the hub gear replaced by a three-speed countershaft gearbox. The Triumph model H was introduced during 1914 with a larger capacity engine and redesigned timing gear and larger diameter valves.

With the declaration of the First World War, various armed forces adopted the smaller Triumph models, but between 1915 and 1918, the Triumph factory concentrated production on the model H and supplied approximately 20,000 to the British military and a further 10,000 to the Allies. The Triumph model H was mainly used for solo despatch rider service, but was also used with various sidecars attached. The illustration features the transportation of pigeons, which were extensively used to maintain front-line communication.

Brief specification

ENGINE TYPE	: Triumph – Vertical single cylinder
DISPLACEMENT	: 550cc (85×97mm)
VALVE DESIGN	: Side valves
COMPRESSION	: 5:1
POWER OUTPUT	: 4HP
ELECTRICS	: 6 volt
CARBURETTOR	: One – Triumph
GEARBOX	: Hand change, 3 speed, separate unit
TRANSMISSION	: Enclosed chain primary drive
	: Exposed belt final drive
FRAME	: Tubular steel construction
SUSPENSION	: Friction damped horizontally sprung front forks
	: No rear suspension
TIRE SIZE	: 26×2.5"
BRAKES	: Mechanical caliper on front wheel rim
	: Block brake on belt wheel rim
DRY WEIGHT	: Solo 91kg
DIMENSIONS	: Wheel base 1321mm
MAX SPEED	: Solo 45mph

1915 TRIUMPH MODEL H & AUSTRALIAN SOLDIER

© DAVID ANSELL

· 1916 ·
HUSQVARNA 145–A
(Sweden)

As with a number of motor cycle factories, the Husqvarna company has a history of armament production and was originally founded as the Royal Arms Company in 1689. After some years of financial difficulty the armaments was reorganised under the name of Husqvarna Vapenfabriks AB in 1876. This company experimented with various proprietory engines at the turn of the century and introduced the first Husqvarna motor cycle in 1903, with a single-cylinder Belgian 1.25HP FN engine mounted vertically in a basic bicycle type frame.

After further tests however, the Husqvarna factory eventually adopted the more powerful V-twin cylinder Swiss 2.5HP and 4HP Moto-Reve engines. At first these machines also had a belt drive and single speed with auxiliary cycle pedals, but between 1909 and 1919 the factory manufactured ten different models with Moto-Reve engines. IN 1916 the Husqvarna 145–A was adopted by the Swedish armed forces, which date the auxiliary cycle pedal and belt drive had been replaced by a three-speed gearbox and chain final drive. These machines were used for solo despatch type service and a total of 486 were supplied during the remaining years of the First World War.

Brief specification

ENGINE TYPE	: Moto-Reve – V-twin cylinder
DISPLACEMENT	: 550cc (65×83mm)
VALVE DESIGN	: Side valves
COMPRESSION	: 5:1
POWER OUTPUT	: 4.25HP
ELECTRICS	: 6 volt
CARBURETTOR	: One – Schebler
GEARBOX	: Hand change, 3 speed, separate unit
TRANSMISSION	: Enclosed chain primary drive
	: Exposed chain final drive
FRAME	: Tubular steel construction
SUSPENSION	: Friction damped parallelogram front forks
	: No rear suspension
TIRE SIZE	: 26×2.25″
BRAKES	: No front wheel brake
	: Block brake on rear wheel dummy rim
DRY WEIGHT	: Solo 150kg
DIMENSIONS	: Wheel base 1397mm
MAX SPEED	: Solo 55mph

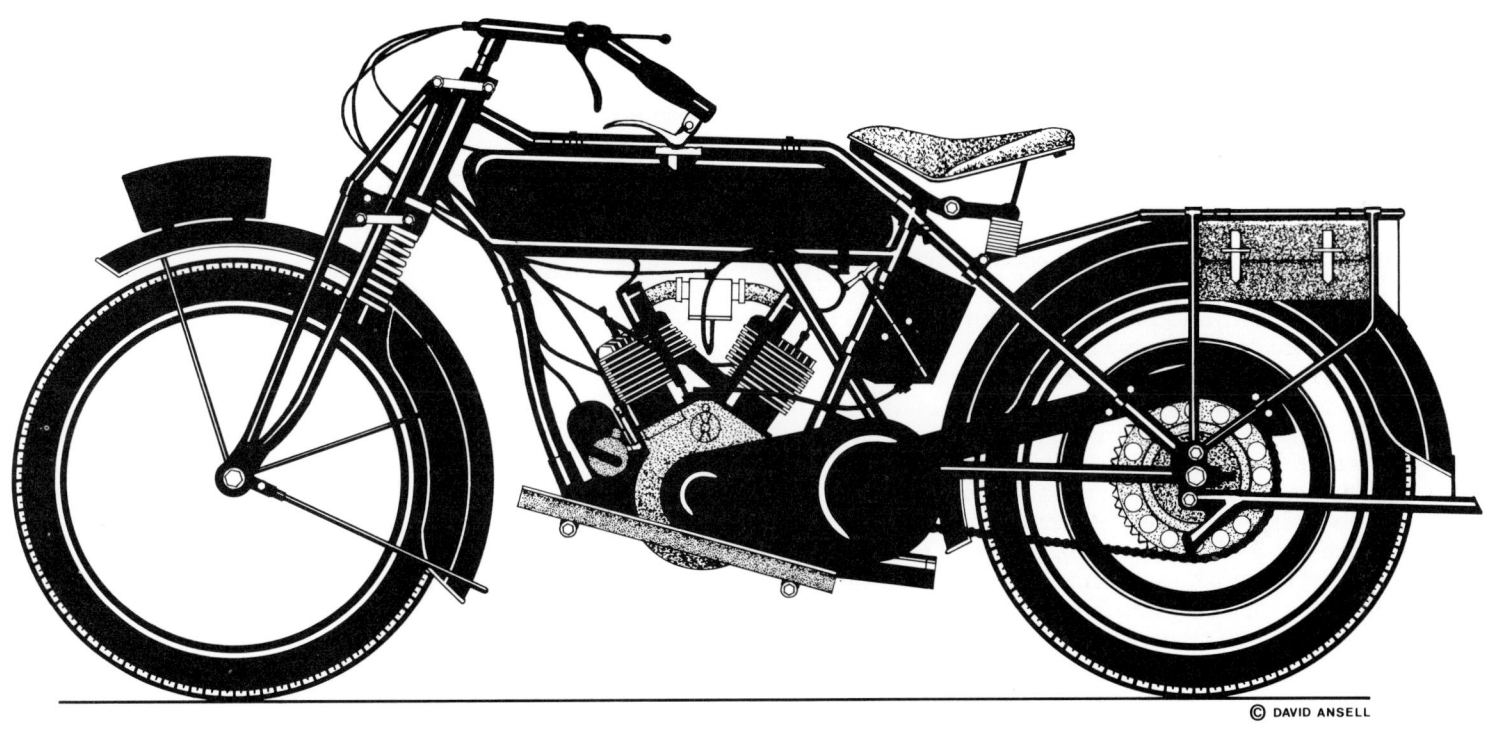

Husqvarna

**1916 HUSQVARNA 145-A
SWEDEN**

· 1917 ·
EXCELSIOR 7–10HP
(America)

From the turn of the century, the American armed forces began to adopt various motor cycles for solo and with sidecar service. The majority of these machines had a single-cylinder engine, but the country's vast expanse quickly resulted in the development of the larger capacity V-twin engine with a gear change and chain drive. The Harley-Davidson and Hendee-Indian factories were the largest producers and set the format for the 45 degree V-twin engines of 750cc and 1000cc displacement.

The Excelsior Supply and Manufacture Company of Chicago, part of the Schwinn bicycle empire, assembled its first motor cycle in 1908. After 5 years of building various models with single-cylinder engines, including the Triumph Junior under license, the first Excelsior 1000cc model was introduced. This machine had an inlet over exhaust valve engine mounted in a tubular frame with leaf sprung trailing link front fork suspension. This model was exported to England as the American X with only minor changes until 1931 when Ignaz Schwinn decided to stop motor cycle production.

Although the majority of motor cycles adopted by the American military during the First World War were supplied by the Harley-Davidson and Hendee-Indian factories, approximately 2,600 Excelsior 1000cc models were also used. The military conversion of these included a reinforced frame, deeper valanced mudguards, and an overall coat of khaki paint.

Brief specification

ENGINE TYPE	: Excelsior – V-twin cylinder
DISPLACEMENT	: 997cc (84.53×88.9mm)
VALVE DESIGN	: Inlet over exhaust valve
COMPRESSION	: 5:1
POWER OUTPUT	: 7–10HP
ELECTRICS	: 6 volt
CARBURETTOR	: One – Schebler model H
GEARBOX	: Hand change, 3 speed, separate unit
TRANSMISSION	: Enclosed chain primary drive
	: Exposed chain final drive
FRAME	: Tubular steel construction
SUSPENSION	: Friction damped trailing link front forks
	: No rear suspension
TIRE SIZE	: 28×3.00"
BRAKES	: No front wheel brake
	: Internal expanding/external contracting rear wheel drum
DRY WEIGHT	: Solo 159kg
DIMENSIONS	: Wheel base 1475mm
MAX SPEED	: Solo 75mph

EXCELSIOR 1917 EXCELSIOR 7-10HP
AMERICA

· 1917 ·
HARLEY-DAVIDSON 7–9HP
(America)

At the turn of the century William Harley and Arthur Davidson began to experiment with powered bicycles. By 1903, they had been joined by Davidson's brothers, Walter and William, and the first Harley-Davidson motor cycle had been assembled. This machine had a single cylinder 400cc engine mounted within a bicycle-type frame with a belt drive and auxiliary cycle pedals. The first Harley-Davidson machine with the latter traditional V-twin engine was introduced in 1909, and this 1000cc model had gained such an excellent reputation by 1914 that a number were immediately adopted with the declaration of the First World War by the Allied armed forces.

When America entered the war in April 1917, the American armed forces also brought the Harley-Davidson 1000cc model to Europe. By this time, the machine featured a rounder shaped petrol tank and had a complete chain drive transmission with a three-speed gearbox. The military conversion was an overall coat of the appropriate service livery; the machines were used both solo and with various sidecars attached. The Harley-Davidson factory supplied a total of 14,666 machines and 14,332 sidecars to the American military during its war-time production.

Brief specification

ENGINE TYPE	: Harley-Davidson – V-twin cylinder
DISPLACEMENT	: 987cc (84.1×88.9mm)
VALVE DESIGN	: Inlet over exhaust valve
COMPRESSION	: 5:1
POWER OUTPUT	: 7–9HP
ELECTRICS	: 6 volt
CARBURETTOR	: One – Schebler
GEARBOX	: Hand change, 3 speed, separate unit
TRANSMISSION	: Enclosed chain primary drive
	: Exposed chain final drive
FRAME	: Tubular steel construction
SUSPENSION	: Friction damped leading link front forks
	: No rear suspension
TIRE SIZE	: 28×3.00″
BRAKES	: No front wheel brake
	: Internal expanding/external contracting rear wheel drum
DRY WEIGHT	: Solo 160kg
DIMENSIONS	: Wheel base 1499mm
MAX SPEED	: Solo 60mph

HARLEY– DAVIDSON

1917 HARLEY-DAVIDSON 7-9HP AMERICA

· 1923 ·
WALTER MODEL 750
(Czechoslovakia)

The Walter motor cycle factory of Praha-Jinonice was developed from a small bicycle business founded by Joseph Walter in Praha-Smichov in 1898. After a number of successful years, Walter left the company and founded another engineering factory in Praha-Kosire in 1922. This business also began motor cycle production in 1926.

In 1923 the Walter factory introduced the advanced design of the company director Plocek: a 750cc V-twin cylinder engine mounted across the frame with tailing link front fork suspension. By this time the factory was also building cars and aircraft engines, and motor cycle production ceased in 1927 to fulfil these further interests. During this short production period the majority of these Walter machines were adopted by the newly formed Czechoslovak armed forces.

While at the Walter factory, the designer Zubaty completed a motor cycle design in 1917 with an opposed twin-cylinder 750cc engine mounted in line with the frame. This was not produced at the Walter factory and the design was sold to the Itar factory of Praha-Radlice, where the machine was manufactured between 1921 and 1929. Like the Walter 750cc design, only a small number of these machines were assembled and the majority of these were adopted by the Czechoslovak military.

Brief specification

ENGINE TYPE	: Walter – Transverse V-twin cylinder
DISPLACEMENT	: 750cc
VALVE DESIGN	: Over head valves
COMPRESSION	: 5:1
POWER OUTPUT	: 7HP
ELECTRICS	: 6 volt
CARBURETTOR	: One
GEARBOX	: Hand change, 3 speed, unit construction
TRANSMISSION	: Exposed chain final drive
FRAME	: Tubular steel construction
SUSPENSION	: Friction damped trailing link front forks
	: No rear suspension
TIRE SIZE	: 26×3.25″
BRAKES	: No front wheel brake
	: Internal expanding rear wheel drum
DRY WEIGHT	: Solo 170kg
DIMENSIONS	: Wheel base 1372mm
MAX SPEED	: Solo 60mph

Walter 1923 WALTER MODEL 750 CZECHOSLOVAKIA

· 1924 ·
RENÉ-GILLET MODEL G
(France)

As the majority of the Allied armed forces, the French military used civilian motor cycles during the First World War, but by the 1920's they had acquired various machines especially designed for military service. The René-Gillet factory of Paris developed a number of motor cycles and sidecars for military use during this period. Their sidecar designs included various machine gun mountings, with and without armour plating, and a fully enclosed radio communication vehicle.

The René-Gillet factory produced motor cycles between 1898 and 1957; and while they did not produce very fast machines they established a reputation for producing models of reliable and lasting design. As a result, the company was favoured by the French police and armed forces throughout its existence.

The René-Gillet motor cycle adopted by the French military during the 1920's included the single cylinder 350cc model H, and the V-twin 759cc model G and 100cc model J. These machines all had side-valve engines with a three-speed gearbox and chain final drive mounted in a tubular frame with trailing link front fork suspension. The V-twin cylinder models were used with a sidecar attached and the single cylinder model for solo despatch type service.

Brief specification

ENGINE TYPE	: René-Gillet – V-twin cylinder
DISPLACEMENT	: 751cc (70×97.7mm)
VALVE DESIGN	: Side valves
COMPRESSION	: 5:1
POWER OUTPUT	: 6HP
ELECTRICS	: 6 volt
CARBURETTOR	: One – Amac
GEARBOX	: Hand change, 3 speed, separate unit
TRANSMISSION	: Enclosed chain primary drive
	: Exposed chain final drive
FRAME	: Tubular construction
SUSPENSION	: Friction damped trailing link front forks
	: No rear suspension
TIRE SIZE	: 27×4.00"
BRAKES	: No front wheel brake
	: Internal expanding rear wheel drum
DRY WEIGHT	: Solo 136kg
DIMENSIONS	: Wheel base 1524mm
MAX SPEED	: Solo 55mph

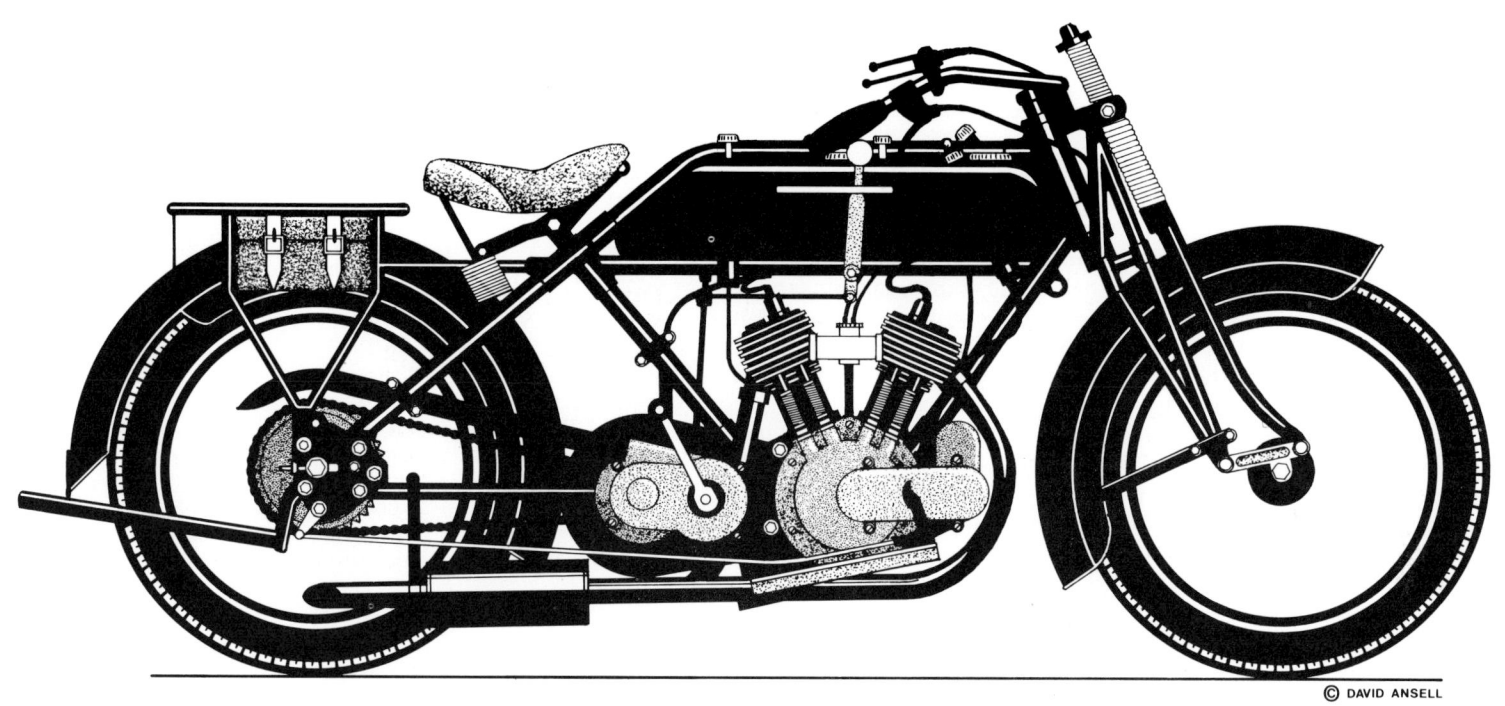

RENÉ GILLET

1924 RENÉ GILLET MODEL G
FRANCE

© DAVID ANSELL

· 1926 ·
HUSQVARNA 180
(Sweden)

In 1922 the Husqvarna factory introduced the model 500 for use with a sidecar. This machine had a side valve 1000cc V-twin cylinder engine and three-speed gearbox with chain drive, mounted in a solid steel tubular frame with girder type front fork suspension. A total of 715 of these machines were manufactured and approximately 150 of these were supplied to the Swedish armed forces. It continued to be developed until 1933 and was also supplied in small numbers to the Swedish military as the model 600 in 1926, the model 610 in 1929, and the model 120 in 1932.

Between 1926 and 1927, the Swedish military also adopted a small number of lighter Husqvarna model 180 for solo despatch rider service. This model was a further development of the Husqvarna model 145A, which had been adopted for Swedish military service during the First World War; improvements included an internal expanding rear wheel drum brake, a shorter wheel base frame, and repositioned electrics.

Brief specification

ENGINE TYPE	: Husqvarna – V-twin cylinder
DISPLACEMENT	: 550cc (65×83mm)
VALVE DESIGN	: Side valves
COMPRESSION	: 4.36:1
POWER OUTPUT	: 15bhp
ELECTRICS	: 6 volt
CARBURETTOR	: One – Schebler
GEARBOX	: Hand change, 3 speed, separate unit
TRANSMISSION	: Enclosed chain primary drive
	: Exposed chain final drive
FRAME	: Tubular steel construction
SUSPENSION	: Friction damped parallelogram front forks
	: No rear suspension
TIRE SIZE	: 26×2.25″
BRAKES	: No front wheel brake
	: Internal expanding rear wheel drum
DRY WEIGHT	: Solo 154kg
DIMENSIONS	: Wheel base 1270mm
MAX SPEED	: Solo 65mph

Husqvarna

**1926 HUSQVARNA 180
SWEDEN**

· 1926 ·
TRIUMPH MODEL P
(Great Britain)

In Great Britain the immediate post-war demand for personal transport ended as quickly as it had begun, and once the free spending boom had passed uncontrollable inflation eventually lead to the General Strike of 1926. During this period, Siegfried Bettmann had asked his Triumph motor cycle drawing office for a machine with the lowest possible price that would make a profit. As a result, the Triumph model P was introduced in 1925.

Although production methods were questionable, the model P quickly became a success as the cheapest 500cc motor cycle on the market. The Triumph factory was committed to a run of 20,000 machines and any improvements could only be made with the start of a second production run. With the introduction of the second version later that year, the expected Triumph workmanship returned. The new model featured caged-roller bearings, an internal expanding front wheel drum brake, and pressed in valve guides.

The British armed forces adopted the second version of the Triumph model P to replace the ageing Triumph model H for solo despatch rider service. Like previous Triumph machines for military use this model was equipped with acetylene lighting, a rear carrier, and a handlebar mounted bulb horn.

Brief specification

ENGINE TYPE	: Triumph – Vertical single cylinder
DISPLACEMENT	: 493cc (84×89mm)
VALVE DESIGN	: Side valves
COMPRESSION	: 5:1
POWER OUTPUT	: 3.5HP
ELECTRICS	: 6 volt
CARBURETTOR	: One – Triumph
GEARBOX	: Hand change, 3 speed, separate unit
TRANSMISSION	: Enclosed chain primary drive
	: Exposed chain final drive
FRAME	: Tubular construction
SUSPENSION	: Friction damped parallelogram front forks
	: No rear suspension
TIRE SIZE	: 26×2.5"
BRAKES	: Internal expanding front wheel drum
	: Block brake on dummy rear wheel rim
DRY WEIGHT	: Solo 91kg
DIMENSIONS	: Wheel base 1321mm
MAX SPEED	: Solo 45mph

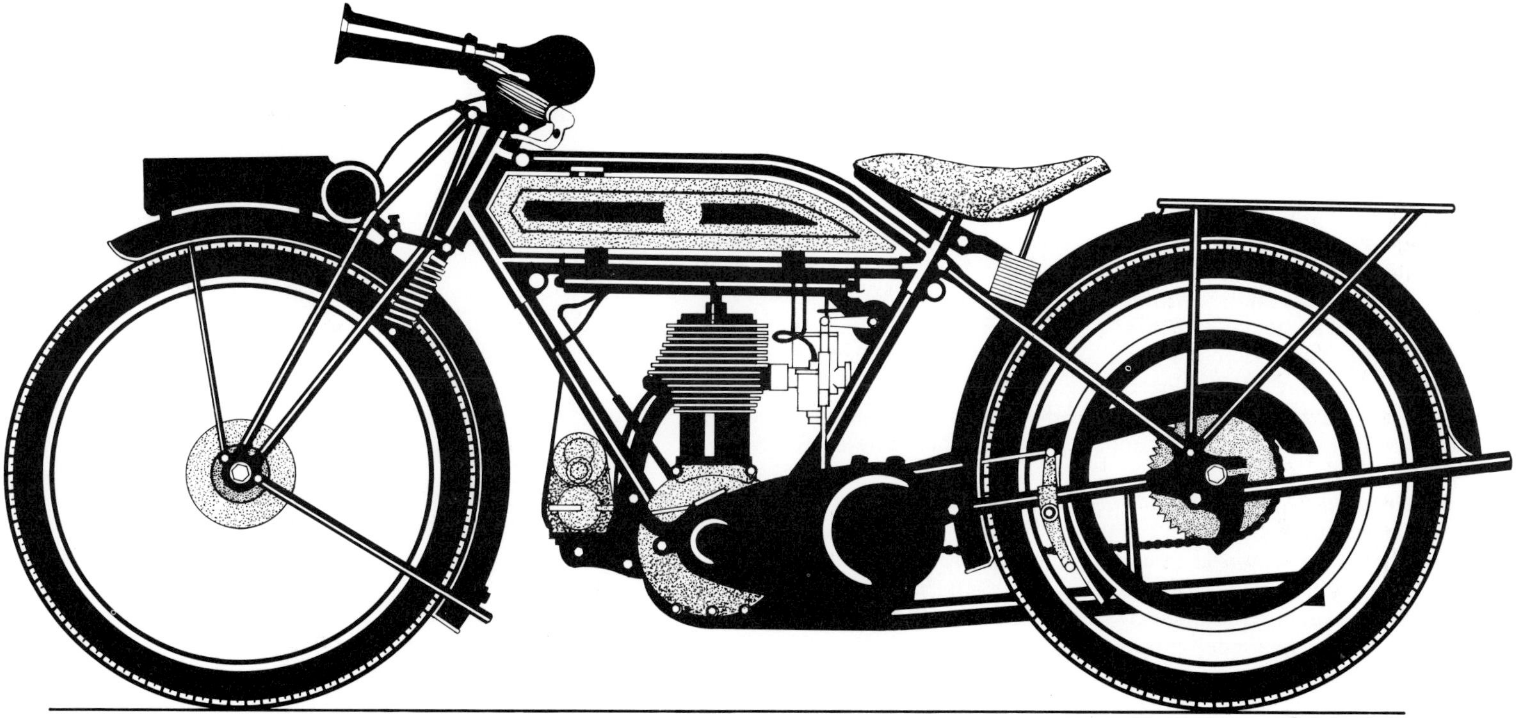

**1926 TRIUMPH MODEL P
GREAT BRITAIN**

· 1928 ·
BMW MODEL R–62
(Germany)

The Bayerische Flugzeugwerke AG was founded in 1916 by the aviation engineers Karl Rapp and Max Friz. After two successful years producing aircraft engines for the German military, the BFW factory combined with the Gustav Otto aircraft factory and formed the Bayerische Motoren Werke GmbH. Under the Treaty of Versailles, the new BMW factory was forced to stop all aircraft production and reluctantly began to manufacture motor cycles in 1920. The first BMW motor cycle was named the Flink and had a forward sloping single-cylinder 150cc two-stroke engine. This was soon followed by the Helios which had an opposed twin-cylinder engine mounted in line with the frame.

After some success with the Helios model, Friz became more interested in motor cycle design and in 1923 the model R–32 was introduced. It also had a side-valve 500cc opposed twin-cylinder engine, but with this model the BMW factory began the tradition of the transverse mounting. In 1925 the overhead valve version model R–37 was introduced. The following year, both machines were superseded by the more powerful side-valve model R–42 and the overhead valve model R–47, and in 1928 these in turn were superseded by the side-valve model R–52 and the overhead valve model R–57. The first BMW motor cycle with a 750cc engine capacity were also introduced in 1928: the side-valve R–62 and the overhead valve model R–63.

Between 1928 and 1929 the BMW factory supplied the German armed forces with a number of the model R–52 and model R–62, both solo and with various sidecars attached, for despatch, escort, and reconnaissance type service. The military conversion included a pillion pan-type saddle mounted on the rear mudguard, a pair of leather pannier bags, and an overall coat of grey paint.

Brief specification

ENGINE TYPE	: BMW – Transverse opposed twin cylinder
DISPLACEMENT	: 745cc (78×78mm)
VALVE DESIGN	: Side valves
COMPRESSION	: 5.5:1
POWER OUTPUT	: 18BHP at 3,400RPM
ELECTRICS	: 6 volt
CARBURETTOR	: One – BMW
GEARBOX	: Hand change, 3 speed, unit construction
TRANSMISSION	: Exposed shaft final drive
FRAME	: Tubular construction
SUSPENSION	: Friction damped leaf sprung front forks
	: No rear suspension
TIRE SIZE	: 26×3.00″
BRAKES	: Internal expanding front wheel drum ⌀ 150mm
	: External contracting transmission drum ⌀ 150mm
DRY WEIGHT	: Solo 155kg
DIMENSIONS	: Wheel base 1400mm, Ground clearance 150mm
MAX SPEED	: Solo 70mph

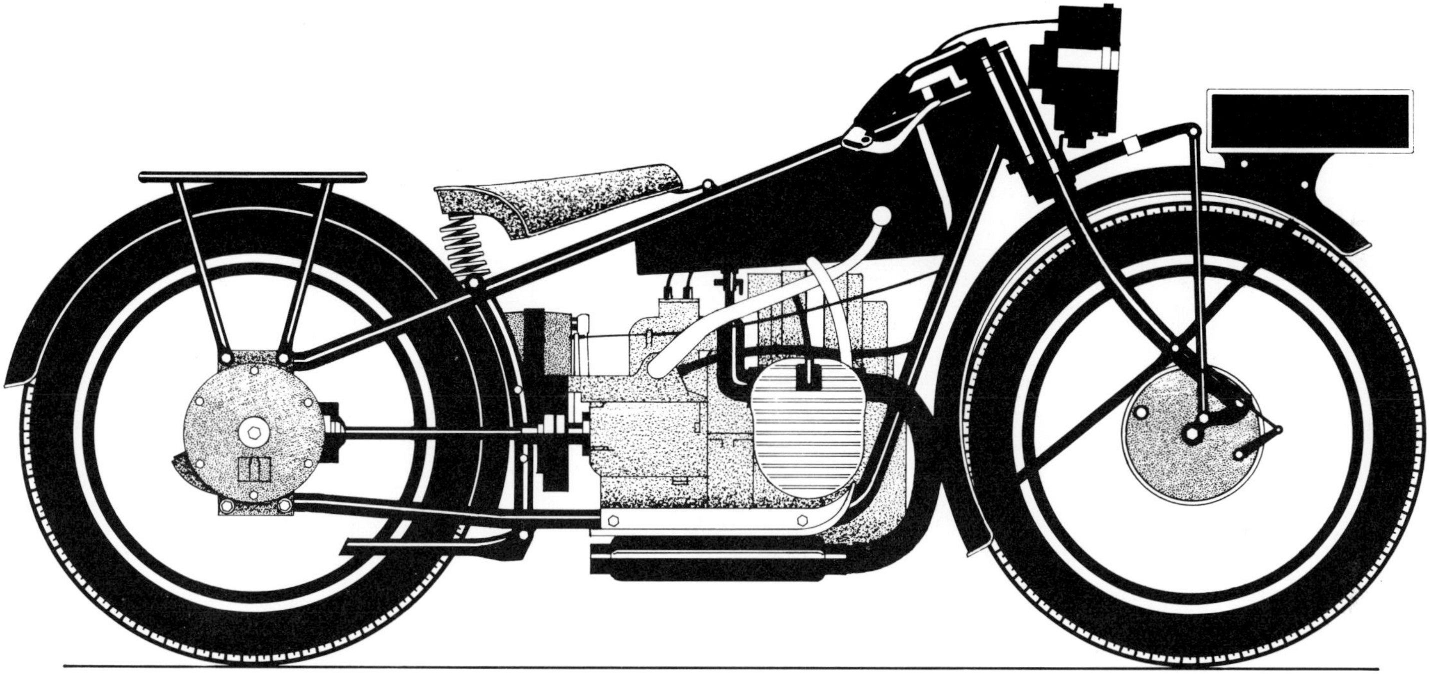

1928 BMW MODEL R-62
GERMANY

· 1929 ·
DOUGLAS MILITARY 350
(Great Britain)

With the reputation gained during the First World War, the Douglas motor cycle factory of Bristol continued to produced their model V until the mid 1920's. By this time, the majority of Douglas machines were equipped with a three-speed gearbox and chain drive transmission. The new Douglas models had a shorter wheel base and lower mounted engines with the option of overhead valves. These relatively light machines were fast: in 1923 Tom Sheard won the Senior TT, and Freddie Dixon won the new sidecar event with a 600cc banking sidecar outfit.

By 1925 the Douglas factory had introduced a semi-automatic dry sump and a flexible band drum brake, but it was the brakeless speedway models that brought Douglas to the height of their fame. Such riders as Australian Vic Huxley took the major awards and helped the factory sell 1,300 speedway machines in 1929 alone. With such a reputation, Douglas also gained a contract to supply the British armed forces with a solo despatch rider machine. The eventual military model provided was combination of the civilian B–29 and L–3 models.

Brief specification

ENGINE TYPE	: Douglas – Longitudinal opposed twin cylinder
DISPLACEMENT	: 348cc (60.8 × 60mm)
VALVE DESIGN	: Side valves
COMPRESSION	: 5:1
POWER OUTPUT	: 3.5HP
ELECTRICS	: 6 volt
CARBURETTOR	: One – Douglas
GEARBOX	: Hand change, 3 speed, separate unit
TRANSMISSION	: Enclosed chain primary drive
	: Exposed chain final drive
FRAME	: Tubular construction
SUSPENSION	: Friction damped parallelogram front forks
	: No rear suspension
TIRE SIZE	: 26 × 3.00″
BRAKES	: Internal expanding front wheel drum
	: Internal expanding rear wheel drum
DRY WEIGHT	: Solo 118kg
DIMENSIONS	: Wheel base 1397mm
MAX SPEED	: Solo 55mph

Douglas

**1929 DOUGLAS MILITARY 350
GREAT BRITAIN**

· 1930 ·
HARLEY-DAVIDSON VL
(America)

During the First World War, the Harley-Davidson factory established an excellent reputation for producing motor cycles of reliable and lasting design. As a result, the Milwaukee company began to supply various armed forces throughout the world with machines for military service after the war. A popular machine during this period with police and military departments was the 1200cc model VL, first introduced in 1922. This machine continued to be developed and was eventually available as the Super Glide in 1980. During which time a number of models were supplied for military service originating from this early 1920's design.

The 1930 Harley-Davidson VL model marked the changeover for the company from the inlet over exhaust valve engine to the side-by-side design. This machine was supplied both solo and with various sidecars attached, and for ease of use the sidecar was equipped with interchangeable wheels and the option of a reverse gear. Further major features included a duplex primary chain, a sprung seat pillar, a lower riding position, and a higher ground clearance. During the Second World War, this machine was adopted by the American and Allied armed forces as the military model UA. The military conversion of this machine included a rear carrier rack, a rifle or machine gun holster mounted on the right front forks, provision for masked lighting, and a crankcase shield.

Brief specification

ENGINE TYPE	: Harley-Davidson – V-twin cylinder
DISPLACEMENT	: 1205cc (86.9 × 106.6mm)
VALVE DESIGN	: Side valves
COMPRESSION	: 6:1
POWER OUTPUT	: 28BHP at 4,000RPM
ELECTRICS	: 6 volt
CARBURETTOR	: One – Schebler
GEARBOX	: Hand change, 3 or 4 speed, separate unit
TRANSMISSION	: Enclosed chain primary drive
	: Exposed chain final drive
FRAME	: Tubular construction
SUSPENSION	: Friction damped leading link front forks
	: No rear suspension
TIRE SIZE	: 27 × 4.00"
BRAKES	: Internal expanding front wheel drum
	: Internal expanding rear wheel drum
DRY WEIGHT	: Solo 182kg
DIMENSIONS	: Wheel base 1499mm
MAX SPEED	: Solo 90mph

· 1932 ·
MOTO GUZZI GT–17
(Italy)

Carlo Guzzi founded his motorcycle factory of Mandello del Lario in 1922, and with the first machines introduced various designs that quickly established an excellent reputation. These motorcycles had a horizontally mounted engine so that the head would receive cooling air while travelling, the flywheel was mounted on the outside to reduce vibration, and the crankcase enclosed the gearbox so that only one lubricating circuit would be required.

A small number of the early civilian Moto Guzzi machines were adopted by the Italian armed forces in 1928, but these were replaced in 1932 by the GT–17, the first Moto Guzzi model to be designed for military service. While these machines were very similar, the GT–17 was supplied with various armament carrying fittings, tool boxes, leg shields, and pillion seating. The GT–17 model remained in production until 1939, by which date a total of 4,810 had been assembled.

With the experience gained from the GT–17, the GT–20 model was introduced in 1938. This military designed machine had a similar engine, but the three-speed gearbox had been replaced with a four-speed design, and the frame had been improved with a higher ground clearance. This was only a transitional model between the GT–17 and Alce military machines, and production ceased the same year after only 248 had been assembled.

Brief specification

ENGINE TYPE	: Moto Guzzi – Horizontal single cylinder
DISPLACEMENT	: 498cc (88×82mm)
VALVE DESIGN	: Inlet over exhaust valves
COMPRESSION	: 4.7:1
POWER OUTPUT	: 13.2bhp at 4,000rpm
ELECTRICS	: 6 volt
CARBURETTOR	: One – Dell'Orto MC 26 F
GEARBOX	: Hand change, 3 speed, unit construction
TRANSMISSION	: Exposed chain final drive
FRAME	: Tubular construction
SUSPENSION	: Friction damped parallelogram front forks
	: Friction damped rear sub-frame
TIRE SIZE	: 19×3.5″
BRAKES	: Internal expanding front wheel drum
	: Internal expanding rear wheel drum
DRY WEIGHT	: Solo 196kg
DIMENSIONS	: Wheel base 1500mm, Ground clearance 165mm
MAX SPEED	: Solo 63mph

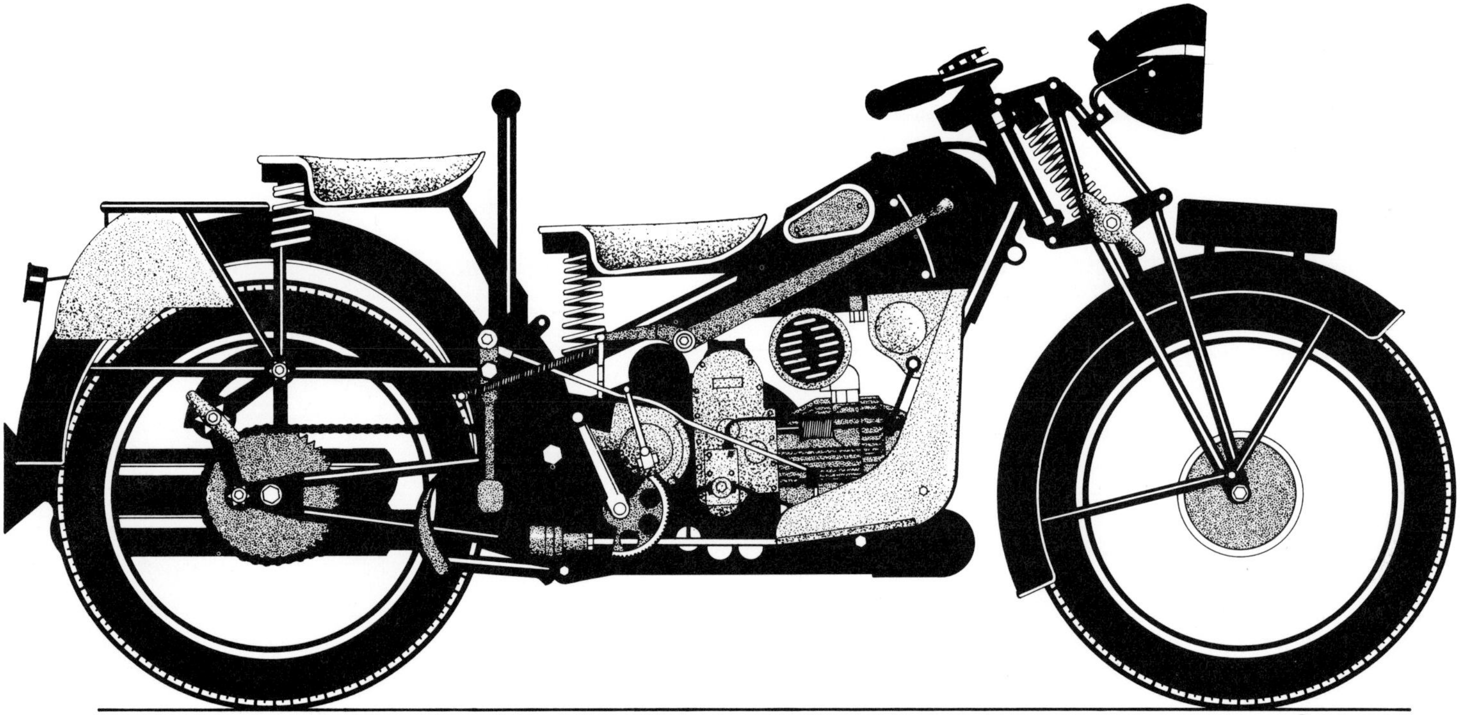

1932 MOTO GUZZI GT-17
ITALY

· 1933 ·

VICTORIA MODEL KR–6
(Germany)

The Victoria factory of Nurnberg was founded by Max Frankenburger and Max Ottenstein to manufacture bicycles in 1886. Within three years, production included a number of powered vehicles, with various proprietary engines. The Victoria KR–I, their first motorcycle of proven design, was not introduced until 1920. This machine had a BMW 500cc engine, with opposed twin cylinders of side-valve layout, mounted in line with the frame. A period of some three years elapsed before BMW began motorcycle production for themselves. The further developed model KR–III, with a similar engine of Victoria overhead valve layout, was adopted by the German armed forces in 1925, and remained in military service until 1927, when superseded by the more powerful model KR–VI.

The Victoria model KR–VI had an opposed twin-cylinder 600cc overhead valve engine, with a three-speed gearbox and chain final drive. This machine was also used as the basis of an experimental model with two rear wheels mounted in tandem. After being tested, the German military did not adopt any three wheeled motor cyles. The model KR–VI was superseded in military service by the KR–6 in 1933. This was a similar machine, but with an improved engine and gearbox, and a saddle-type petrol tank. The Victoria model KR–6 remained in military service until 1938, by which date approximately 30,000 had been supplied, for solo despatch rider type use.

Brief specification

ENGINE TYPE	: Victoria – Longitudinal opposed twin cylinder
DISPLACEMENT	: 596cc (77×64mm)
VALVE DESIGN	: Overhead valves
COMPRESSION	: 6.2:1
POWER OUTPUT	: 20bhp at 4,000rpm
ELECTRICS	: 6 volt, 30 watt
CARBURETTOR	: One – Graetzin
GEARBOX	: Hand change, 4 speed, separate unit
TRANSMISSION	: Enclosed chain primary drive
	: Exposed chain final drive
FRAME	: Tubular construction
SUSPENSION	: Friction damped parallelogram front forks
	: No rear suspension
TIRE SIZE	: 19×4.00″
BRAKES	: Internal expanding front wheel drum
	: Internal expanding rear wheel drum
DRY WEIGHT	: Solo 160kg
DIMENSIONS	: Wheel base 1480mm, Ground clearance 120mm
MAX SPEED	: Solo 60mph

VICTORIA

**1933 VICTORIA MODEL KR-6
GERMANY**

· 1934 ·
BMW MODEL R–4
(Germany)

During the world economic crisis of the late 1920's and early 1930's, the BMW factory had to introduce a cheaper motor cycle to remain in production. As a result, the first BMW single-cylinder models were assembled. The BMW model R–4 was introduced in 1932 and remained in production until 1938 by which date a total of 15,200 had been manufactured. This machine had a unit construction 400cc engine, mounted in a pressed steel frame, with leaf sprung trailing link front fork suspension.

The BMW model R–4 was adopted by the German armed forces in 1934, but only remained in military service for two years, when it was superseded by more powerful BMW R–35. This machine had a 350cc engine, mounted in a similar pressed steel frame, but with undamped telescopic front fork suspension, and remained in service throughout the Secondon World War. The military conversion of these machines included a pair of leather pannier bags, a rear carrier rack, and an overall coat of grey.

Brief specification

ENGINE TYPE	: BMW – Vertical single cylinder
DISPLACEMENT	: 401cc (78×84mm)
VALVE DESIGN	: Overhead valves
COMPRESSION	: 5.2:1
POWER OUTPUT	: 12BHP at 3,400rpm
ELECTRICS	: 6 volt, 45 watt
CARBURETTOR	: One – Sum or Amal
GEARBOX	: Hand change, 4 speed, unit construction
TRANSMISSION	: Exposed shaft final drive
FRAME	: Pressed steel construction
SUSPENSION	: Friction damped trailing link front forks
	: No rear suspension
TIRE SIZE	: 19×3.5"
BRAKES	: Internal expanding front wheel drum ⌀ 200mm
	: Internal expanding rear wheel drum ⌀ 200mm
DRY WEIGHT	: Solo 165kg
DIMENSIONS	: Wheel base 1320mm, Ground clearance 130mm
MAX SPEED	: Solo 65mph

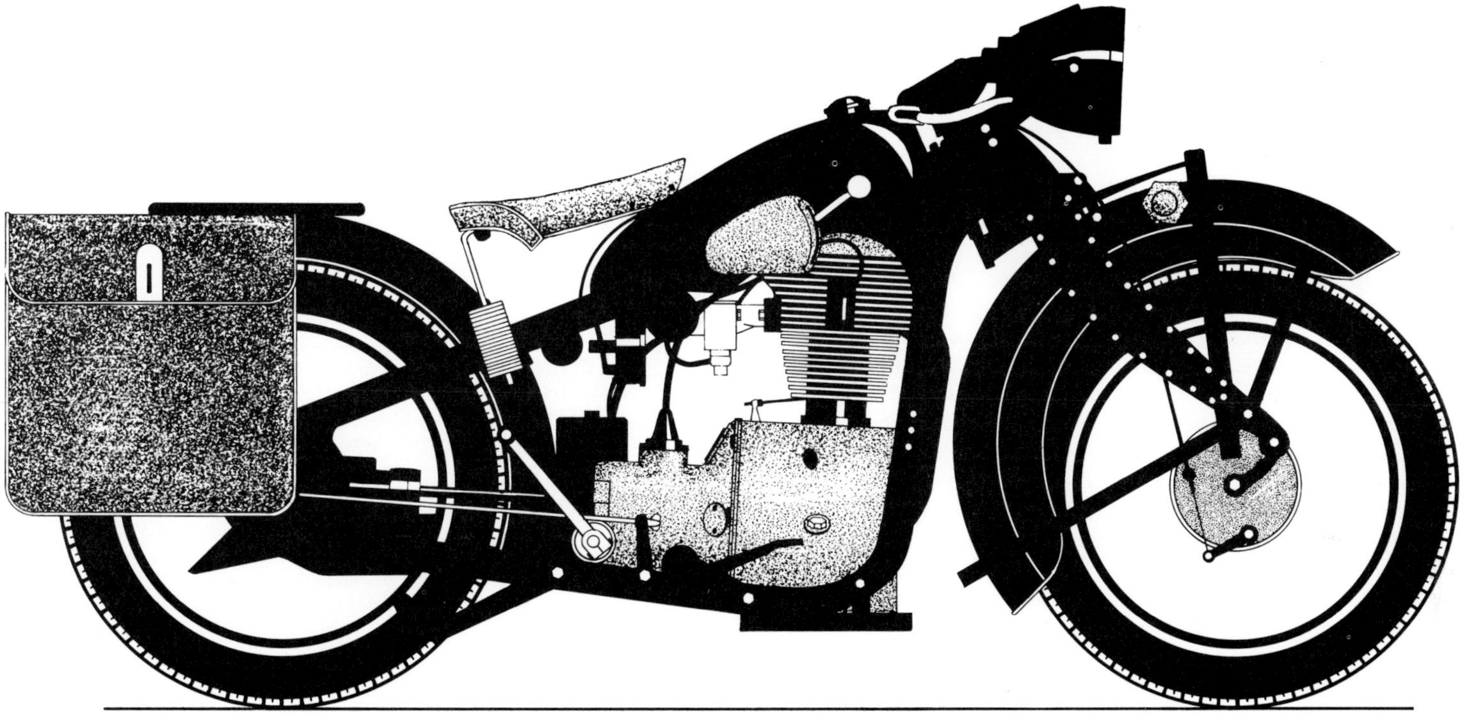

 **1934 BMW MODEL R-4 GERMANY**

· 1934 ·
JAWA MODEL 350–SV
(Czechoslovakia)

With the fall in demand for armaments after the First World War, the Janeck Arms Manufacturing Company of Prague began motor cycle production in 1928. The following year, the Jawa 500–OHV model was introduced. This had a unit construction engine and gearbox with a shaft final drive, mounted in a pressed steel frame with a trailing link front fork suspension. This design was built under license from the German factory of Wanderer and the name Jawa was taken from the first two letters of Janeck and Wanderer. The machine was not successful and design work began on a simpler model.

At first, the Janeck factory introduced a number of two-stroke machines, but in 1934 the Jawa 350–SV model was produced. This machine had a single cylinder 350cc side-valve engine, mounted in a pressed steel frame with pressed steel girder-type front fork suspension. With an interest in producing racing machines, a parts kit was also produced a few years later to convert this engine into an overhead camshaft design. A small number of the Jawa 350–SV model were adopted by the Czechoslovak armed forces from 1934 for solo and with sidecar service. This machine remained in production until the Second World War, during which time it was also used by the German military.

Brief specification

ENGINE TYPE	: Jawa – Vertical single cylinder
DISPLACEMENT	: 346cc (70×90mm)
VALVE DESIGN	: Side valves
COMPRESSION	: 6:1
POWER OUTPUT	: 14BHP at 4,200rpm
ELECTRICS	: 6 volt
CARBURETTOR	: One – Amal
GEARBOX	: Hand change, 4 speed, separate unit
TRANSMISSION	: Enclosed chain primary drive
	: Exposed chain final drive
FRAME	: Pressed steel construction
SUSPENSION	: Friction damped parallelogram front forks
	: No rear suspension
TIRE SIZE	: 19×3.5″
BRAKES	: Internal expanding front wheel drum
	: Internal expanding rear wheel drum
DRY WEIGHT	: Solo 125kg
DIMENSIONS	: Wheel base 1295mm
MAX SPEED	: Solo 60mph

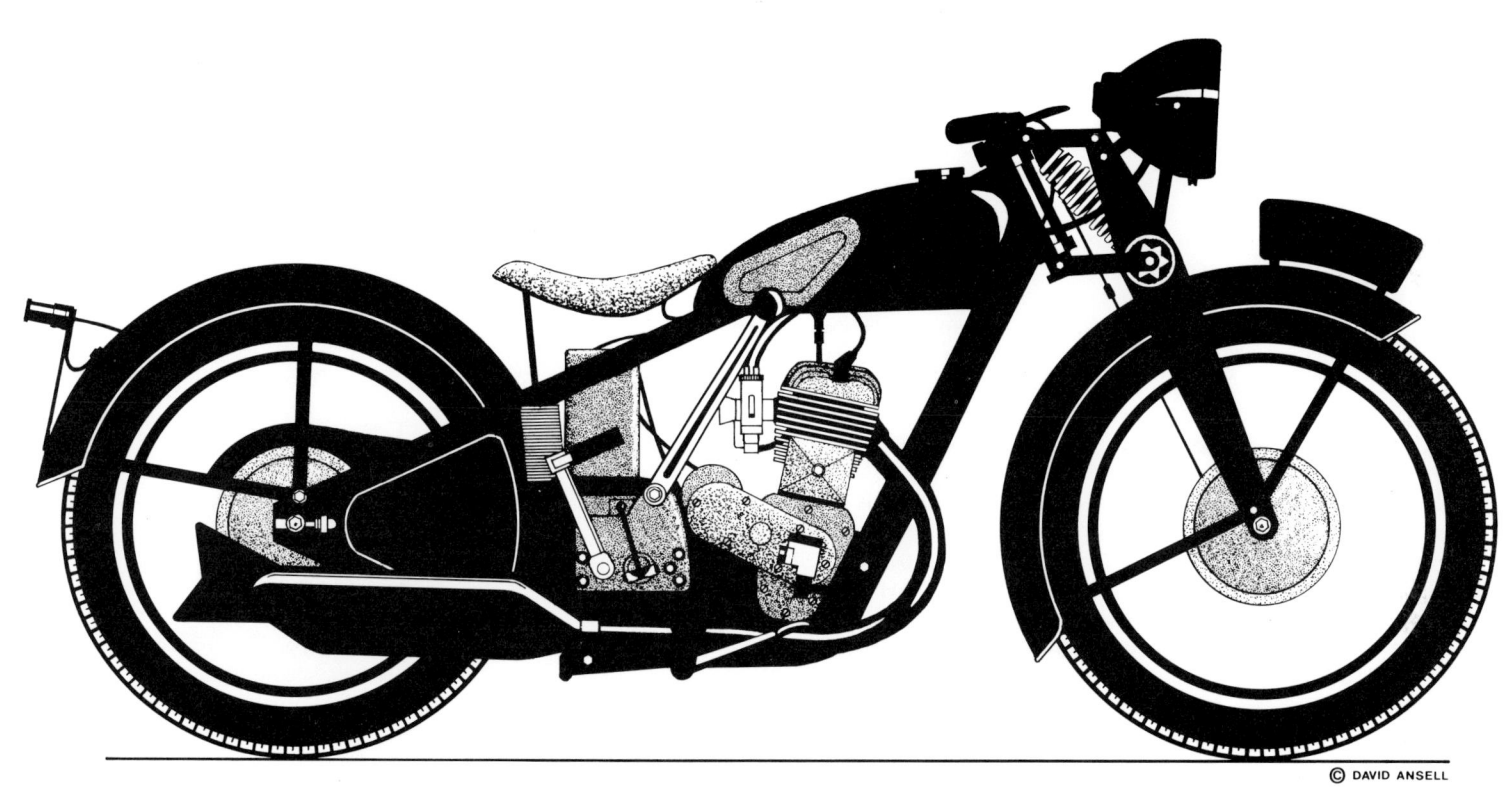

JAWA — 1934 JAWA MODEL 350-SV CZECHOSLOVAKIA

· 1934 ·
ZÜNDAPP K–500–W
(Germany)

The munitions business of Zünder and Apparatebau GmbH was founded in Nürnberg in 1917. This factory became Zündapp Gesellschaft after the First World War and began to manufacture heavy transport equipment. The first Zündapp motorcycle was introduced as the model K–22 in 1922. This machine had a single-cylinder 211cc two-stroke engine with a single speed and belt final drive. Though a very basic design, this model established motor cycle production at the factory, and within two years more than 10,000 Zündapp motor cycles had been assembled.

With this success, the Zündapp factory introduced a complete 'K' model range at the Berlin Motor Show in 1933. These machines featured unit construction engine and gearbox designs with shaft final drive and pressed steel cycle frames with pressed steel front fork suspension. The following year, the Zündapp K–500 model was adopted by the German armed forces for solo despatch type service. The military version designated with a 'W' for Wehrmacht remained in production until 1939. This machine had a pillion pan-type saddle mounted on the rear mudguard, a pair of leather pannier bags, and an overall coat of grey paint.

Brief specification

ENGINE TYPE	: Zündapp – Transverse opposed twin cylinder
DISPLACEMENT	: 498cc (69×66.6mm)
VALVE DESIGN	: Side valves
COMPRESSION	: 5.8:1
POWER OUTPUT	: 16BHP at 4,800rpm
ELECTRICS	: 6 volt, 50/70 watt
CARBURETTOR	: One – Bing or Amal 22mm
GEARBOX	: Hand change, 4 speed, unit construction
TRANSMISSION	: Exposed shaft final drive
FRAME	: Pressed steel construction
SUSPENSION	: Friction damped parallelogram front forks
	: No rear suspension
TIRE SIZE	: 19×3.5/4.00"
BRAKES	: Internal expanding front wheel drum
	: Internal expanding rear wheel drum
DRY WEIGHT	: Solo 190kg
DIMENSIONS	: Wheel base 1390mm, Ground clearance 110mm
MAX SPEED	: Solo 60mph

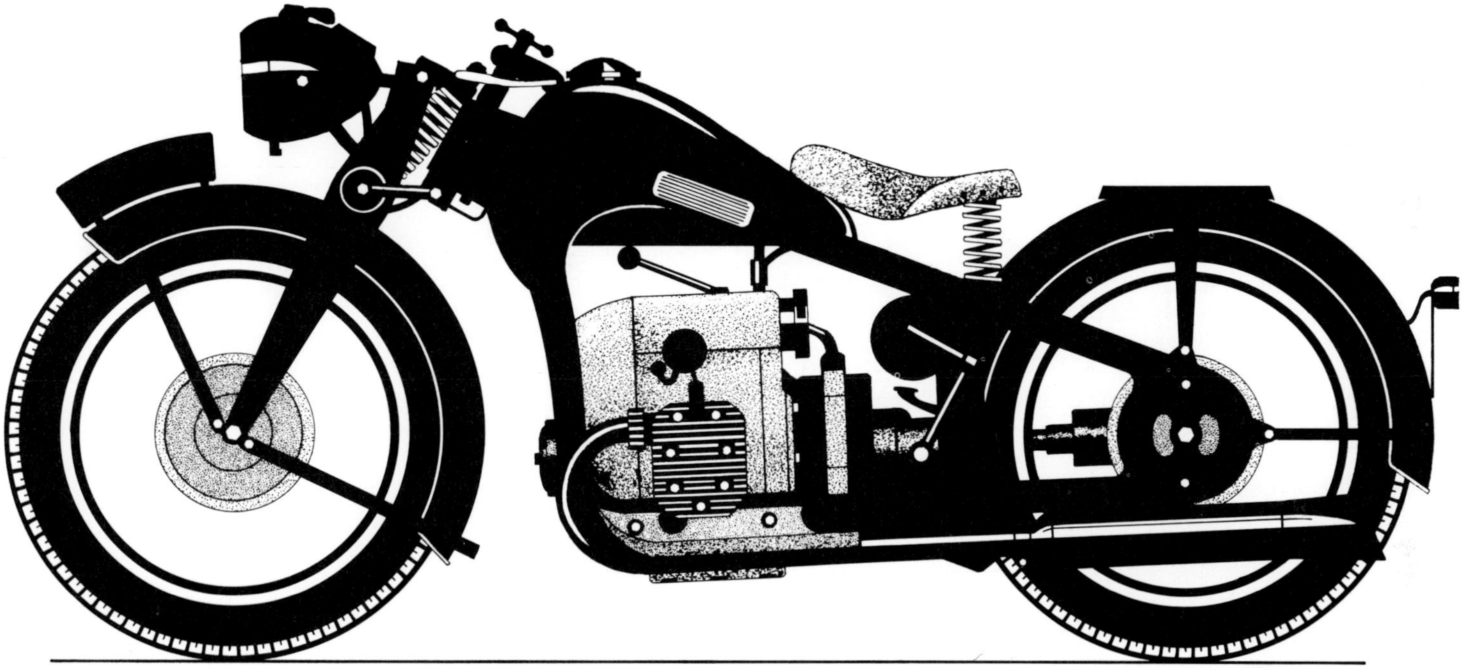

1934 ZÜNDAPP K-500-W
GERMANY

· 1934 ·
ZÜNDAPP K–800–W
(Germany)

The Zündapp factory of Nürnburg introduced their 'K' model range at the Berlin Motor Show of 1933. The K–200 had a vertical mounted single-cylinder two-stroke engine, the K–400 and K–500 models had transverse mounted opposed twin-cylinder side-valve engines, and the K–600 and K–800 models had transverse mounted opposed four-cylinder side-valve engines. All of these machines had a unit construction engine and gearbox design, with a shaft final drive, mounted within a pressed steel cycle frame with pressed steel front fork suspension.

The following year the K–500 and K–800 models were adopted by the German armed forces for solo and sidecar military service. The K–800 model continued to be supplied until production ceased in 1938, when one of the last modifications included the use of hydraulic damping on the front fork suspension. Even with insufficient cooling to the rear two cylinders, this model alone matched the reputation of the BMW model R–12, also in service during this period. The military version K–800 was designated 'W' for Wehrmacht, and had a pillion pan-type saddle mounted on the rear mudguard, a pair of leather pannier bags, and an overall coat of grey paint. These machines remained in service throughout the Second World War, by which date approximately 5,00 had been provided, and still continues to be the only four-cylinder machine to be adopted by the German armed forces.

Brief specification

ENGINE TYPE	: Zündapp – Transverse opposed four cylinder
DISPLACEMENT	: 804cc (62×66.6mm)
VALVE DESIGN	: Side valves
COMPRESSION	: 5.8:1
POWER OUTPUT	: 22BHP at 4,300rpm
ELECTRICS	: 6 volt, 50/70 watt
CARBURETTOR	: One – Pallas or Amal 22mm
GEARBOX	: Hand change, 4 speed, unit construction
TRANSMISSION	: Exposed shaft final drive
FRAME	: Pressed steel construction
SUSPENSION	: Friction damped parallelogram front forks
	: No rear suspension
TIRE SIZE	: 19×3.5/4.00″
BRAKES	: Internal expanding front wheel drum
	: Internal expanding rear wheel drum
DRY WEIGHT	: Solo 215kg
DIMENSIONS	: Wheel base 1405mm, Ground clearance 120mm
MAX SPEED	: Solo 70mph, W/SC 60mph

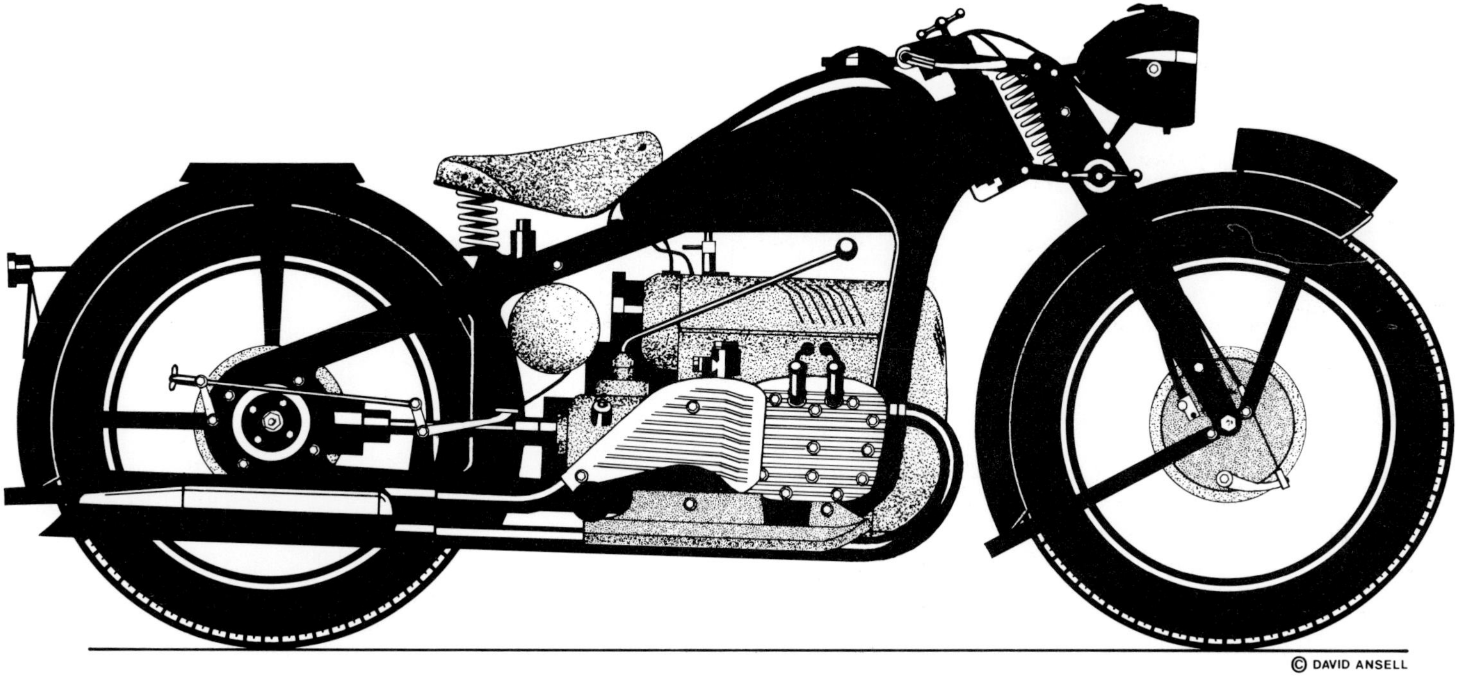

**1934 ZÜNDAPP K-800-W
GERMANY**

· 1935 ·

CZ MODEL 175
(Czechoslovakia)

The Ceska Zbrojovka company of Strakonice was originally founded for the manufacture of armaments in 1918. It was not until 1930 that the factory became interested in two-wheeled transport and began to manufacture bicycles. Within a few years, a simple motor cycle was assembled with a small two-stroke engine mounted within a standard bicycle frame. Although the factory continued to produce armaments, the management became more interested in the motor cycle area of businees, as the CZ developed. As a result, the CZ model 175 was introduced at the Prague Trade Fair of 1935. This machine had a unit construction single cylinder two stroke 175cc engine and 3 speed gearbox, mounted within a pressed steel frame with pressed steel front fork suspension.

From its introduction, the CZ model 175 began to gain the factory a creditable success competitive events, so it is not surprising that a number of these advanced machines were also adopted by the Czechoslovak armed forces. The model remained in active miltary service until the Second World War, when a number were also adopted by the German Wehrmacht. The CZ model 175 was used with little military conversion, which included a rear carrier rack, a pair of canvas pannier bags, and an overall coat of the appropriate service livery.

Brief specification

ENGINE TYPE	: CZ – Vertical single cylinder
DISPLACEMENT	: 172cc (60×61mm)
VALVE DESIGN	: Two stroke
COMPRESSION	: 5:1
POWER OUTPUT	: 5.5BHP at 3,800rpm
ELECTRICS	: 6 volt
CARBURETTOR	: One – Kf 20 S
GEARBOX	: Foot change, 3 speed, unit construction
TRANSMISSION	: Exposed chain final drive
FRAME	: Pressed steel construction
SUSPENSION	: Friction damped parallelogram front forks
	: No rear suspension
TIRE SIZE	: 19×3.00″
BRAKES	: Internal expanding front wheel drum
	: Internal expanding rear wheel drum
DRY WEIGHT	: Solo 95kg
DIMENSIONS	: Wheel base 1372mm
MAX SPEED	: Solo 50mph

**1935 CZ MODEL 175
CZECHOSLOVAKIA**

· 1935 ·
MOTO GUZZI GTV
(Italy)

The Moto Guzzi GTV model was first introduced in 1934 and adopted by the Italian armed forces the following year. It was originally intended as a civilian sports model, and although mounted within the traditional Moto Guzzi cycle frame, was one of the first models from the Mandello del Lario factory to feature an overhead valve engine design. The GTV model was supplied to the Italian military for solo internal use only, and, apart from the green colour, without any further military modification.

Between 1934 and 1940 the Moto Guzzi GTS model was also in production. While the cycle parts of this machine were virtually identical to the GTV model, the engine had an inlet over exhaust valve design very similar to the Moto Guzzi GT-17 model of two years before. From 1934 the GTS model was adopted by the Milizia della Strada, and in 1940 was used to demonstrate various handlebar mounted machine guns. After being tested, however, the Italian military did not adopt any of these designs.

Brief specification

ENGINE TYPE	: Moto Guzzi – Horizontal single cylinder
DISPLACEMENT	: 498cc (88×82mm)
VALVE DESIGN	: Overhead valves
COMPRESSION	: 5.5:1
POWER OUTPUT	: 18.9bhp at 4,300rpm
ELECTRICS	: 6 volt
CARBURETTOR	: One – Amal
GEARBOX	: Foot change, 4 speed, unit construction
TRANSMISSION	: Exposed chain final drive
FRAME	: Tubular construction
SUSPENSION	: Friction damped parallelogram front forks
	: Friction damped rear sub-frame
TIRE SIZE	: 19×3.25/3.5″
BRAKES	: Internal expanding front wheel drum
	: Internal expanding rear wheel drum
DRY WEIGHT	: Solo 160kg
DIMENSIONS	: Wheel base 1400mm
MAX SPEED	: Solo 75mph

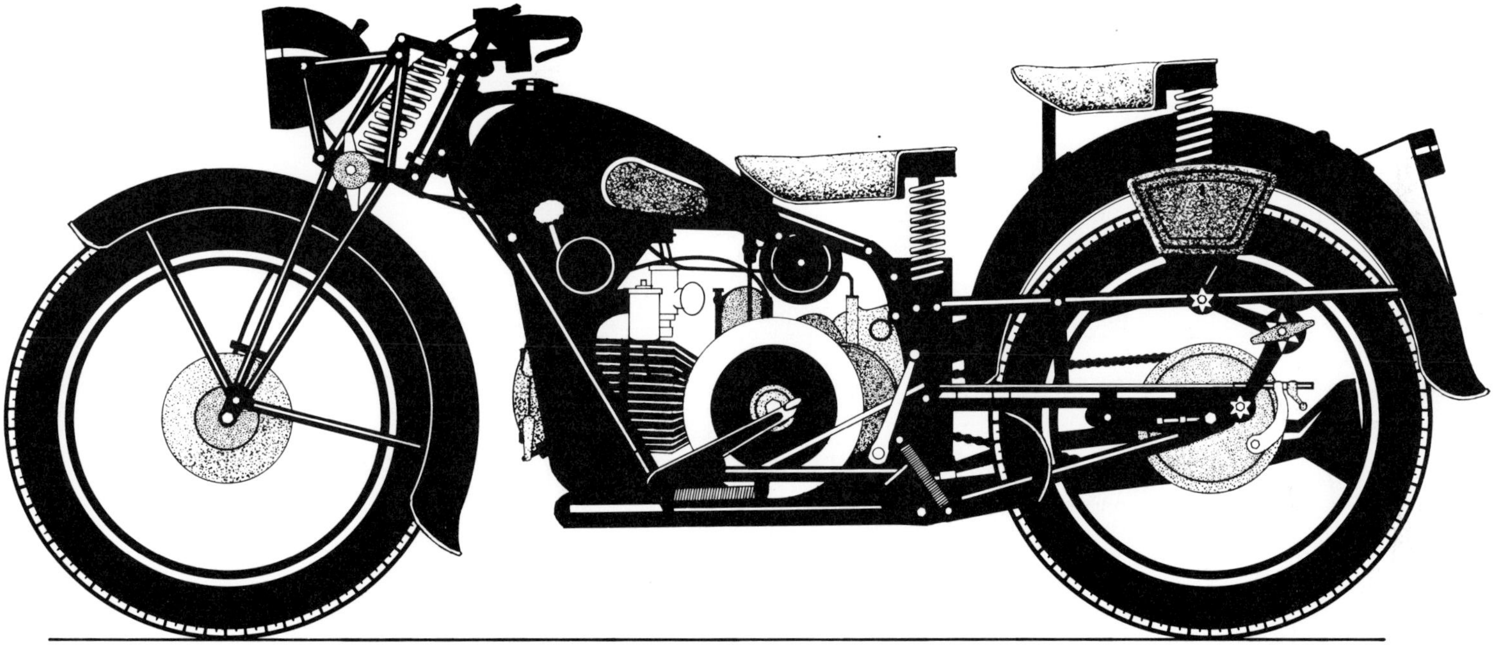

1934 MOTO GUZZI G.T.V.
ITALY

· 1936 ·

FN MILITARY MODEL 86
(Belgium)

The FN factory of Herstal resumed production of the pre-war single- and four-cylinder models during the early 1920's. The FN model 60 was introduced in 1924, and this single-cylinder 350cc machine proved to be as quick as the further developed four-cylinder model. As a result, the four-cylinder design was eventually discontinued in 1926. The FN factory continued to establish a reputation for speed and introduced the model 86 in 1933. The following year René Milhoux gained the world two-wheel speed record on this FN 500 machine.

Within a few years, the FN model 86 was available with an engine of 500cc or 600cc displacement and side- or overhead valve design. A variety of these machines were first adopted by the Belgian military during 1936, and later supplied to allied armed forces throughout the world. The military conversion included a pillion pan-type mounted on the rear mudguard, a pair of pannier bags, provision for masked lighting, and and overall coat of appropriate service livery. This machine was used both solo and with various sidecars attached, for despatch, escort, and general reconnaissance type service. The sidecar variants included ammunition carrying, wireless communications, and armoured machine gun mounting.

Brief specification

ENGINE TYPE	: FN – Vertical single cylinder
DISPLACEMENT	: 499cc (86×86mm)
VALVE DESIGN	: Overhead valves
COMPRESSION	: 6:1
POWER OUTPUT	: 20BHP at 4,800rpm
ELECTRICS	: 6 volt
CARBURETTOR	: One – Amal type 29
GEARBOX	: Foot change, 4 speed, unit construction
TRANSMISSION	: Exposed chain final drive
FRAME	: Tubular construction
SUSPENSION	: Friction damped parallelogram front forks
	: No rear suspension
TIRE SIZE	: 20×3.25″
BRAKES	: Internal expanding front wheel drum
	: Internal expanding rear wheel drum
DRY WEIGHT	: Solo 175kg
DIMENSIONS	: Wheel base 1380mm, Ground clearance 200mm
MAX SPEED	: Solo 80mph

1936 FN MILITARY MODEL 86 BELGIUM

· 1936 ·
PUCH TYPE 800
(Austria)

The Puch factory merged with the car manufacturer Austro-Daimler in 1928, and, with the military equipment ban in Austria after the First World War, the Steyr armaments factory joined Puch and Daimler in 1934. Although the Steyr factory had been producing cars since 1920, the general world depression had proved too difficult to overcome alone, so the three companies formed the Steyr-Daimler-Puch organisation. The Daimler factory was closed down, the four-wheeled production concentrated at the Steyr factory, and the two-wheeled production at that of Puch.

The type 800 was one of the first motor cycles to be introduced by the new company. This unusual machine had a transverse mounted opposed four-cylinder engine, with the cylinders set in a slight V angle and a clutch in the rear wheel hub. A total of 550 of these machines were produced between 1936 and 1938, and the majority were adopted by the newly formed Austrian armed forces. They were supplied both solo and vaious sidecars attached and were used with only minor military modifications.

Brief specification

ENGINE TYPE	: Puch – Transverse opposed four cylinder
DISPLACEMENT	: 791cc (60×70mm)
VALVE DESIGN	: Side valves
COMPRESSION	: 5:1
POWER OUTPUT	: 20BHP at 4,000rpm
ELECTRICS	: 6 volt, 50/70 watt
CARBURETTOR	: One – Puch
GEARBOX	: Hand change, 4 speed, unit construction
TRANSMISSION	: Exposed chain final drive
FRAME	: Tubular construction
SUSPENSION	: Friction damped parallelogram front forks
	: No rear suspension
TIRE SIZE	: 19×4.00″
BRAKES	: Internal expanding front wheel drum
	: Internal expanding rear wheel drum
DRY WEIGHT	: Solo 195kg
DIMENSIONS	: Wheel base 1427mm, Ground clearance 170mm
MAX SPEED	: Solo 75mph, W/SC 60mph

**1936 PUCH TYPE 800
AUSTRIA**

· 1937 ·

FN MILITARY MODEL 12
(Belgium)

As the threat of the Second World War became more apparent, a number of countries began to prepare their armed forces. Large scale motorization of the Belgian military began in 1936, and the FN military model M–12 motor cycle was introduced and adopted the following year. This machine was designed for multi-terrain use with a sidecar attached. For this purpose, the model had a shaft driven sidecar wheel and four-speed with reverse and ratio-change gearbox. Further specification included large section tires, high clearance mudguards, a carburettor sand filter, high level exhaust system, and a high ground clearance.

The FN military model M–12 was used with various sidecar designs, with and without different mobil machine gun mountings. Experiments with various partly or completely enclosed armour protection were also undertaken. From 1939, a number of tricycle derivatives were also adopted for military service. Known as the FN Tricar, this model could carry a payload of 600g or five people. These two FN military models were only used by the Belgian armed forces until 1940 when the factory and machines were commandeered by the German military during their occupation of Belgium. The FN military model M–12 was adopted by the German armed forces, and used for general reconnaissance type duties throunghout this period.

Brief specification

ENGINE TYPE	: FN – Transverse opposed twin cylinder
DISPLACEMENT	: 992cc (90×78mm)
VALVE DESIGN	: Side valves
COMPRESSION	: 5:1
POWER OUTPUT	: 22BHP
ELECTRICS	: 6 volt
CARBURETTOR	: One – Amal
GEARBOX	: Hand change, 4/R×2 speed, unit construction
TRANSMISSION	: Enclosed shaft final drive
FRAME	: Tubular construction
SUSPENSION	: Friction damped parallelogram front forks
	: No rear suspension
TIRE SIZE	: 16×4.75″
BRAKES	: Internal expanding front wheel drum
	: Internal expanding rear wheel drum
DRY WEIGHT	: W/SC 300kg
DIMENSIONS	: Wheel base 1510mm, Ground clearance 200mm
MAX SPEED	: W/SC 55mph

**1937 FN MILITARY MODEL 12
BELGIUM**

· 1937 ·

JAWA MODEL 175
(Czechoslovakia)

With the failure to gain a market with their first attempt at motor cycle production in 1929, the Janeck factory of Prague introduced the inexpensive Jawa model 175 in 1932. This machine had a single-cylinder 175cc two-stroke engine mounted in a pressed steel frame with front fork suspension. The engine was built under license from the British Villiers company, but as the Czechoslovak factory became more competent, the Villiers engine was replaced with a unit of their own design and built under the Schnurle patent.

Within a few years, the Jawa model 175 dominated domestic sales. it is not surprising therefore that the machine was also adopted by the newly formed Czechoslovak armed forces in 1937. The military conversion included a pair of pannier bags or rear carrier rack, provision for masked lighting, and an overall coat of khaki paint. This machine remained in production until the Second World War, during which period a number were also used by the German military.

Brief specification

ENGINE TYPE	: Jawa – Vertical single cylinder
DISPLACEMENT	: 172cc (57.2×67mm)
VALVE DESIGN	: Two stroke
COMPRESSION	: 5.8:1
POWER OUTPUT	: 5.5BHP at 3,750rpm
ELECTRICS	: 6 volt
CARBURETTOR	: One – Villiers
GEARBOX	: Hand change, 3 speed, separate unit
TRANSMISSION	: Enclosed chain primary drive
	: Exposed chain final drive
FRAME	: Pressed steel construction
SUSPENSION	: Friction damped parallelogram front forks
	: No rear suspension
TIRE SIZE	: 19×3.00″
BRAKES	: Internal expanding front wheel drum
	: Internal expanding rear wheel drum
DRY WEIGHT	: Solo 90kg
DIMENSIONS	: Wheel base 1295mm
MAX SPEED	: Solo 50mph

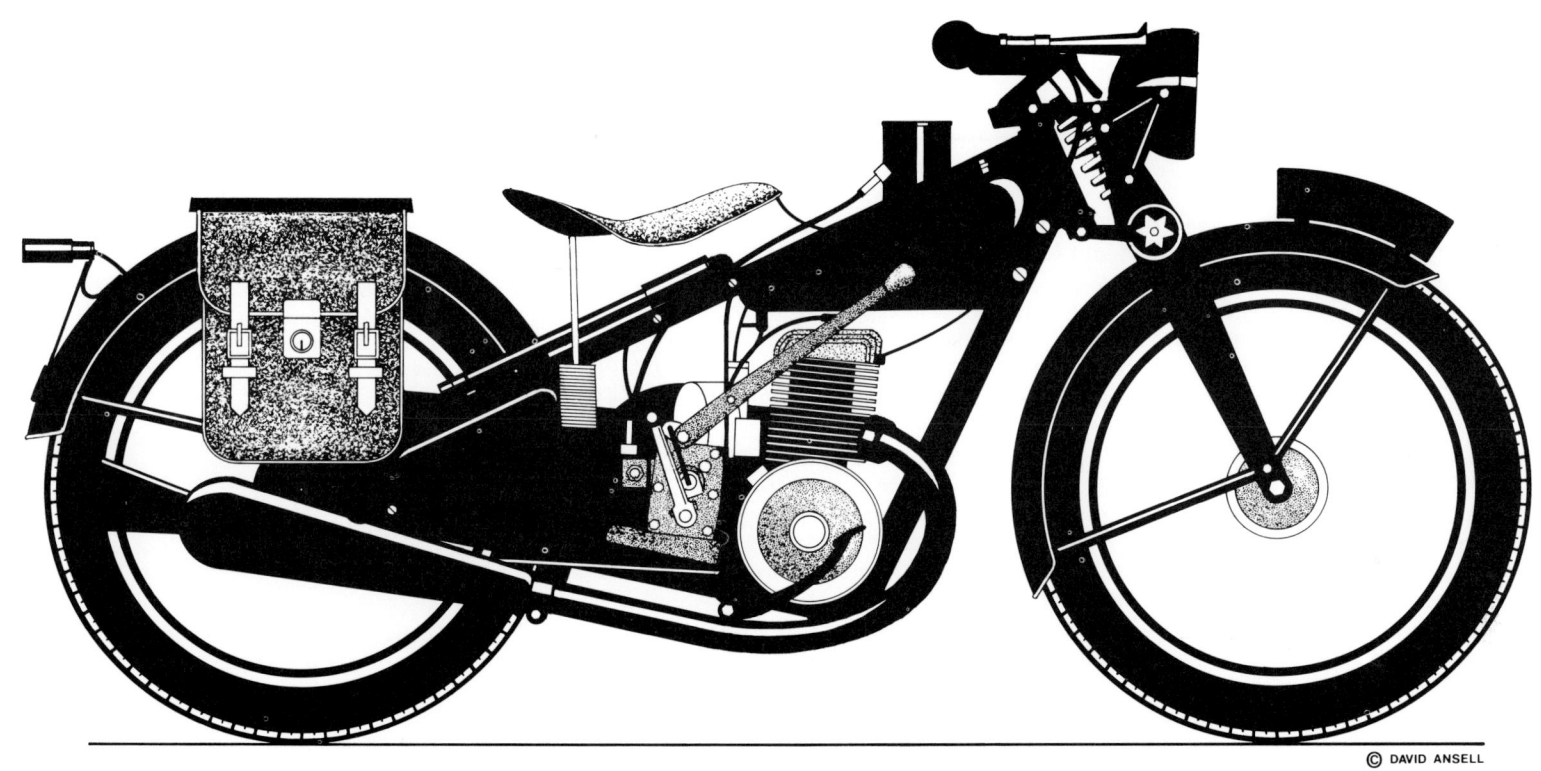

JAWA 1937 JAWA MODEL 175 CZECHOSLOVAKIA

· 1937 ·
NIMBUS MODEL 750
(Denmark)

The Fisker and Nielsen factory of Copenhagen manufactured their second Nimbus motor cycle design between 1934 and 1959. This machine featured a unit construction in-line four-cylinder 750cc engine and three-speed gearbox with a shaft final drive, mounted within a pressed steel cycle frame with telescopic front fork suspension. While quite advanced when first introduced, this model remained virtually unchanged during its entire production period. The major developments were introduced in 1936, when a foot gear change, heavier telescopic front forks, and larger drum brakes were adopted.

Although not produced in any great numbers, about 20 per cent of the 12,715 Nimbus machines produced during this period were adopted by the Danish armed forces between 1937 and 1955. These machines were used both solo and with various sidecars attached with little military modification. The military conversion included a pair of convas pannier bags, a carrier rack or pillion pan-type saddle mounted on the rear mudguard, and an overall coat of khaki paint. A number of these machines adopted before the Second World War were also equipped with a machine gun carrying sidecar. Their general characteristics were well suited to military service, and a number were still being used during the late 1970's.

Brief specification

ENGINE TYPE	: Fisker & Nielsen – Vertical four cylinder
DISPLACEMENT	: 746cc (60×66mm)
VALVE DESIGN	: Overhead valves
COMPRESSION	: 5.4:1
POWER OUTPUT	: 22BHP at 4,500rpm
ELECTRICS	: 6 volt, 70 watt
CARBURETTOR	: One
GEARBOX	: Foot change, 3 speed, unit construction
TRANSMISSION	: Exposed shaft final drive
FRAME	: Pressed steel construction
SUSPENSION	: Hydraulic damped telescopic front forks
	: No rear suspension
TIRE SIZE	: 19×3.5″
BRAKES	: Internal expanding front wheel drum ∅ 180mm
	: Internal expanding rear wheel drum ∅ 180mm
DRY WEIGHT	: Solo 185kg
DIMENSIONS	: Wheel base 1397mm
MAX SPEED	: Solo 75mph

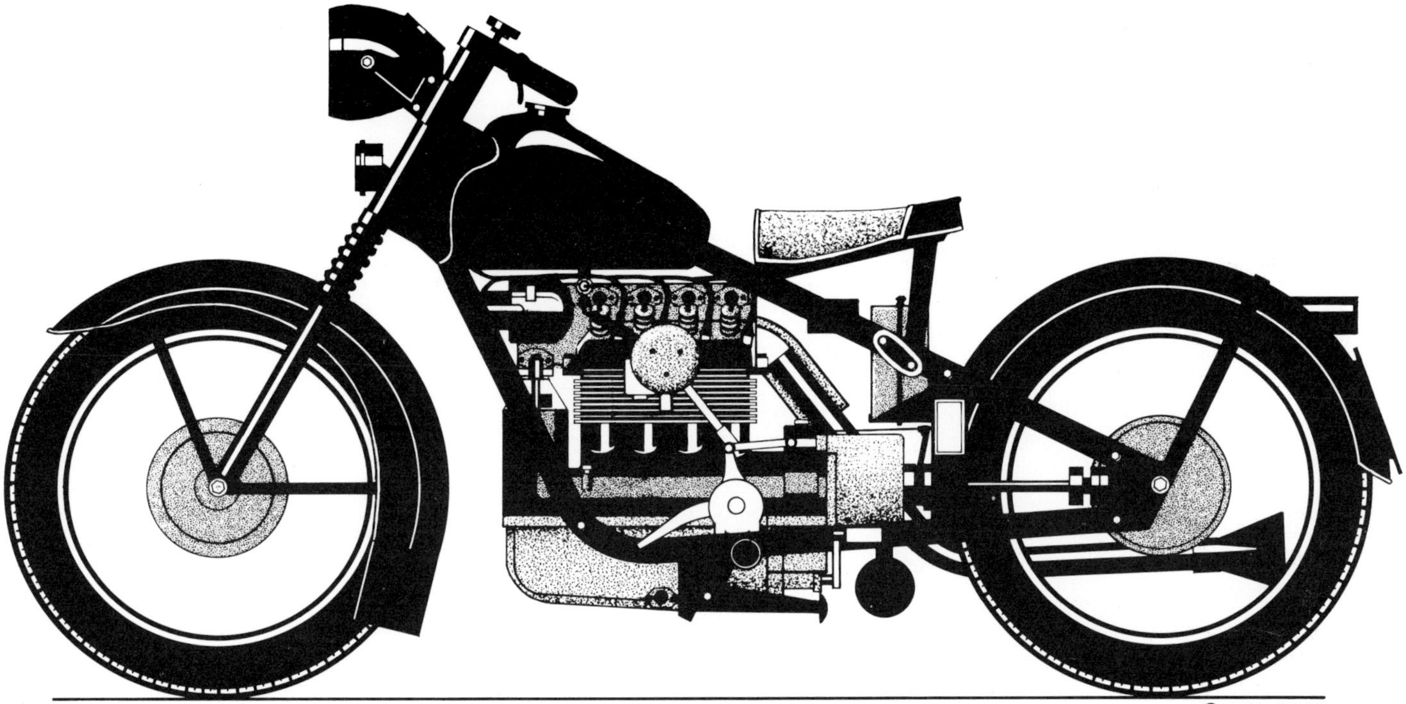

**1937 NIMBUS MODEL 750
DENMARK**

· 1937 ·
SUECIA MILITARY 500
(Sweden)

The Suecia Verken Motor AB factory was founded by Axel Lofstrom, in the small village of Orelljunga, in 1928. During the limited production period of this company, these machines were equipped with a variety of proprietory engine and gearbox units. The first Suecia models adopted the British single-cylinder Blackburn engines of 350cc, and 500cc, and 600cc capacity, with the British three-speed Sturmey-Archer gearbox. These machines were designated 'Sport' models with the overhead valve design, and 'Tourist' models with the side-valve engine lay-out. By the mid 1930's, however, the Suecia factory replaced the Blackburn units with engines from the British JAP and Swiss MAG companies, and the Sturmey-Archer unit with the British four-speed Burman gearbox.

The manufacture of Suecia motor cycles ceased with the declaration of the Second World War. By this time, approximately 5,000 machines had been assembled and the factory had established an excellent reputation, within various competitive events in Sweden. It is not surprising that a number of Suecia machines were supplied to the Swedish armed forces during this period. The Suecia military 500cc was basically a civilian 'Tourist' model with an overall coat of khaki paint; it was supplied both solo, and with a purpose-built Suecia military sidecar attached.

Brief specification

ENGINE TYPE	: MAG – Vertical single cylinder
DISPLACEMENT	: 496cc (82×94mm)
VALVE DESIGN	: Side valves
COMPRESSION	: 5:1
POWER OUTPUT	: 11BHP at 4,000rpm
ELECTRICS	: 6 volt
CARBURETTOR	: One – Amal 76/001
GEARBOX	: Foot change, 4 speed, separate unit
TRANSMISSION	: Enclosed chain primary drive
	: Exposed chain final drive
FRAME	: Tubular construction
SUSPENSION	: Friction damped parallelogram front forks
	: No rear suspension
TIRE SIZE	: 26×3.00″
BRAKES	: Internal expanding front wheel drum
	: Internal expanding rear wheel drum
DRY WEIGHT	: Solo 165kg
DIMENSIONS	: Wheel base 1420mm
MAX SPEED	: Solo 50mph

SUECIA — 1937 SUECIA MILITARY 500 SWEDEN

· 1938 ·
BMW MODEL R–61
(Germany)

The BMW factory of Munich introduced the model R–61 and the similar R–71 machines during 1938. These models had transverse mounted opposed twin-cylinder engines of 600cc and 750cc capacity respectively. While they were the last BMW machines to use the side-valve lay-out, they were also the first to feature a plunger-type rear wheel suspension. Twin-cylinder BMW models were also equipped with two carburettors for the first time during this period.

Although originally designed as civilian machines, the R–61 and R–71 were both adopted by the German armed forces in 1938 to replace the ageing BMW model R–12. They were supplied both solo and with various sidecars attached for escort, despatch, and general reconnaissance service. The military conversion included a pillion pan-type saddle or carrier rack mounted on the rear mudguard, a pair of leather pannier bags, the provision for masked lighting, and an overall coat of grey paint. These machines remained in production until 1941, by which date a total of 13,000 of the model R–61 and 2,000 of the model R–71 had been assembled.

Brief specification

ENGINE TYPE	: BMW – Transverse opposed twin cylinder
DISPLACEMENT	: 600cc (70×78mm)
VALVE DESIGN	: Side valves
COMPRESSION	: 5.7:1
POWER OUTPUT	: 18BHP at 4,800rpm
ELECTRICS	: 6 volt
CARBURETTOR	: Two – Amal or Bing
GEARBOX	: Foot change, 4 speed, unit construction
TRANSMISSION	: Exposed shaft final drive
FRAME	: Tubular construction
SUSPENSION	: Hydraulic damped telescopic front forks
	Undamped plunger rear wheel
TIRE SIZE	: 19×3.5″
BRAKES	: Internal expanding front wheel drum ⌀ 200mm
	: Internal expanding rear wheel drum ⌀ 200mm
DRY WEIGHT	: Solo 184kg
DIMENSIONS	: Wheel base 1400mm, Ground clearance 160mm
MAX SPEED	: Solo 70mph, W/SC 60mph

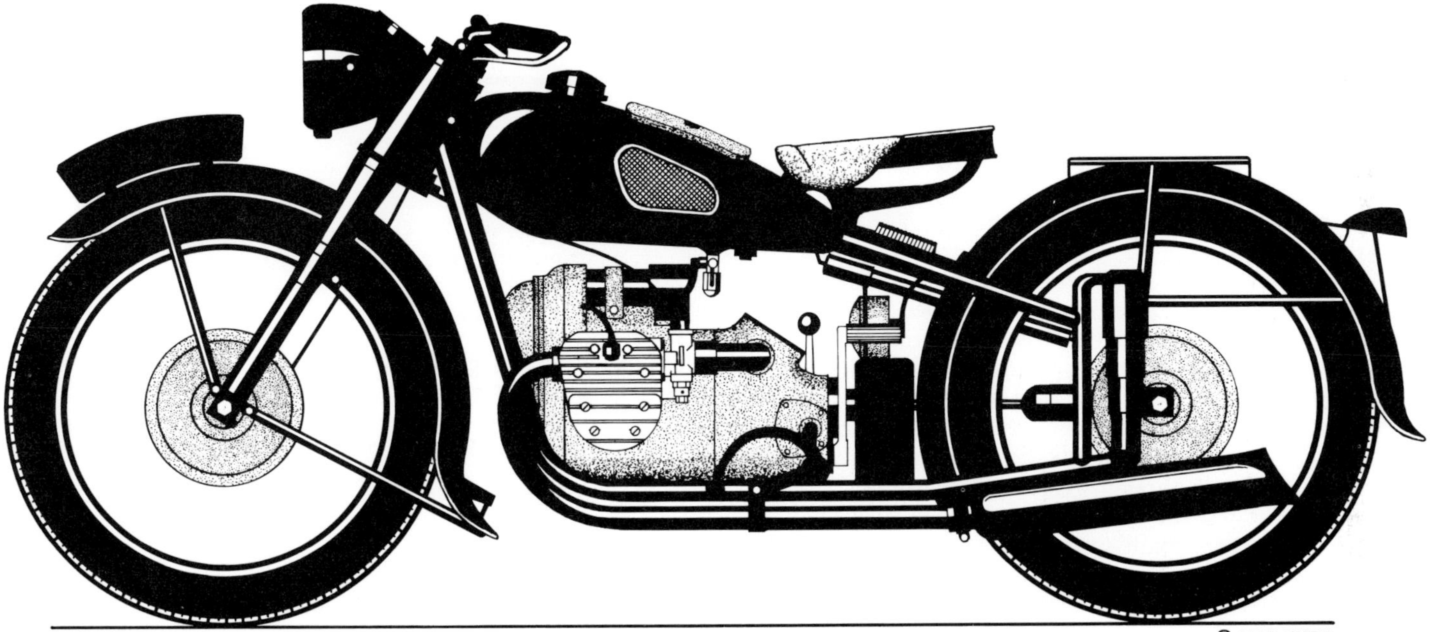

**1938 BMW MODEL R-61
GERMANY**

· 1938 ·
BSA MODEL M20
(Great Britain)

During the year before the Second World War was declared the BSA factory of Birmingham supplied various motorcycle models to a number of armed forces throughout the world – Great Britain, India, S. Africa, Netherlands, etc. The largest overseas order came from the Government of the Netherlands, but the majority of military BSA machines were supplied to the British, and these were basically civilian model M20. The military conversion included a pillion seat or carrier rack mounted on the rear mudguard, a pair of canvas pannier bags, the provision for masked lighting, the adopteion of a carburettor sand filter, and an overall coat of khaki paint.

Although an order for 10,000 machines with a 350cc engine was placed with the BSA factory during the first months of the war by the British War Office, this was soon changed to the 500cc model M20 already in service. It was decided that there would be complications in spares and maintenance if two different BSA models were in service. The BSA model M20 therefore became the most common motor cycle used by the British armed forces during the Second World War, and the BSA factory supplied approximately one third of all the motor cycles supplied by British manufacturers. The majority of these machines were used for solo despatch rider service, while a number were also used with various sidecars attached.

Brief specification

ENGINE TYPE	: BSA – Vertical single cylinder
DISPLACEMENT	: 496cc (82×94mm)
VALVE DESIGN	: Side valves
COMPRESSION	: 4.9:1
POWER OUTPUT	: 13BHP at 4,000rpm
ELECTRICS	: 6 volt
CARBURETTOR	: Two – Amal 76/014
GEARBOX	: Foot change, 4 speed, separate unit
TRANSMISSION	: Enclosed chain primary drive
	: Exposed chain final drive
FRAME	: Tubular construction
SUSPENSION	: Friction damped parallelogram front forks
	: No rear suspension
TIRE SIZE	: 19×3.25″
BRAKES	: Internal expanding front wheel drum ⌀ 7″
	: Internal expanding rear wheel drum 7″
DRY WEIGHT	: Solo 175kg
DIMENSIONS	: Wheel base 1370mm, Ground clearance 110mm
MAX SPEED	: Solo 60mph

BSA

1938 BSA MODEL M20
GREAT BRITAIN

· 1938 ·
NSU MODEL 251–OSL
(Germany)

The NSU factory of Neckarsulm did not return to full production until 1922, and these machines remained basically pre-war designs until 1924, when a range of unit construction models was introduced. It was with these designs that the NSU factory successfully pioneered line production in 1929. That year the Norton racing engine designer Walter Moore also joined the factory and a range of racing models were introduced, but, due to the world depression, these expensive machines were discontinued within a few years, and the NSU factory concentrated on their utility models.

With the recovery of the German economy, the Neckarsulm factory began to assemble larger machines and the NSU model 251–OSL was introduced in 1934. This machine quickly became successful within domestic sales, and was supplied to the German armed forces between 1938 and 1940. The military conversion included a crankcase shield, a larger carburettor filter, a pair of leather pannier bags, and an overall coat of grey paint. The NSU model 251–OSL remained in military service throughout the Second World War for solo despatch type duties.

Brief specification

ENGINE TYPE	: NSU – Vertical single cylinder
DISPLACEMENT	: 241cc (64×75mm)
VALVE DESIGN	: Overhead valves
COMPRESSION	: 6.8:1
POWER OUTPUT	: 10.5BHP at 5,300rpm
ELECTRICS	: 6 volt
CARBURETTOR	: One – Graetzin or Amal
GEARBOX	: Foot change, 4 speed, separate unit
TRANSMISSION	: Enclosed chain primary drive
	: Enclosed chain final drive
FRAME	: Tubular construction
SUSPENSION	: Friction damped parallelogram front forks
	: No rear suspension
TIRE SIZE	: 19×3.00″
BRAKES	: Internal expanding front wheel drum
	: Internal expanding rear wheel drum
DRY WEIGHT	: Solo 144kg
DIMENSIONS	: Wheel base 1320mm, Ground clearance 120mm
MAX SPEED	: Solo 60mph

**1938 NSU MODEL 251-OSL
GERMANY**

· 1938 ·
NSU MODEL 601–OSL
(Germany)

With the recovery of the German economy, the NSU factory of Neckarsulm began to introduce larger capacity motor cycles during the mid 1930's. During this period the OSL range of machines was assembled and, after continued development and an increase in engine performance, the NSU model 601–OSL was introduced in 1938. As other examples of this model range, the 601–OSL featured a fully enclosed chain drive, and was offered with either a standard or the popular high-level exhaust system. This machine quickly proved successful within domestic sales, and remained in production during the pre-war period.

The NSU model 601–OSL was first adopted by the German armed forces in 1938, and remained in active military service throughout the Second World War. It was used both solo and with various sidecars attached, for despatch, escort, and general reconnaissance duties. A number of the sidecars were also used with various mounted machine guns. The majority of these machines were used with the standard level exhaust system to enable the use of large pannier bags. The military conversion included a crankcase shield, a larger carburettor filter, a pair of leather pannier bags, and an overall coat of grey paint.

Brief specification

ENGINE TYPE	: NSU – Vertical single cylinder
DISPLACEMENT	: 561cc (85×99mm)
VALVE DESIGN	: Overhead valves
COMPRESSION	: 6.5:1
POWER OUTPUT	: 20BHP at 3,800rpm
ELECTRICS	: 6 volt, 45/70 watt
CARBURETTOR	: One – Amal M76/434
GEARBOX	: Foot change, 4 speed, separate unit
TRANSMISSION	: Enclosed chain primary drive
	: Enclosed chain final drive
FRAME	: Tubular construction
SUSPENSION	: Friction damped parallelogram front forks
	: No rear suspension
TIRE SIZE	: 19×3.5 or 4.00″
BRAKES	: Internal expanding front wheel drum
	: Internal expanding rear wheel drum
DRY WEIGHT	: Solo 185kg
DIMENSIONS	: Wheel base 1420mm, Ground clearance 105mm
MAX SPEED	: Solo 60mph

**1938 NSU MODEL 601-OSL
GERMANY**

· 1938 ·
ZÜNDAPP KS–600–W
(Germany)

After continued development and expanding sales, the Zündapp factory was renamed Zündapp GmbH in 1938. With the declaration of the Second World War, all civilian production ceased the following year, and only machines adopted by the German armed forces were manufactured. A number of civilian Zündapp models were found to be suitable for military use with only minor modifications.

The Zündapp model KS–600 was introduced and adopted by the German armed forces in 1938. The military version was designated with a 'W' for Wehrmacht and remained in production until 1941, by which date more than 18,000 had been supplied, almost a quarter of the total Zündapp military motor cycle production during this period. The military conversion included a pillion pan-type saddle mounted on the rear mudguard, a pair of leather pannier bags, a larger carburettor filter, provision for masked lighting, and an overall coat of grey paint. This machine remained in military service throughout the Second World War and was used both solo and with various sidecars attached for escort, despatch, and general reconnaissance.

Brief specification

ENGINE TYPE	: Zündapp – Transverse opposed twin cylinder
DISPLACEMENT	: 597cc (75×67.6mm)
VALVE DESIGN	: Overhead valves
COMPRESSION	: 6.5:1
POWER OUTPUT	: 28BHP at 4,700rpm
ELECTRICS	: 6 volt, 50/70 watt
CARBURETTOR	: One – Amal 25.4mm
GEARBOX	: Hand change, 4 speed, unit construction
TRANSMISSION	: Exposed shaft final drive
FRAME	: Pressed steel construction
SUSPENSION	: Friction damped parallelogram front forks
	: No rear suspension
TIRE SIZE	: 19×3.5 or 4.00″
BRAKES	: Internal expanding front wheel drum
	: Internal expanding rear wheel drum
DRY WEIGHT	: Solo 205kg
DIMENSIONS	: Wheel base 1390mm, Ground clearance 125mm
MAX SPEED	: Solo 75mph, W/SC 60mph

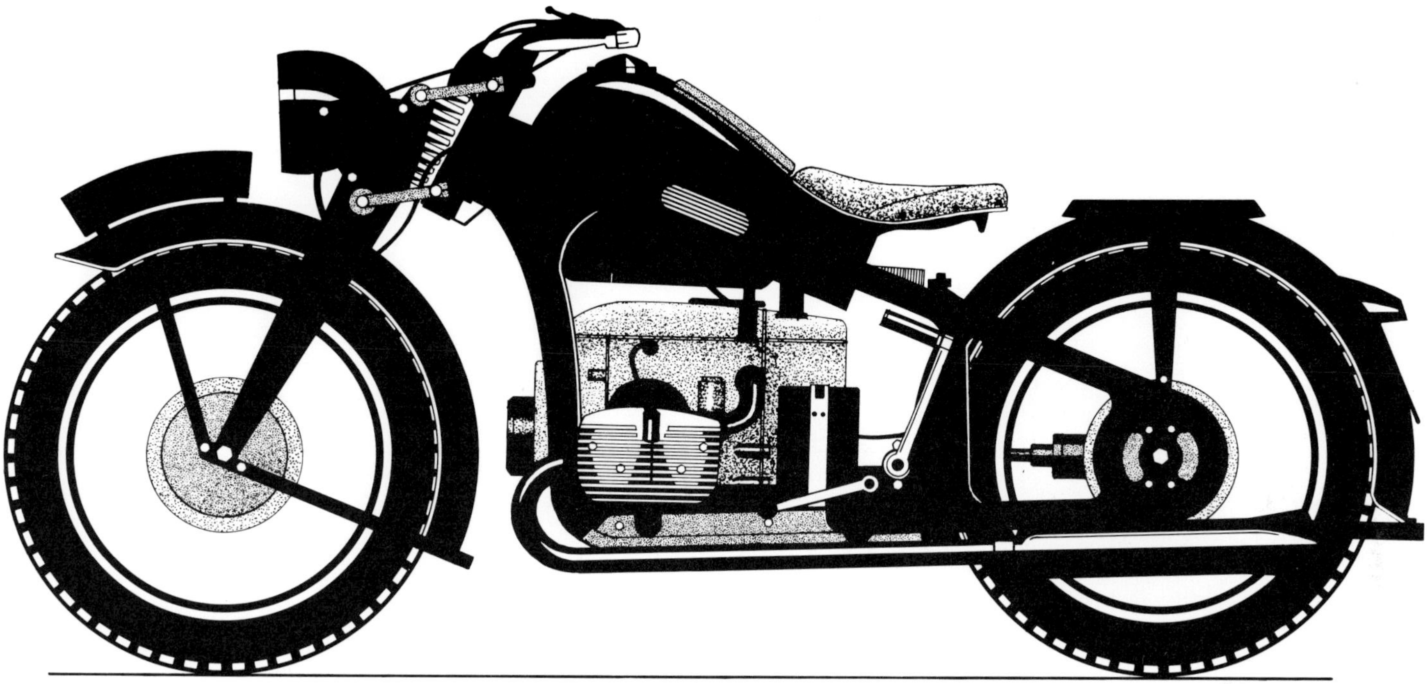

1938 ZÜNDAPP KS-600-W GERMANY

· 1939 ·
BENELLI MODEL 500
(Italy)

The Italian armed forces used a variety of civilian motor cycles during the First World War, and by 1918 had a total of 6,420 of these machines in their possession. The majority were manufactured by the Bianchi and Frera factories. During the 1930's, however, the Italian military adopted a number of motor cycles and their advantages, designed for military service, which were mainly produced by the Benelli, Gilera, and Moto Guzzi factories.

The Benelli factory of Pesaro supplied a number of military machines during the Second World War. The majority of these had a single-cylinder 500cc overhead valve engine, mounted in a tubular frame with girder type front fork suspension. They were used both solo and with various sidecars attached, for escort, despatch, and general reconnaissance duties. A number of tricycle machines derived from this model were also adopted by the Italian military for general load carrying and as a mobile platform for a heavy machine gun mounting.

Brief specification

ENGINE TYPE	: Benelli – Vertical single cylinder
DISPLACEMENT	: 500cc
VALVE DESIGN	: Overhead valves
COMPRESSION	: 5:1
POWER OUTPUT	: 12BHP
ELECTRICS	: 6 volt
CARBURETTOR	: One
GEARBOX	: Foot change, 4 speed, separate unit
TRANSMISSION	: Exposed shaft final drive
	: Exposed chain final drive
FRAME	: Tubular construction
SUSPENSION	: Friction damped parallelogram front forks
	: No rear suspension
TIRE SIZE	: 19×3.5"
BRAKES	: Internal expanding front wheel drum
	: Internal expanding rear wheel drum
DRY WEIGHT	: Solo 182kg
DIMENSIONS	: Wheel base 1397mm
MAX SPEED	: Solo 80mph

BENELLI 1939 BENELLI MODEL 500
ITALY

· 1939 ·

MOTO GUZZI ALCE
(Italy)

The Moto Guzzi Alce was introduced and adopted by the Italian armed forces in 1939. This military designed machine was developed from the Moto Guzzi GT–20 model of the previous year, and equipped with armament carrying fittings, pillion seating or general load carrying, and weather protection for the rider. The 19″ wheels were interchangeable, and the chain drive featured a ratchet, to prevent going backwards when climbing steep hills. Experiments with ski attachments for service on snow were also undertaken.

The Alce (Elk) model was used both solo and with various sidecars attached, and remained in production until 1945, by which date a total of 6,390 solo machines and 669 combinations had been supplied. These machines were used on all fronts during the Second World War, and became the major part of the Italian military motor cycle strength. From 1940 a number of tricycle machines derived from this model were also used by the Italian military for general load carrying and a mobil heavy machine gun mounting.

From 1946 the Moto Guzzi Superalce was introduced and adopted by various Italian police and military departments. This had been developed from the Alce and GTV models during the war years. While the cycle parts of the new model were similar to the Alce, the engine had the overhead valve design of the GTV. The Superalce remained in productions until 1957 with few variations, and was also used both solo and with various sidecars attached.

Brief specification

ENGINE TYPE	: Moto Guzzi – Horizontal single cylinder
DISPLACEMENT	: 498cc (88×82mm)
VALVE DESIGN	: Inlet over exhaust valve
COMPRESSION	: 4.7:1
POWER OUTPUT	: 13.2BHP at 4,000rpm
ELECTRICS	: 6 volt
CARBURETTOR	: One – Dell'Orto MC 26 F
GEARBOX	: Hand change, 4 speed, unit construction
TRANSMISSION	: Exposed chain final drive
FRAME	: Tubular construction
SUSPENSION	: Friction damped parallelogram front forks
	: Friction damped rear sub-frame
TIRE SIZE	: 19×3.5″
BRAKES	: Internal expanding front wheel drum
	: Internal expanding rear wheel drum
DRY WEIGHT	: Solo 179kg
DIMENSIONS	: Wheel base 1455mm, Ground clearance 225mm
MAX SPEED	: Solo 55mph

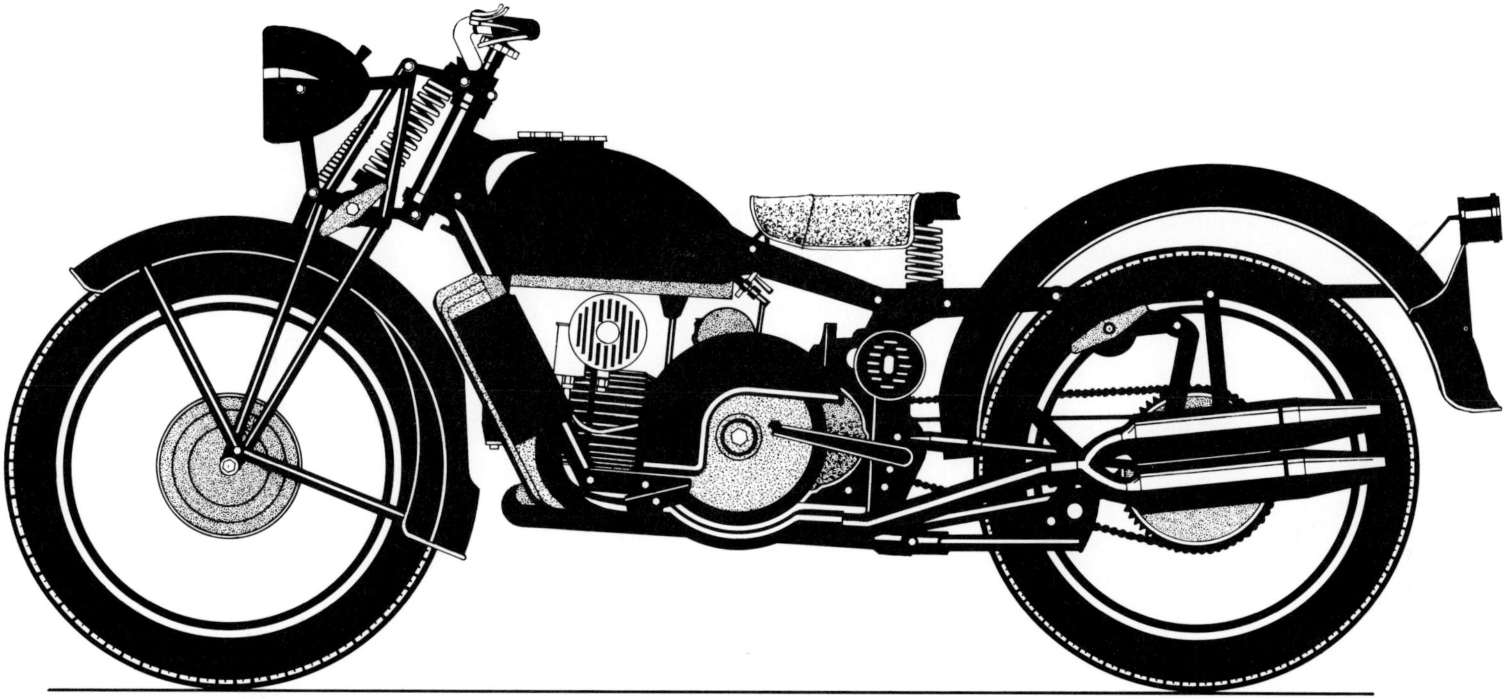

1939 MOTO GUZZI ALCE
ITALY

· 1939 ·

NORTON MODEL 16–H
(Great Britain)

With the declaration of the Second World War, the Norton factory of Birmingham began to supply their 16–H and Big Four models to the British and Allied armed forces. These were basically civilian machines with a little modification. The military conversion of he model 16–H mainly included a crankcase shield, a pillion seat or rear carrier rack, a pair of canvas pannier bags, provision for masked lighting, and an overall coat of khaki paint. The Norton model 16H was used both solo and with various sidecars attached for escort, despatch, and general reconnaissance duties throughout the world, and remained in active military service during the immediate post-war years in a number of armed forces such as Belgium, Canada, France, Great Britain, and the Netherlands.

The Norton Big Four model was a very similar machine, but with an increased engine capacity. This machine had an established reputation as a sidecar machine and the military version continued this tradition and was fitted with a sidecar wheel drive. The military conversion also included a crankcase shield, extra frame support for a pillion seat, large section tires and mudguards, provision for masked lighting, and an overall coat of khaki paint. The sidecar was used with various machine gun mountings, and a sidecar mounted mortar was also experimented with. These machines were used for multi-terrain reconnaissance and general personnel carrying throughout the world.

Brief specification

ENGINE TYPE	: Norton – Vertical single cylinder
DISPLACEMENT	: 490cc (79×100mm)
VALVE DESIGN	: Side valve
COMPRESSION	: 4.9:1
POWER OUTPUT	: 14BHP at 4,500rpm
ELECTRICS	: 6 volt
CARBURETTOR	: One – Amal 276/AE/IBE
GEARBOX	: Foot change, 4 speed, separate unit
TRANSMISSION	: Enclosed chain primary drive
	: Exposed chain final drive
FRAME	: Tubular construction
SUSPENSION	: Friction damped parallelogram front forks
	: No rear suspension
TIRE SIZE	: 19×3.25″
BRAKES	: Internal expanding front wheel drum $\varnothing$ 7″
	: Internal expanding rear wheel drum $\varnothing$ 7″
DRY WEIGHT	: Solo 167kg
DIMENSIONS	: Wheel base 1384mm, Ground clearance 110mm
MAX SPEED	: Solo 65mph

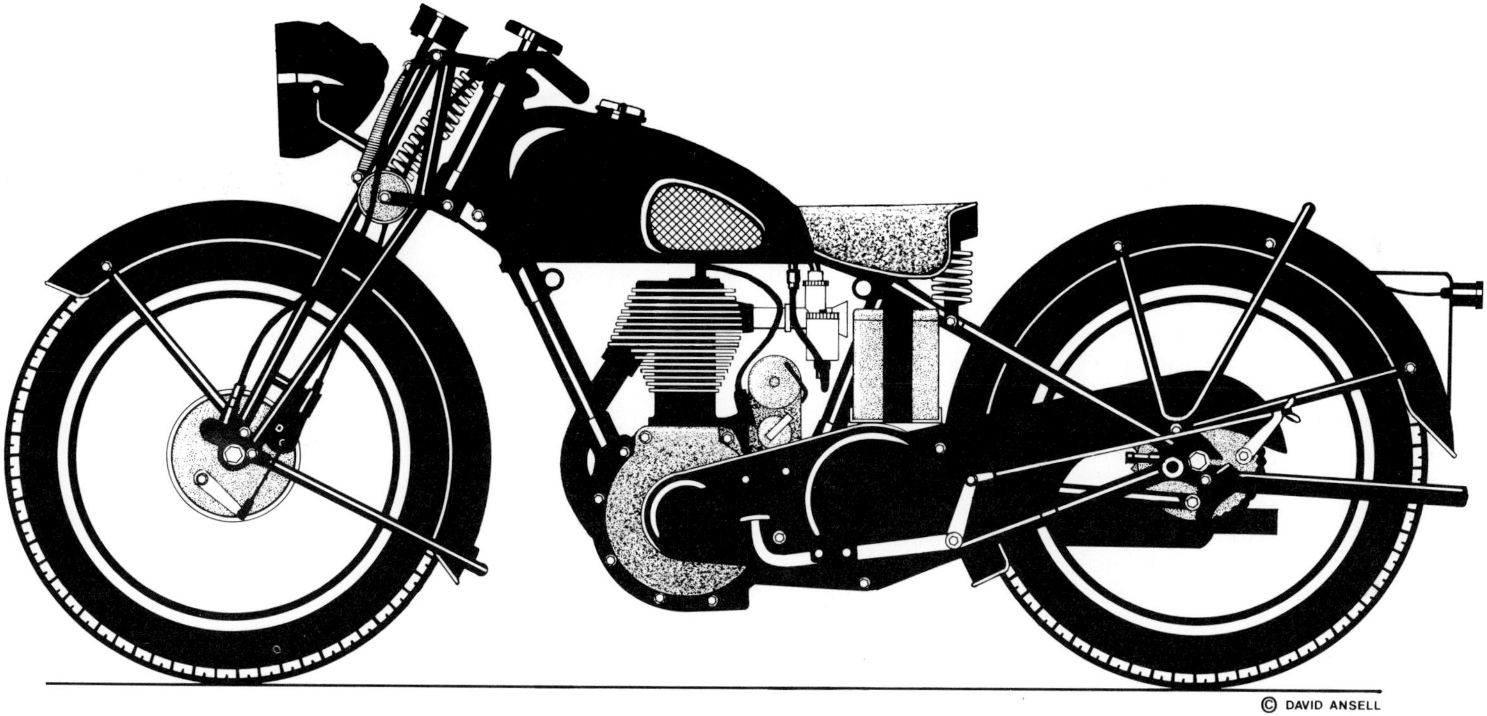

Norton

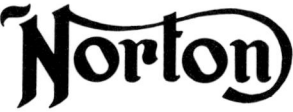

1939 NORTON MODEL 16-H
GREAT BRITAIN

· 1939 ·

SERTUM MODEL 500
(Italy)

The Sertum factory of Milan was founded by Fausto Alberti during the early 1920's for the manufacture of precision instruments. By 1924 the first Sertum motor cycle had been assembled. This machine had a single cylinder 175cc side valve engine and three-speed gearbox of unit construction. With the success of this machine the Sertum factory began to develop further motor cycles, and during the remaining years before the Second World War established a reputation for producing models of simple but lasting design. These machines utilized the majority of engine valve designs, and even a small three-wheel car was produced.

It was not until the late 1930's that the Sertum factory introduced a motor cycle with an engine of more than 250cc capacity; this had a twin cylinder 500cc side valve engine and 4 speed gearbox of unit construction, mounted in a tubular frame with girder-type front fork suspension. The option for a sprung rear sub-frame similar to other contemporary Italian motor cycle manufactures was also available. This machine was adopted by the Italian armed forces during the Second World War, and was used both solo and with various sidecars attached. The military conversion included various armament carrying fittings, pillion seating or general load carrying rack, provision for masked lighting, and a coat of appropriate service livery.

Brief specification

ENGINE TYPE	: Sertum – Vertical twin cylinder
DISPLACEMENT	: 496cc
VALVE DESIGN	: Side valves
COMPRESSION	: 5:1
POWER OUTPUT	: 19BHP at 4,000rpm
ELECTRICS	: 6 volt
CARBURETTOR	: One
GEARBOX	: Hand change, 4 speed, unit construction
TRANSMISSION	: Exposed chain final drive
FRAME	: Tubular construction
SUSPENSION	: Friction damped parallelogram front forks
	: No rear suspension
TIRE SIZE	: 19×3.5″
BRAKES	: Internal expanding front wheel drum
	: Internal expanding rear wheel drum
DRY WEIGHT	: Solo 181kg
DIMENSIONS	: Wheel base 1397mm
MAX SPEED	: Solo 60mph

Sertum

1939 SERTUM MODEL 500 ITALY

· 1939 ·
TERROT TYPE HDA
(France)

From 1901 the Terrot factory of Dijon began to establish a reputation for producing motor cycles of reliable and lasting design. As a result, the company supplied a purpose built military machine to the French armed forces during the First World War. This model had a Swiss built MAG V-twin 500cc engine, and a three-speed gearbox, mounted within a tubular frame with girder-type front fork suspension. These machines were used solo, and with various sidecars attached, for general despatch duties.

The factory introduced its first completely Terrot engineered motor cycle during the mid 1920's. This was known as the type H, and had a single-cylinder 350cc engine, with a three-speed gearbox that featured a pressed steel enclosure. Like a number of manufacturers of this period, the Terrot factory offered both side- and overhead valve versions of their models, with each machine also available with various specifications. In this way, Terrot were able to offer 21 different models by the mid 1930's, and have sold 200,000 machines since 1918. Almost one sixth of this total were the type H machines with the side valve engine design.

It is not surprising therefore that the Terrot type HD was adopted by the French armed forces during the Second World War. The military version was designated with an "A" for Army, and was equipped with a pair of canvas pannier bags, provision for masked lighting, and an overall coat of khaki paint. These machines were used for solo despatch duties.

Brief specification

ENGINE TYPE	: Terrot – Vertical single cylinder
DISPLACEMENT	: 346cc (70×90mm)
VALVE DESIGN	: Side valves
COMPRESSION	: 5.2:1
POWER OUTPUT	: 9BHP at 4,200rpm
ELECTRICS	: 6 volt
CARBURETTOR	: One – Amal 5/012
GEARBOX	: Hand change, 3 speed, separate unit
TRANSMISSION	: Enclosed chain primary drive
	: Exposed chain final drive
FRAME	: Tubular construction
SUSPENSION	: Friction damped parallelogram front forks
	: No rear suspension
TIRE SIZE	: 26×3.5″
BRAKES	: Internal expanding front wheel drum
	: Internal expanding rear wheel drum
DRY WEIGHT	: Solo 136kg
DIMENSIONS	: Wheel base 1346mm
MAX SPEED	: Solo 55mph

TERROT

1939 TERROT TYPE HDA FRANCE

· 1939 ·
TRIUMPH MODEL 3SW
(Great Britain)

Though the Second World War was inevitable, the British armed forces had no military motor cycles prepared for 1939, so the majority of machines adopted at this time were basically civilian models with a khaki finish. At the outbreak of the war the Triumph factory immediately supplied a number of their 3SW and 5SW models. These had single cylinder side-valve engines of 350cc and 500cc displacement respectively. If the Triumph factory of Coventry not been bombed and destroyed in November 1940 these machines would have been replaced by the miliary designed 3TW model, which had a quite different twin-cylinder overhead valve engine of 350cc displacement.

The Triumph 3TW model did not go into production, and when a new factory was completed at Meriden in 1942 manufacture concentrated on the 3HW model. This was an overhead valve version of the 3SW model. A number of the 3HW machines were also built at a temporary Triumph factory at Warwick between late 1940 and early 1942. Although the 3SW and 3HW models were not produced in sufficient numbers for 'front line' service they continued the Triumph tradition of being popular with those to use them. The military conversion of these machines included a carrier rack or pillion seat mounted on the rear mudguard, a pair of canvas pannier bags, the provision for masked lighting, and an overall coat of khaki paint.

Brief specification

ENGINE TYPE	: Triumph – Vertical single cylinder
DISPLACEMENT	: 342cc (70×89mm)
VALVE DESIGN	: Side valves
COMPRESSION	: 5:1
POWER OUTPUT	: 12BHP at 4,800rpm
ELECTRICS	: 6 volt
CARBURETTOR	: One – Amal
GEARBOX	: Foot change, 4 speed, separate unit
TRANSMISSION	: Enclosed chain primary drive
	: Exposed chain final drive
FRAME	: Tubular construction
SUSPENSION	: Friction damped parallelogram front forks
	: No rear suspension
TIRE SIZE	: 19×3.25"
BRAKES	: Internal expanding front wheel drum ⌀ 7"
	: Internal expanding rear wheel drum ⌀ 7"
DRY WEIGHT	: Solo 144kg
DIMENSIONS	: Wheel base 1334mm, Ground clearance 140mm
MAX SPEED	: Solo 60mph

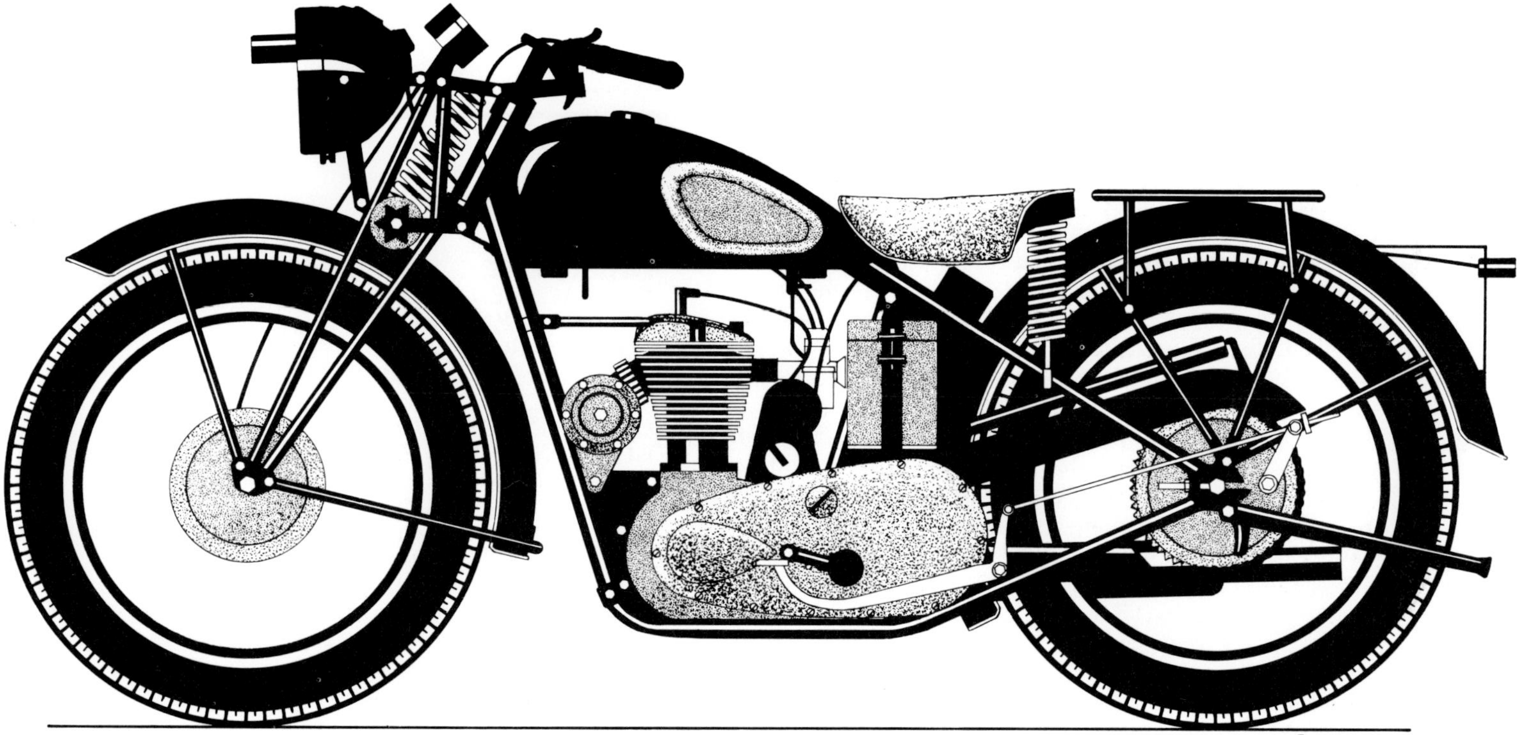

© DAVID ANSELL

TRIUMPH

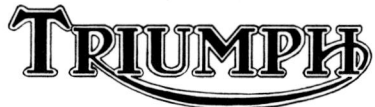

1939 TRIUMPH MODEL 3SW
GREAT BRITAIN

· 1939 ·
ZÜNDAPP DB–200–W
(Germany)

While the Zündapp factory of Nürnburg supplied a number of motor cycles for heavy-duty military service, a large number of the lightweight DB–200 model were also adopted by the German armed forces during the Second World War. This machine had a single cylinder 198cc two-stroke engine and three-speed gearbox in a unit construction, mounted in a tubular frame with pressed steel front fork suspension. This was also one of the few Zündapp models to have a chain final drive during this period.

The Zündapp DB–200 model was introduced in 1935, remained in production until 1940, and was re-introduced after the war between 1947 and 1951. The military version was designated 'W' for Wehrmacht, and was equipped with a pair of leather pannier bags, a rear carrier rack, the provision for masked lighting, and an overall coat of grey paint. This machine was used for solo despatch and general reconnaissance type duties.

Brief specification

ENGINE TYPE	: Zündapp – Vertical single cylinder
DISPLACEMENT	: 198cc (60×70mm)
VALVE DESIGN	: Two stroke
COMPRESSION	: 6:1
POWER OUTPUT	: 7BHP at 4,000rpm
ELECTRICS	: 6 volt, 50 watt
CARBURETTOR	: One – Bing 20mm
GEARBOX	: Hand change, 3 speed, unit construction
TRANSMISSION	: Exposed chain final drive
FRAME	: Tubular construction
SUSPENSION	: Friction damped parallelogram front forks
	: No rear suspension
TIRE SIZE	: 19×3.00″
BRAKES	: Internal expanding front wheel drum
	: Internal expanding rear wheel drum
DRY WEIGHT	: Solo 117kg
DIMENSIONS	: Wheel base 1300mm, Ground clearance 130mm
MAX SPEED	: Solo 50mph

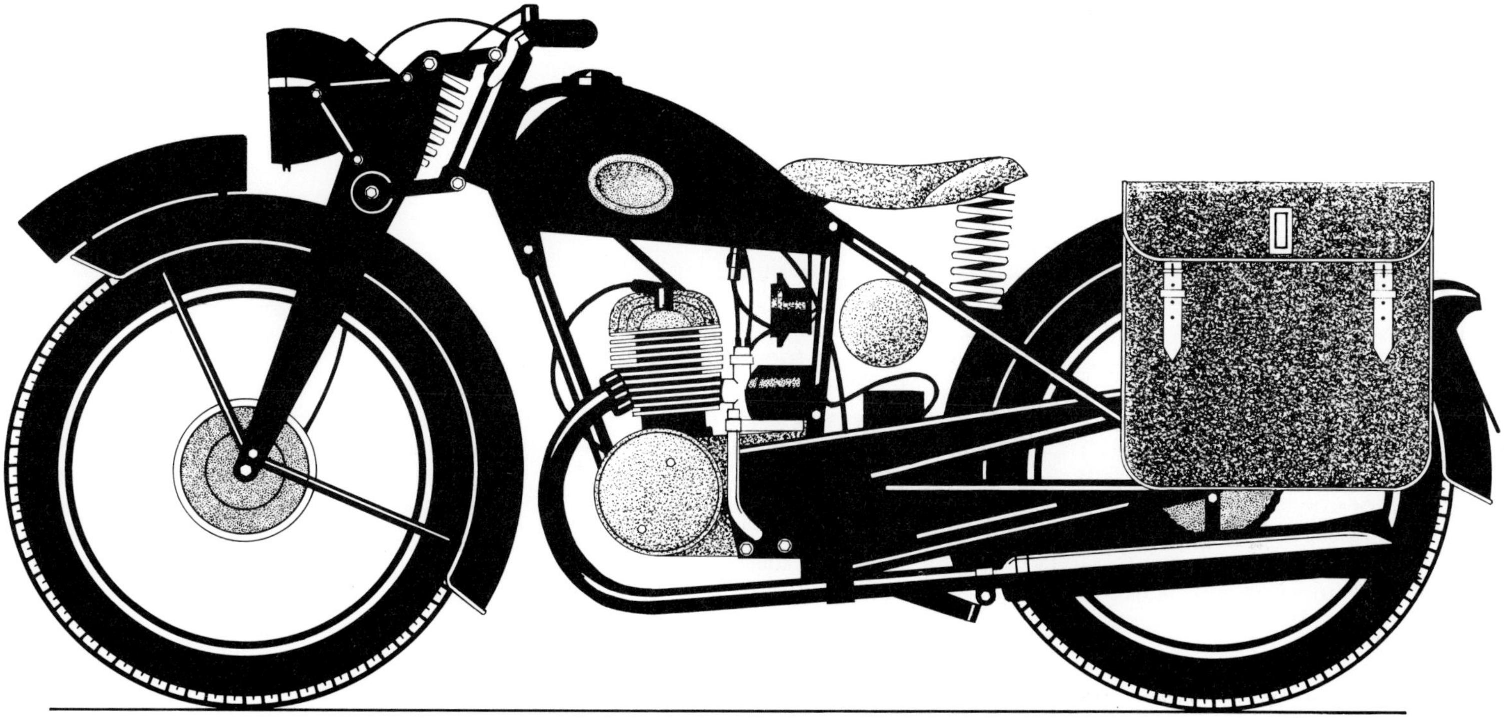

1939 ZÜNDAPP DB-200-W GERMANY

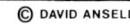

· 1940 ·
ARIEL MODEL W–NG
(Great Britain)

While the Ariel factory of Birmingham continued to manufacture civilian machines into 1940 it also began to supply motor cycles for military service from the outbreak of the Second World War. The British government commandeered all Ariel single-cylinder machines until 1940 when the more suitable W–NG model was introduced. This machine was based upon the successful trials model that had been ridden by Fred Povey in the 1938 Scottish Six Days Trial.

The military conversion of this machine included the removal of the instrument panel from the petrol tank, the adoption of a large bronze bush instead of rollers for the gearbox selector, the removal of the adjustable oil valve, and a repositioned prop stand. The same frame and girder-type front forks were retained, and the machine was given a pillion seat mounted on the rear mudguard, a pair of canvas pannier bags, provision for masked lighting, an extra tool box, and an overall coat of khaki paint.

The Ariel model W–NG remained in production until 1945, by which date a total of 47,599 had been assembled, and it became the most numerous British military motor cycle with an overhead valve type engine. It was used for solo despatch rider duties while on 'front line' service, and a number were used with a machine gun mounted sidecar by the Home Guard.

Brief specification

ENGINE TYPE	: Ariel – Vertical single cylinder
DISPLACEMENT	: 346cc (72×85mm)
VALVE DESIGN	: Overhead valves
COMPRESSION	: 6.5:1
POWER OUTPUT	: 15BHP at 4,800rpm
ELECTRICS	: 6 volt
CARBURETTOR	: One – Amal 275
GEARBOX	: Foot change, 4 speed, separate unit
TRANSMISSION	: Enclosed chain primary drive
	: Exposed chain final drive
FRAME	: Tubular construction
SUSPENSION	: Friction damped parallelogram front forks
	: No rear suspension
TIRE SIZE	: 19×3.25"
BRAKES	: Internal expanding front wheel drum
	: Internal expanding rear wheel drum
DRY WEIGHT	: Solo 159kg
DIMENSIONS	: Wheel base 1360mm, Ground clearance 130mm
MAX SPEED	: Solo 70mph

ARIEL 1940 ARIEL MODEL W-NG
GREAT BRITAIN

· 1940 ·

VELOCETTE MDD–WD
(Great Britain)

With the outbreak of the Second World War, the Veloce motor cycle factory of Birmingham received an order 13,000 machines for the French armed forces. As a result, the pre-war model MAC was modified and supplied as the model MDD. The military conversion included a lower compression, a cylindrical fishtail silencer, a crankcase guard, a lower first gear ratio, and an overall coat of khaki paint. When France fell to the German army, the British government accepted an outstanding 1,200 machines, though no further, required.

After the retreat from Dunkirk the British government re-assessed the usefulness of the motor cycle and placed an order for a further 2,000 military Velocettes. The Veloce factory improved the model MDD and assembled the more suitable model MAF. This machine had the steel crankcase shield replaced by a large alloy forging, and the timing chest cover and gearbox end plate were made in cast iron. To give the same sequence as other British military motor cycles the gearbox operation was also reversed. The Velocette model MAF was equipped with a pillion seat, a pair of canvas pannier bags, and a guard for the lower run of the chain final drive. Approximately 5,000 were produced, a large number being supplied to the RAF.

Brief specification

ENGINE TYPE	: Veloce – Vertical single cylinder
DISPLACEMENT	: 349cc (68×96mm)
VALVE DESIGN	: Overhead valves
COMPRESSION	: 6:1
POWER OUTPUT	: 14BHP at 5,000rpm
ELECTRICS	: 6 volt
CARBURETTOR	: One – Amal
GEARBOX	: Foot change, 4 speed, separate unit
TRANSMISSION	: Enclosed chain primary drive
	: Exposed chain final drive
FRAME	: Tubular construction
SUSPENSION	: Friction damped parallelogram front forks
	: No rear suspension
TIRE SIZE	: 19×3.25″
BRAKES	: Internal expanding front wheel drum ⌀ 6″
	: Internal expanding rear wheel drum ⌀ 6″
DRY WEIGHT	: Solo 154kg
DIMENSIONS	: Wheel base 1327mm, Ground clearance 127mm
MAX SPEED	: Solo 70mph

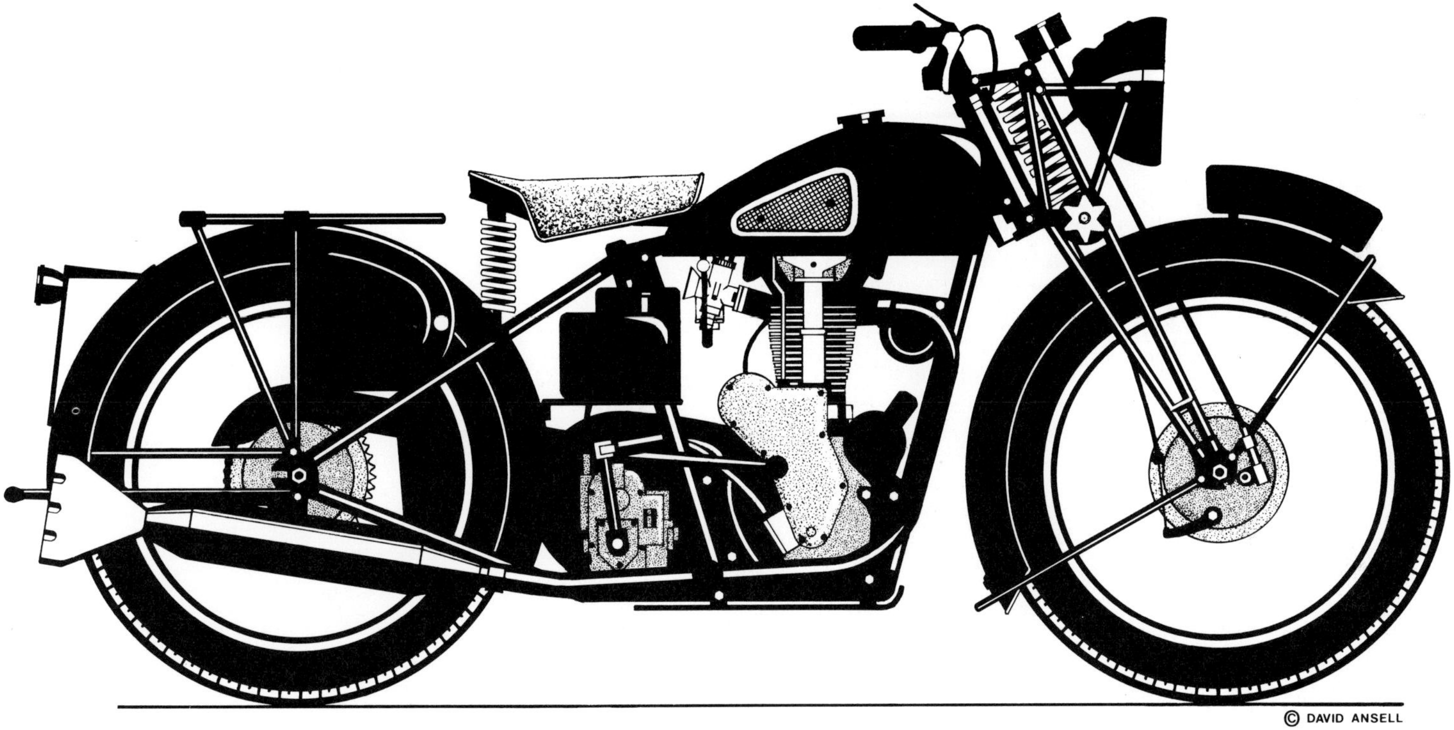

1940 VELOCETTE MDD-WD
GREAT BRITAIN

· 1940 ·
ZÜNDAPP KS–750–W
(Germany)

The Zündapp KS–750–W was first introduced within the desert war of North Africa during the Autumn of 1940. Though quite able during the most severe conditions, it had originally been intended as a toweing vehicle for a light gun of the airborne troops. The towbar had been found to lift the front wheel clear of the ground, and so the model became a multi-terrain fighting machine as an afterthought. While the KS–750 fulfiled these duties beyond all expectations, its cost was double that of the VW jeep, which could offer greater versatility and better weather protection. Even so, these machines remained in service throughout the war, by which time a total of 18,635 had been supplied.

As on earlier Zündapp machines the KS–750 model had a pressed steel cycle frame, but for the first time telescopice front forks replaced the previously used parallelogram suspension. Like other German military motor cycles of this period, the KS–750 had a pillion pan-type saddle mounted on the rear mudguard, a pair of leather pannier bags, provsions for masked lighting, and an overall coat of the appropriate service livery. The Steib designed sidecar also had pannier-type bags mounted forward of the passenger, a spare wheel behind, and was often used as a mobile machine gun mounting. Further specifications to enable multi-terrain use included a ratio change 4 speed and reverse gearbox, sidecar wheel drive, large section tires, and a high ground clearance.

Brief specification

ENGINE TYPE	: Zündapp – Transverse opposed twin cylinder
DISPLACEMENT	: 751cc (75×85mm)
VALVE DESIGN	: Overhead valves
COMPRESSION	: 6.2:1
POWER OUTPUT	: 26BHP at 4,000rpm
ELECTRICS	: 6 volt, 50/70 watt
CARBURETTOR	: One – Solex 30 BFR (H)
GEARBOX	: Hand change, 2×4/R speed, unit construction
TRANSMISSION	: Exposed shaft final drive
FRAME	: Press steel construction
SUSPENSION	: Hydraulic damped telescopic front forks
	: No rear suspension
TIRE SIZE	: 16×4.5 or 4.75"
BRAKES	: Internal expanding front wheel drum
	: Internal expanding rear wheel drum
DRY WEIGHT	: W/SC 400kg
DIMENSIONS	: Wheel base 1410mm, Ground clearance 160mm
MAX SPEED	: W/SC 60mph

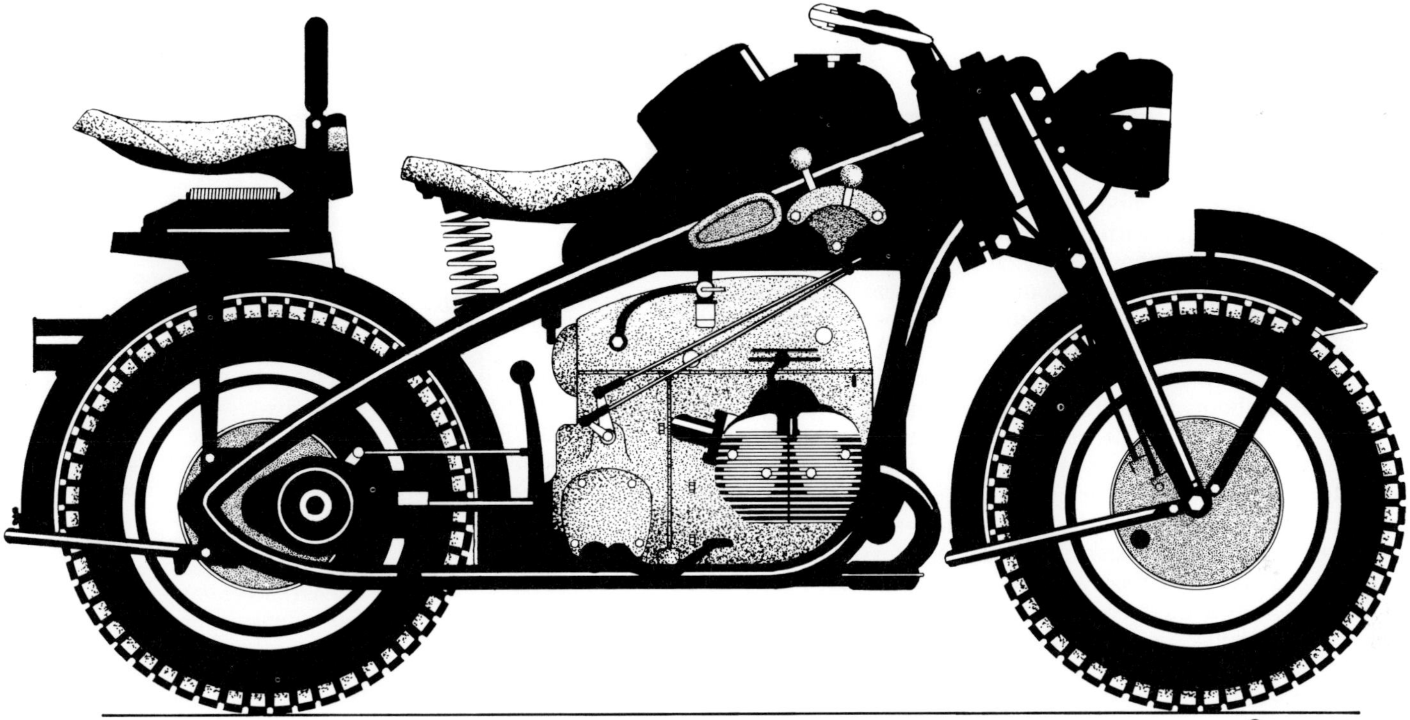

1940 ZÜNDAPP KS-750-W GERMANY

· 1941 ·
BMW MODEL R–75
(Germany)

The specially developed BMW model R–75 had originally been intended as a towing vehicle for a light gun within the airborne troops, but this idea was abandoned when it was found that the towbar weight lifted the front wheel of the ground. While this shortcoming could not be corrected, the machine was adopted as a multi-terrain fighting vehicle by the army. With a ratio change four-speed and reverse gearbox, and a lockable differential to the sidecar wheel, it was found the R–75 could be used almost anywhere. At first, only limited numbers were supplied to operations in North Africa, but as its excellent reputation grew the machine was used throughout Europe and the Russian front.

Like other German military motor cycles of the period, the R–75 had a pillion pan-type saddle mounted on the rear mudguard, a pair of leather pannier bags, the provision for masked lighting, and an overall coat of the appropriate service livery. The Steib designed sidecar also had pannier-type bags mounted forward of the passenger, a spare wheel behind, and was often used as a mobile machine gun mounting. Further specifications to enable multi-terrain use included a high-level exhaust system, large section tires with high clearance mudguards, and replaceable carburettor air filter.

While the R–75 fulfiled its duties beyond all expectations, its cost was double that of the VW jeep, which could offer greater versatility and better weather protection. Even so, these machines remained in service throughout the war, by which date a total of 16,500 had been supplied.

Brief specification

ENGINE TYPE	: BMW – Transverse opposed twin cylinder
DISPLACEMENT	: 745cc (78×78mm)
VALVE DESIGN	: Overhead valves
COMPRESSION	: 5.6 or 5.8:1
POWER OUTPUT	: 26BHP at 4,000rpm
ELECTRICS	: 6 volt, 50 watt
CARBURETTOR	: One – Graetzin Sa 24/1
GEARBOX	: Hand change, 2×4/R speed, unit construction
TRANSMISSION	: Exposed shaft final drive
FRAME	: Tubular construction
SUSPENSION	: Hydraulic damped telescopic front forks
	: No rear suspension
TIRE SIZE	: 16×4.5"
BRAKES	: Internal expanding front wheel drum
	: Internal expanding rear wheel drum
DRY WEIGHT	: W/SC 420kg
DIMENSIONS	: Wheel base 1444mm, Ground clearance 275mm
MAX SPEED	: W/SC 56mph

1941 BMW MODEL R-75 & GERMAN SOLDIERS
© DAVID ANSELL

· 1941 ·
GILERA MILITARY MODEL
(Italy)

Giuseppe Gilera asssembled his first motor cycle in a small workshop in Milan in 1909. Demand for this reliable single-cylinder machine soon forced him to move to larger premises in Arcore, and during the First World War the new factory gained the prestige of officially supplying the Italian military. The Gilera business continued to expand after the war and by 1930 had established an international reputation within competitive events. During the late 1930's the Gilera factory also introduced the 'Planet' model range. These were standard road machines of reliable and lasting design, with both side- and overhead valve engine lay-out and chain or shaft final drive. In Italy, shaft drive was considered more suitable for utility machines and chains were reserved for the more sporting models.

During the Second World War, the Gilera factory supplied a number of machines to the Italian armed forces for various kinds of military service. From 1941, Gilera supplied a military solo model with a chain final drive, and a military combination model with a shaft and sidecar wheel drive. These machines were based upon the pre-war Gilera Mars model, and used the same single-cylinder side-valve engine of 500cc displacement. Further military conversion included various armament carrying fittings, a pillion saddle and carrying rack mounted on the rear mudguard, leg shields with extra tool boxes inside, provision for masked lighting, and an overall coat of the appropriate service livery. These machines were probably also produced by other firms under license, and used throughout Europe and North Africa.

Brief specification

ENGINE TYPE	: Gilera – Vertical single cylinder
DISPLACEMENT	: 498cc (84×90mm)
VALVE DESIGN	: Side valves
COMPRESSION	: 5:1
POWER OUTPUT	: 12BHP at 3,800rpm
ELECTRICS	: 6 volt
CARBURETTOR	: One – Dell'Orto MC 26 F
GEARBOX	: Hand change, 4 speed, separate unit
TRANSMISSION	: Enclosed chain primary drive
	: Exposed chain final drive
FRAME	: Tubular construction
SUSPENSION	: Friction damped parallelogram front forks
	: Friction damped rear sub-frame
TIRE SIZE	: 19×3.5"
BRAKES	: Internal expanding front wheel drum
	: Internal expanding rear wheel drum
DRY WEIGHT	: Solo 190kg
DIMENSIONS	: Wheel base 1450mm, Ground clearance 140mm
MAX SPEED	: Solo 55mph

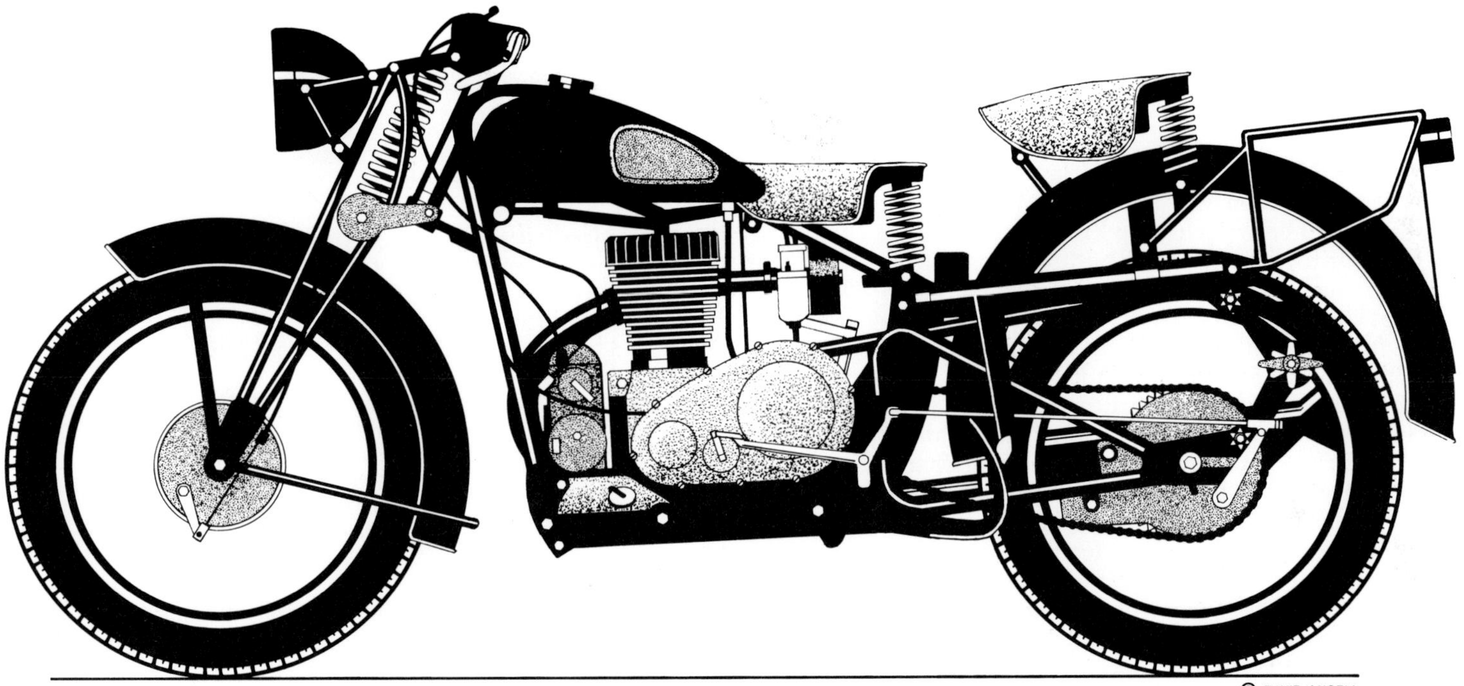

1941 GILERA MILITARY MODEL
ITALY

· 1941 ·
MATCHLESS MODEL G3L
(Great Britain)

When the Second World War was declared, the Matchless motor cycle factory of South London was better able to produce machines for the military than it had been during the First. From 1939 the company began to supply the British armed forces with their civilian G3 model for solo despatch rider use. This machine had a single-cylinder 350cc overhead valve engine and four-speed gearbox, mounted in a tubular cycle frame with girder-type front fork suspension. The military version was designated the W39/G3, and the conversion included a lower compression engine, provision for masked lighting, a rear carrier rack, a pair of canvas pannier bags, a reinforced side stand, and an overall coat of khaki paint.

While this machine was certainly liked by the military riders, from 1941 it was equipped with 'teledraulic' front forks and became the most popular British WD model available. Designated the W41/G3L, this was the first British manufactured motorcycle to feature hydraulic damped telescopic front fork suspension. Other minor differences included the mounting positions of the footrests, the speedometer drive, the rear lights and lifting handles, and the make of pillion seat when fitted. It has been estimaed that the Matchless factory assembled more than 80,000 of these two G3 military models. The Matchless model G3L was used throughout the world during the Second World War, and a large number remained in active military service in various armed forces during the post-war years, e.g. Belgium, Great Britain, Netherlands.

Brief specification

ENGINE TYPE	: Matchless – Vertical single cylinder
DISPLACEMENT	: 347cc (69×93mm)
VALVE DESIGN	: Overhead valves
COMPRESSION	: 6:1
POWER OUTPUT	: 16BHP at 5,500rpm
ELECTRICS	: 6 volt
CARBURETTOR	: One – Amal 275/1
GEARBOX	: Foot change, 4 speed, separate unit
TRANSMISSION	: Enclosed chain primary drive
	: Exposed chain final drive
FRAME	: Tubular construction
SUSPENSION	: Hydraulic damped telescopic front forks
	: No rear suspension
TIRE SIZE	: 19×3.25″
BRAKES	: Internal expanding front wheel drum ⌀ 5.5″
	: Internal expanding rear wheel drum ⌀ 5.5″
DRY WEIGHT	: Solo 149kg
DIMENSIONS	: Wheel base 1340mm, Ground clearance 140mm
MAX SPEED	: Solo 70mph

MATCHLESS — 1941 MATCHLESS MODEL G3L GREAT BRITAIN

· 1942 ·
HARLEY-DAVIDSON WLA
(America)

The Harley-Davidson WL model was adopted by the American and Allied armed forces during the Second World War for solo escort, despatch, and general police duties. The military version was designated with an 'A' for army, and although the WLA model varied a little from one contract to another it remained very similar to the civilian machine. The main differences were a more substantial rear carrying rack, a rifle or machine gun holster mounted on the right front fork, provision for masked lighting, and a crankcase shield. The military specifications also included a pair of leather pannier bags, front and rear crash bars, a handlebar mounted screen, and an overall coat of the appropriate service livery.

For the Canadian armed forces Harley-Davidson produced a variant of the WLA model designated the WLC model. These featured a clutch lever on the left handlebar, a right foot gear change lever, and the horn mounted on top of the headlight rather than beneath it. The Canadian machines were also produced with a pillion saddle, an auxiliary box mounted on top of the front mudguard, and special gear ratios for use with a sidecar. Further military specifications were the same as the WLA.

The WLA and WLC models remained in service throughout the war, during which time almost 80,000 were produced. A large number of these machines continued in military service after the war in various armed forces around the world, e.g. Australia, Belgium, Canada, France, Great Britain, Netherlands, South Africa. Although the American military only retained a relatively small number of motor cycles after 1945, they also adopted a number of the further developed WL model in 1947.

Brief specification

ENGINE TYPE	: Harley-Davdison – V-twin cylinder
DISPLACEMENT	: 742cc (69.85×96.83mm)
VALVE DESIGN	: Side valves
COMPRESSION	: 4.32:1
POWER OUTPUT	: 23BHP at 4,600rpm
ELECTRICS	: 6 volt
CARBURETTOR	: One – Schebler
GEARBOX	: Hand change, 3 speed, separate unit
TRANSMISSION	: Enclosed chain primary drive
	: Exposed chain final drive
FRAME	: Tubular construction
SUSPENSION	: Friction damped leading link front forks
	: No rear suspension
TIRE SIZE	: 18×4.00"
BRAKES	: Internal expanding front wheel drum
	: Internal expanding rear wheel drum
DRY WEIGHT	: Solo 243kg
DIMENSIONS	: Wheel base 1461mm, Ground clearance 102mm
MAX SPEED	: Solo 65mph

HARLEY– DAVIDSON

1942 HARLEY-DAVIDSON WLA AMERICA

· 1942 ·

HARLEY-DAVIDSON XA
(America)

When America entered the Second World War in 1942, the Harley-Davidson factory of Wilwaukee diverted all production to the manufacture of motor cycles for the American and Allied armed forces. At the request of the American military, work also began on a military machine specified for use in North Africa, and the XA model was developed. This machine had a close copy of an early BMW engine with shaft final drive, mounted within a tubular frame with leading link front forks and plunger-type rear wheel suspension. Further major features included, a foot-operated gear change, a carburettor for each cylinder, and an upswept exhaust system.

The Harley-Davidson XA model was designed for both solo and with a sidecar service. The military equipment for this machine included a handlebar mounted screen, front and rear crash bars, an auxiliary box mounted on the left front fork, a pair of leather pannier bags, and the provision for masked lighting. The sidecar was equipped with a large storage compartment and interchangeable spare wheel. Although about 1,000 of these machines were assembled they remained experimental only, as the African phase of the war was almost over when the model went into production. Further factors for this decision included the limited number of interchangeable parts with other Harley-Davidson military models, and the extra training that would have been required for the military mechanics.

Brief specification

ENGINE TYPE	: Harley-Davdison – Transverse opposed twin
DISPLACEMENT	: 739cc (77.8×77.8mm)
VALVE DESIGN	: Side valves
COMPRESSION	: 5.7:1
POWER OUTPUT	: 23BHP at 4,500rpm
ELECTRICS	: 6 volt
CARBURETTOR	: Two – Schebler
GEARBOX	: Hand/Foot change, 4 speed, unit construction
TRANSMISSION	: Exposed shaft final drive
FRAME	: Tubular construction
SUSPENSION	: Friction damped leading link front forks
	: Undamped plunger rear wheel
TIRE SIZE	: 18×4.00″
BRAKES	: Internal expanding front wheel drum
	: Internal expanding rear wheel drum
DRY WEIGHT	: Solo 238kg
DIMENSIONS	: Wheel base 1511mm
MAX SPEED:	: Solo 70mph

Harley– Davidson

1942 HARLEY-DAVIDSON XA AMERICA

· 1942 ·

MONARK MC–42
(Sweden)

The Monark motor cycle factory of Varberg was originally founded as the Svenska Cykeldepoten business, and introduced a single cylinder 3hp model in 1913 known as the Sleipner. These almost forgotten names were replaced shortly after the First World War, when production continued under the name of Esse until the mid 1920's. The machines manufactured at this time were not very successful and, with a further name change to Monark, the factory began the tradition of adopting proprietory components. After experimenting with numerous engine designs of 250 to 600cc capacity from various manufacturers, Monark adopted the products of the German IL0 factory in 1936, but with the declaration of the Second World War, this also became a short term arrangement.

In December 1940, the Swedish armed forces requested a number of the Husqvarna 112 model, for solo despatch rider service. As this factory was heavily committed to other military production at this time, the contract was placed with the Monark and Albin-Motor factories in June 1941. The design, tools, and equipment, were supplied by Husqvarna, the engine was produced by the Albin-Motor business of Kristinehamn, and the final assembly took place at the Monark factory. The result was the Monark MC-42 model. This machine was manufactured in two versions, with either a side- or over-head valve engine design. The military equipment included a pillion pan-type saddle mounted on the rear mudguard, the provision for masked lighting, crankcase shield, and an overall coat of khaki paint.

Brief specification

ENGINE TYPE	: Albin – Vertical single cylinder
DISPLACEMENT	: 495cc (79×101mm)
VALVE DESIGN	: Overhead valves
COMPRESSION	: 6.4:1
POWER OUTPUT	: 20BHP at 4,000rpm
ELECTRICS	: 6 volt, 175 watt
CARBURETTOR	: One
GEARBOX	: Foot change, 3 speed, separate unit
TRANSMISSION	: Enclosed chain primary drive
	: Exposed chain final drive
FRAME	: Tubular construction
SUSPENSION	: Hydraulic damped parallelogram front forks
	: Hydraulic damped plunger rear wheel
TIRE SIZE	: 19×3.5"
BRAKES	: Internal expanding front wheel drum
	: Internal expanding rear wheel drum
DRY WEIGHT	: Solo 200kg
DIMENSIONS	: Wheel base 1410mm, Ground clearance 145mm
MAX SPEED:	: Solo 70mph

Monark   1942 MONARK MC-42
SWEDEN

· 1942 ·

ROYAL ENFIELD WD–RE
(Great Britain)

The Royal Enfield factory of Redditch supplied various motor cycles for military service during the Second World War. These mainly comprised the WD–RE model (a 125cc two-stroke machine), the WD–C model (a 350cc side-valve machine), and the WD–CO model (a 350cc overhead valve machine). All of these models were basically civilian machines with a little military modification. Most numerous was the Royal Enfield WD–CO model: a total of 29,037 were supplied between March 1942 and November 1944, a little more than half of the total motor cycle production at the Redditch factory during the war years. The military conversion of the WD–C and WD–CO models included a pair of canvas pannier bags, a pillion seat or rear carrier rack mounted on the rear mudguard, the provision for masked lighting, and an overall coat of the appropriate service liver. These machines were used for solo despatch rider services throughout the world, and a number remained in active use during the immediate post-war years, in armed forces such as Belgium, France, Great Britain.

Perhaps a better known military machine to be supplied by Royal Enfield during the war was their lightweight WD–RE. Apart from a small increase in engine capacity, this machine was a close copy of the DKW RT–100 model of Germany. It had been developed during the immediate pre-war years as a result of the DKW termination of deliveries to a particular DKW and Royal Enfield agent (Stokvis & Zonen) in the Netherlands. This production was halted until its military potential was realised in late 1942, and the machine eventually gained the name of the Flying Flea after servicing with British and Allied airborne troops. It was also carried into battle on various tracked vehicles.

Brief specification

ENGINE TYPE	: Royal Enfield – Vertical single cylinder
DISPLACEMENT	: 125cc (53.8×55mm)
VALVE DESIGN	: Two stroke
COMPRESSION	: 5.5:1
POWER OUTPUT	: 4.5BHP at 4,500rpm
ELECTRICS	: 6 volt
CARBURETTOR	: One – Villiers
GEARBOX	: Hand change, 3 speed, unit construction
TRANSMISSION	: Exposed chain final drive
FRAME	: Tubular construction
SUSPENSION	: Rubber damped parallelogram front forks
	: No rear suspension
TIRE SIZE	: 19×2.5"
BRAKES	: Internal expanding front wheel drum
	: Internal expanding rear wheel drum
DRY WEIGHT	: Solo 63.5kg
DIMENSIONS	: Wheel base 1219mm
MAX SPEED:	: Solo 40mph

Royal Enfield

1942 ROYAL ENFIELD WD-RE
GREAT BRITAIN

· 1944 ·
INDIAN MODEL 148
(America)

With the increasing reports of Allied and Axis military use of motor cycles, the American military placed contracts with the Indian and Harley-Davidson companies for as many suitable machines as they could manufacture. At the Indian factory, this resulted in the conversion of the 500cc Junior and 750cc Scout models. Originally designated 640A and 640B respectively, these machines became 741A and 741B military models the following year. The 1200cc Chief model was also designated the 340 military model for use with a sidecar. These three Indian models were used throughout the world during the war, and a large number remained in active military service within various armed forces during the post-war years, e.g. Australia, Belgium, Canada, France, Great Britain, Netherlands, South Africa.

A further military motor cycle to be supplied to the American armed forces during the Second World War was the Indian model 148. This lightweight machine had a single-cylinder side-valve engine mounted in a tubular frame with girder-type front fork suspension and was equipped with parachute rings for use with airborne troops. The model 148 remained in active military service until the early 1950's when it was superseded by the more powerful Indian model 149. This machine had a single-cylinder overhead valve engine mounted in a tubular frame with telescopic front fork suspension.

Brief specification

ENGINE TYPE	: Indian – Vertical single cylinder
DISPLACEMENT	: 221cc (63.5×69.85mm)
VALVE DESIGN	: Side valves
COMPRESSION	: 4.75:1
POWER OUTPUT	: 6.3BHP at 4,800rpm
ELECTRICS	: 6 volt
CARBURETTOR	: One
GEARBOX	: Hand change, 3 speed, separate unit
TRANSMISSION	: Enclosed chain primary drive
	: Exposed chain final drive
FRAME	: Tubular construction
SUSPENSION	: Friction damped parallelogram front forks
	: No rear suspension
TIRE SIZE	: 18×3.00″
BRAKES	: Internal expanding front wheel drum
	: Internal expanding rear wheel drum
DRY WEIGHT	: Solo 113kg
DIMENSIONS	: Wheel base 1270mm
MAX SPEED:	: Solo 45mph

Indian 1944 INDIAN MODEL 148 AMERICA

· 1947 ·
JAWA 250 PERAK
(Czechoslovakia)

The Janeck factory of Prague was used to repair German military motor cycles during the Second World War occupation of Czechoslovakia. At the same time, the Jawa designers were secretly developing a new motor cycle model. This machine had a unit construction single-cylinder 250cc two-stroke engine and four-speed gearbox with a semi-automatic clutch. This was mounted within a pressed steel and tubular cycle frame with telescopic front forks and plunger-type rear wheel suspension. This advanced design was introduced as the Jawa 250 Perak.

With this machine the Janeck factory started to establish an international reputation for producing motor cycles of reliable and lasting design, and, as a result, produced approximately 60,000 a year during the immediate post-war period. This achivement was certainly noted by the Czechoslovakia military and the Jawa 250 Perak was adopted for despatch and general police duties in 1947. This machine was used both solo and with various sidecars attached, and remained in service for ten years when superseded by the more powerful Jawa 350 Kyvacka. The military conversion included a pair of pannier bags, and an overall coat of khaki paint.

Brief specification

ENGINE TYPE	: Jawa – Vertical single cylinder
DISPLACEMENT	: 248cc (65×75mm)
VALVE DESIGN	: Two stroke
COMPRESSION	: 6:1
POWER OUTPUT	: 9BHP at 4,200rpm
ELECTRICS	: 6 volt
CARBURETTOR	: One – Jikov
GEARBOX	: Foot change, 4 speed, unit construction
TRANSMISSION	: Exposed chain final drive
FRAME	: Pressed steel & Tubular construction
SUSPENSION	: Hydraulic damped telescopic front forks
	: Hydraulic damped plunger rear wheel
TIRE SIZE	: 19×3.25″
BRAKES	: Internal expanding front wheel drum
	: Internal expanding rear wheel drum
DRY WEIGHT	: Solo 113kg
DIMENSIONS	: Wheel base 1295mm
MAX SPEED:	: Solo 60mph

JAWA

**1947 JAWA 250 PERAK
CZECHOSLOVAKIA**

· 1948 ·
CONDOR MODEL A–580
(Switzerland)

For many years the Swiss armed forces converted various commercial motor cycles for military service, both solo and with various sidecars attached. A number of two-wheeled trailers were also adopted. After the Second World War, the majority of Swiss military motor cycles were built to army specifications, and a number were also assembled by more than one manufacturer.

From 1945 the Condor motor cycle factory of Courfaivre began to concentrate production on machines for military service. The Condor model A–580 was introduced and adopted by the Swiss armed forces in 1948. This machine had a unit construction opposed twin cylinder 580cc side-valve engine and four-speed with a ratio change gearbox. For multi-terrain use a high ground clearance was maintained with the exhaust system mounted above the lowest frame members and the silencer between the upper and lower rear frame forks. This machine was used both solo and with various sidecars attached, for despatch, escort, and general police duties. The military equipment included a pair of canvas pannier bags, a pan-type saddle mounted on the rear mudguard, and an overall coat of khaki paint.

Within a few years, this machine was superseded by the Condor model A–580–1. The new machine featured improved telescopic front forks and plunger-type rear wheel suspension, and a redesigned exhaust system. Further military equipment also included an auxiliary masked headlight mounted on the front mudguard. The Condor '580' series remained in service until 1977 by which date a total of 4,420 had been supplied.

Brief specification

ENGINE TYPE	: Condor – Transverse opposed twin cylinder
DISPLACEMENT	: 578cc (70×75.2mm)
VALVE DESIGN	: Side valves
COMPRESSION	: 6:1
POWER OUTPUT	: 19.8BHP at 4,400rpm
ELECTRICS	: 6 volt
CARBURETTOR	: One – OBA type 20
GEARBOX	: Foot change, 4× speed, unit construction
TRANSMISSION	: Enclosed shaft final drive
FRAME	: Tubular construction
SUSPENSION	: Hydraulic damped telescopic front forks
	: No suspension
TIRE SIZE	: 19×3.5"
BRAKES	: Internal expanding front wheel drum
	: Internal expanding rear wheel drum
DRY WEIGHT	: Solo 195kg
DIMENSIONS	: Wheel base 1450mm, Ground clearance 160mm
MAX SPEED:	: Solo 75mph

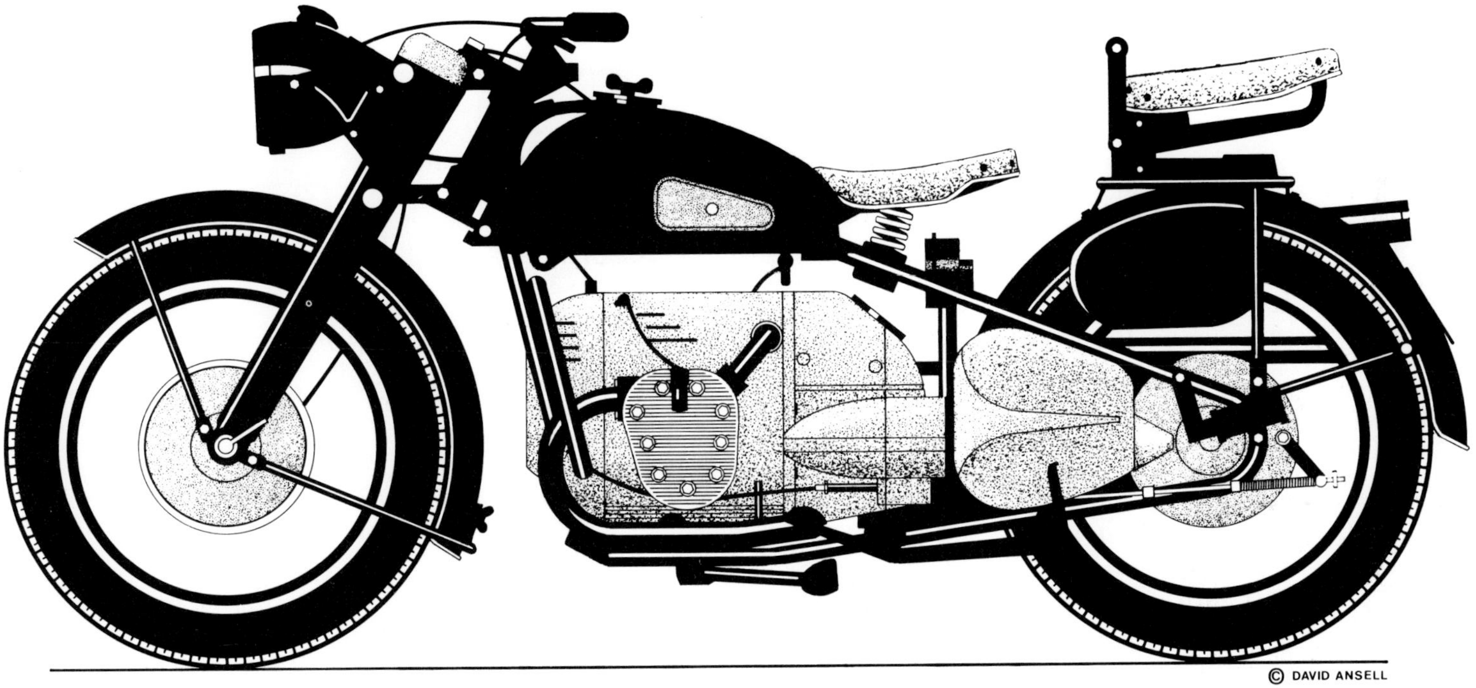

1948 CONDOR MODEL A-580
SWITZERLAND

· 1948 ·
TRIUMPH MODEL TRW
(Great Britain)

During the latter years of the Second World War the British Ministry of Supply prepared a list of minimum requirements for the ideal military motor cycle. These included a weight of not more than 136 Kg, a ground clearance of 153mm, a petrol consumption of 80mpg at 30mph, and to be inaudible from half a mile. In response Edward Turner designed the model TRW and the prototype was assembled at the Triumph factory in 1944. This machine was very similar to the Bert Hopwood designed model 5TW of 1942, but with a lighter aluminium engine with spur timing gears instead of a chain and a fully enclosed chain drive. The model 5TW had been the first Triumph motorcycle to feature telescopic front fork suspension.

Neither of these machines went into production, and in 1948 the Ministry of Supply stated that the TRW was too expensive. To reduce cost, the Triumph factory assembled the TRW engine within the civilian cycle components then in production. In this way the hybrid model looked like a Triumph Trophy with the engine modified for side valve design. A similar second version was later introduced with a cast iron cylinder head. With so many unwanted motor cycles after the war and British army only bought twelve of these machines. From the early 1950's, a number of the Triumph model TRW were supplied to other British and armed forces throughout the world, and the machine remained in production until the early 1960's.

Brief specification

ENGINE TYPE	: Triumph – Vertical twin cylinder
DISPLACEMENT	: 498cc (63×80mm)
VALVE DESIGN	: Side valves
COMPRESSION	: 6:1
POWER OUTPUT	: 16.8BHP at 5,000rpm
ELECTRICS	: 6 volt
CARBURETTOR	: One – Solex WH–2
GEARBOX	: Foot change, 4 speed, separate unit
TRANSMISSION	: Enclosed chain primary drive
	: Exposed chain final drive
FRAME	: Tubular construction
SUSPENSION	: Hydraulic damped telescopic front forks
	: No suspension
TIRE SIZE	: 19×3.25/4.00″
BRAKES	: Internal expanding front wheel drum ⌀ 7″
	: Internal expanding rear wheel drum ⌀ 7″
DRY WEIGHT	: Solo 145kg
DIMENSIONS	: Wheel base 1346mm, Ground clearance 159mm
MAX SPEED:	: Solo 75mph

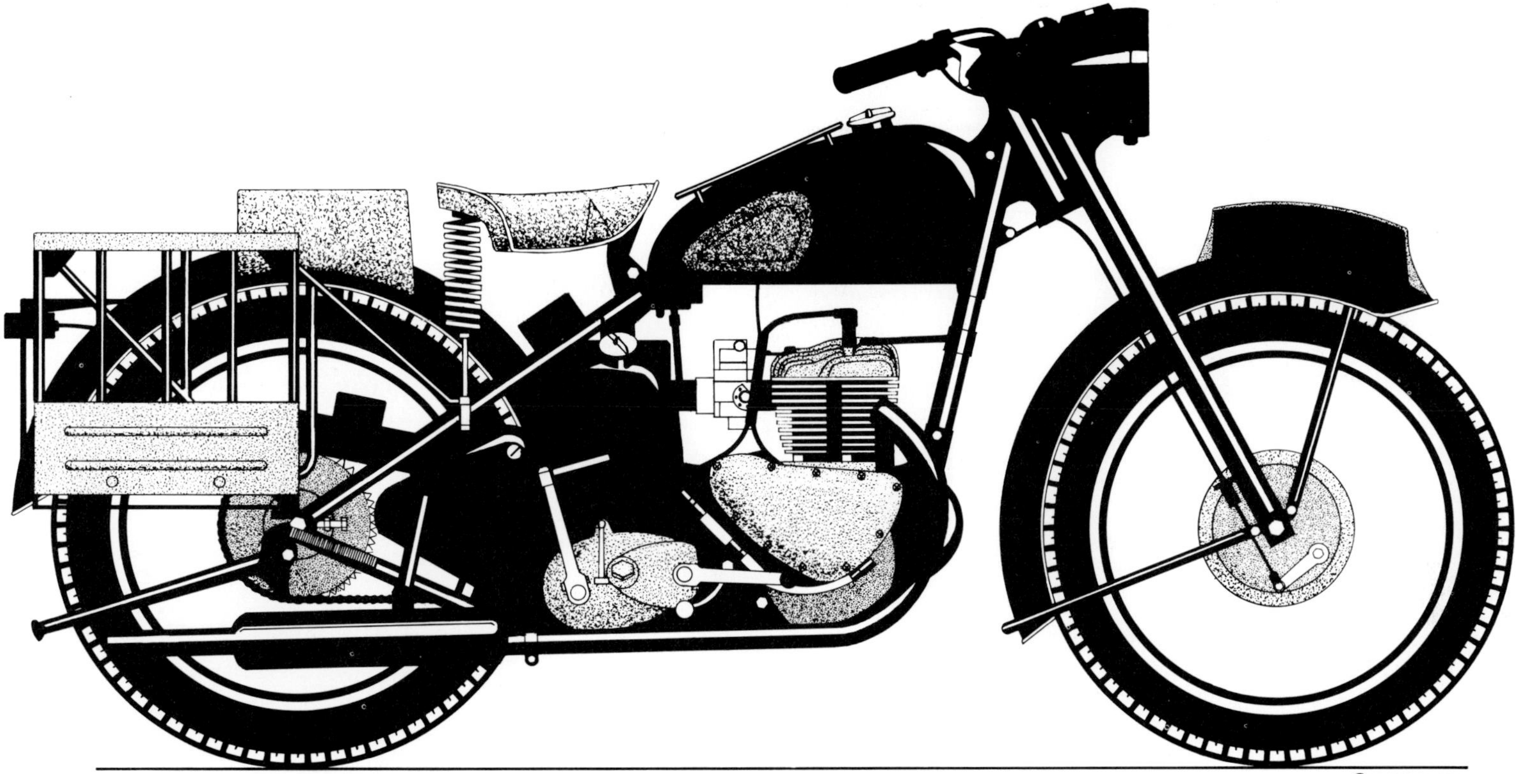

TRIUMPH

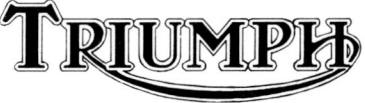

1949 TRIUMPH MODEL TRW
GREAT BRITAIN

· 1950 ·

GILERA MILITARY 500
(Italy)

As a result of the ban on super-charged racing engines from 1947, the Gilera factory discontinued production of their famous four cylinder 500cc machine. As a result, the pre-war Saturno model was developed and re-introduced in competitive events. This machine had a single-cylinder 500cc engine, and was equipped with either standard road, moto cross, or racing trim. The Saturno model continued to be improved for various events until 1952, and remained in production for general use until 1960.

During the early 1950's the Gilera Saturno model was also adopted by the Italian armed forces, for solo despatch, escort, and general police duties. This machine was very similar to the Saturno Sport model of the period, but was equipped with a rear carrier-rack, a pan-type saddle mounted on the rear mudguard, frame mounted leg shields, and an overall coat of khaki paint. The Gilera Saturno model remained in service until the early 1960's, when Italian policy introduced far smaller models for despatch rider type duties.

Brief specification

ENGINE TYPE	: Gilera – Vertical single cylinder
DISPLACEMENT	: 498cc (84×90mm)
VALVE DESIGN	: Overhead valves
COMPRESSION	: 5.5:1
POWER OUTPUT	: 19BHP at 4,500rpm
ELECTRICS	: 6 volt
CARBURETTOR	: One – Dell'Orto RDF 28
GEARBOX	: Foot change, 4 speed, unit construction
TRANSMISSION	: Enclosed chain primary drive
FRAME	: Tubular construction
SUSPENSION	: Hydraulic damped telescopic front forks
	: Hydraulic damped trailing rear forks
TIRE SIZE	: 19×3.25″
BRAKES	: Internal expanding front wheel drum ⌀ 185mm
	: Internal expanding rear wheel drum ⌀ 185mm
DRY WEIGHT	: Solo 198kg
DIMENSIONS	: Wheel base 1450mm, Ground clearance 140mm
MAX SPEED:	: Solo 75mph

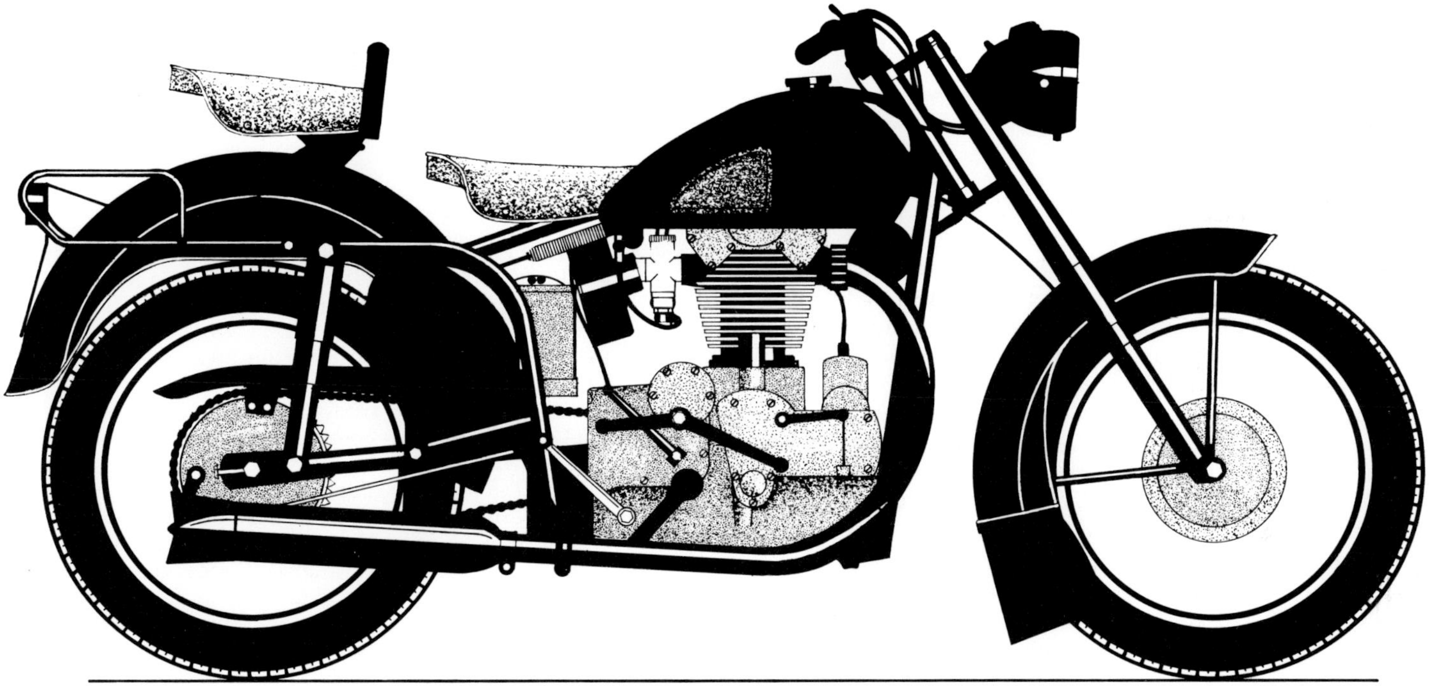

**1950 GILERA MILITARY 500
ITALY**

· 1950 ·
MOTO GUZZI FALCONE
(Italy)

The Moto Guzzi Falcone Sport and Turismo models were introduced and adopted by the Italian armed forces in 1950. These machines were used both solo and with various sidecars attached, for despatch, escort, and general police duties. Apart from the colour, at first amaranth-red and later grey-green, standard production machines were supplied with only minor military modifications. The military conversion included various weather protection screens, additional lighting mounted on the crash bars, and various pillion seats mounted on the rear mudguard.

In particular, special care was taken in preparing the machines for the Corazzieri (Presidential Guard). They had deeply valanced mudguards, a pressed steel gearbox enclosure, chromium plated leg shields, and additional side lighting. The technical specifications were left unchanged from the basic model. A few machines used by the Guardia di Finanza (Financial Police), were assembled to go slightly faster than the standard production machines. The Moto Guzzi Falcone models remained in production until 1967, by which date they had become the most common motor cycle adopted within the Italian military service.

Brief specification

ENGINE TYPE	: Moto Guzzi – Horizontal single cylinder
DISPLACEMENT	: 498cc (88×82mm)
VALVE DESIGN	: Overhead valves
COMPRESSION	: 5.5:1
POWER OUTPUT	: 18.9BHP at 4,300rpm
ELECTRICS	: 6 volt
CARBURETTOR	: One – Dell'Orto MD 27 F
GEARBOX	: Foot change, 4 speed, unit construction
TRANSMISSION	: Exposed chain final drive
FRAME	: Tubular construction
SUSPENSION	: Hydraulic damped telescopic front forks
	: Hydraulic damped rear sub-frame
TIRE SIZE	: 19×3.5"
BRAKES	: Internal expanding front wheel drum
	: Internal expanding rear wheel drum
DRY WEIGHT	: Solo 170kg
DIMENSIONS	: Wheel base 1500mm
MAX SPEED:	: Solo 75mph

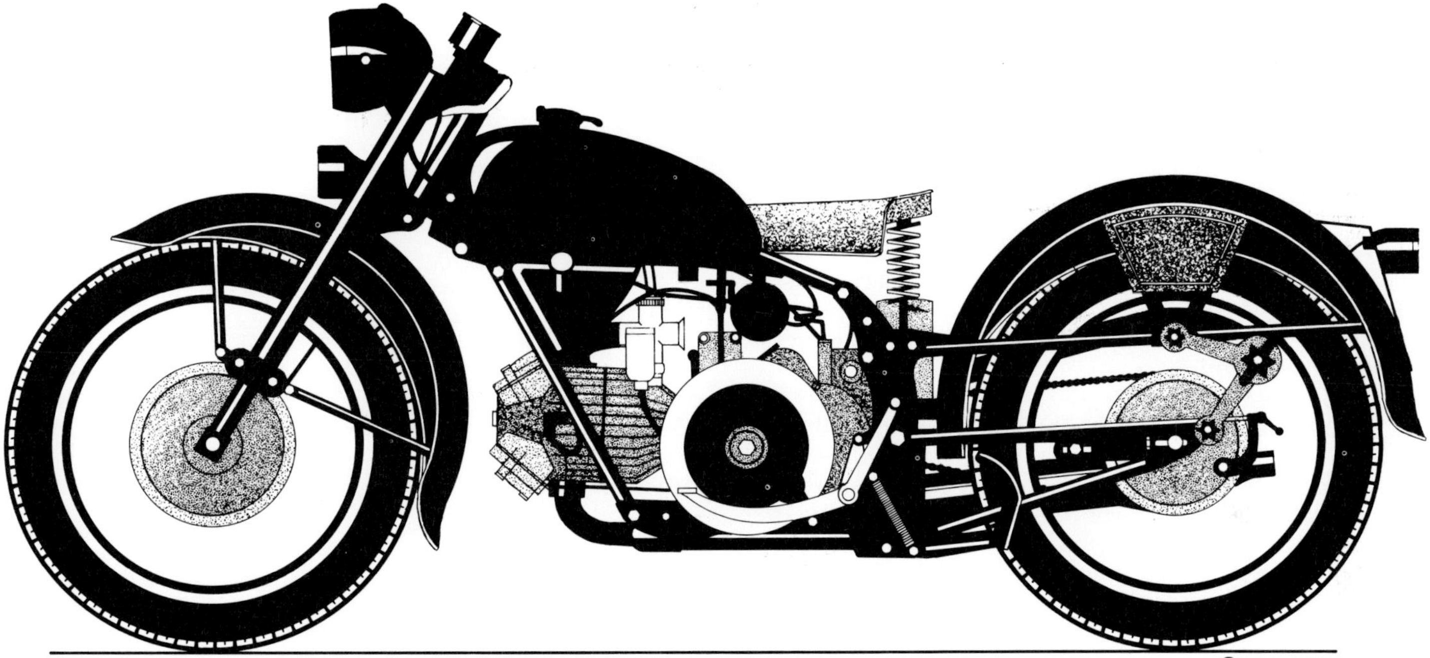

1950 MOTO GUZZI FALCONE
ITALY

· 1950 ·
TERROT TYPE HCT
(France)

Like the majority of motor cycle manufactures, the Terrot factory of Dijon resumed production after the Second World War, with machines of basically pre-war design. The H series was continued and the type HCT was introduced during the late 1940's. With this version, the earlier hand change three-speed gearbox was replaced with a foot change four-speed, and the elegant fishtail silencer was replaced with a cylindrical design. Although the rear wheel was still without suspension, the girder-type front forks were replaced with hydraulic damped telescopic units.

The Terrot type HCT was adopted by the French military to replace the ageing BSA, Harley-Davidson, Indian, Norton, and Royal-Enfield machines that had been in service since 1945. While still basically a civilian model, the military conversion included a pair of leather pannier bags, various pillion seating, frame mounted crash bars, and an overall coat of the appropriate service livery. The type HCT remained in military service for despatch and general reconnaissance duties until the early 1960's, when it was replaced by various BMW models.

Brief specification

ENGINE TYPE	: Terrot – Vertical single cylinder
DISPLACEMENT	: 346cc (70×90mm)
VALVE DESIGN	: Side valves
COMPRESSION	: 5.2:1
POWER OUTPUT	: 9BHP at 4,200rpm
ELECTRICS	: 6 volt
CARBURETTOR	: One – Amac 5/012
GEARBOX	: Foot change, 4 speed, separate unit
TRANSMISSION	: Enclosed chain primary drive
	: Exposed chain final drive
FRAME	: Tubular construction
SUSPENSION	: Hydraulic damped telescopic front forks
	: No rear suspension
TIRE SIZE	: 26×3.5″
BRAKES	: Internal expanding front wheel drum ⌀ 170mm
	: Internal expanding rear wheel drum ⌀ 170mm
DRY WEIGHT	: Solo 160kg
DIMENSIONS	: Wheel base 1400mm, Ground clearance 110mm
MAX SPEED:	: Solo 60mph

· 1950 ·
TERROT TYPE RGST
(France)

Following the success of their type 'H' series during the late 1920's, the Terrot factory introduced the type 'R' series in the early 1930's. This was a similar machine with an increase in engine capacity. Both of these model types became popular machines and were continually developed until Terrot ceased production during the early 1960's. During the Second World War the type HD was designated 'A' for army and supplied to the French armed forces for solo despatch rider service, and the type RD became the RDA and was supplied for military service with various sidecars attached. The Terrot type RDA with a sidecar attached had a dry weight of about 280kg, and could maintain a speed of 55mph.

During the late 1940's the Terrot type R series was introduced with an overhead valve engine design, and by 1950 a telescopic front fork and plunger-type rear wheel suspension. Known as the type RGST, this machine was adopted by the French military for solo despatch, escort, and general police duties. This model was used to replace the ageing ex-American and British WD machines adopted by the French since 1946. The military equipment included a pair of leather pannier bags, various pillion seats mounted on the rear mudguard, a frame mounted front crash bar, and an overall coat of the appropriate service livery. The Terrot type RGST remained in service until the early 1960's when, due to poor financial condition of the Terrot factory, the French military contracts were lost to the German BMW factory. The Terrot business was eventually taken over by Cycles Peugeot who assembled the last Terrot 175cc machines.

Brief specification

ENGINE TYPE	: Terrot – Vertical single cylinder
DISPLACEMENT	: 498cc (84×90mm)
VALVE DESIGN	: Overhead valves
COMPRESSION	: 6.6:1
POWER OUTPUT	: 21BHP at 5,500rpm
ELECTRICS	: 6 volt, 35 watt
CARBURETTOR	: One – Amac 6/024
GEARBOX	: Foot change, 4 speed, unit construction
TRANSMISSION	: Exposed chain final drive
FRAME	: Tubular construction
SUSPENSION	: Hydraulic damped telescopic front forks
	: Hydraulic damped plunger rear wheel
TIRE SIZE	: 26×3.25/27×3.75"
BRAKES	: Internal expanding front wheel drum ⌀ 170mm
	: Internal expanding rear wheel drum ⌀ 200mm
DRY WEIGHT	: Solo 180kg
DIMENSIONS	: Wheel base 1460mm, Ground clearance 120mm
MAX SPEED:	: Solo 80mph

TERROT

**1950 TERROT TYPE R.G.S.T.
FRANCE**

· 1951 ·
FN MILITARY MODEL 13
(Belgium)

The FN motor cycle factory of Herstal resumed production after the Second World War with the introduction of the M–13 in 1947. This machine remained available for several years with a single-cylinder 350cc and 450cc side-valve engine and 250cc and 350cc overhead valve design. All these engines had an 80mm piston stroke. The M–13 machines featured an unusual rubber band front and rear suspension until 1951 when more conventional telescopic front and trailing rear forks were fitted.

The FN military model 13 was adopted by the Belgian armed forces in 1951 for solo despatch, escort, and general police duties. This machine had a unit construction single-cylinder 450cc side-valve engine with a four-speed gearbox. The military equipment included a pair of leather pannier bags, a pillion seat mounted on the rear mudguard, front mounted crash bar, a fire extinguisher, and an overall coat of khaki paint. This machine was used to replace the ageing ex-British WD Ariel, BSA, Matchless Norton, Royal Enfield, and Triumph models, and between June and December 1951 a total of 1,030 were supplied to the Belgium military.

Brief specification

ENGINE TYPE	: FN – Vertical single cylinder
DISPLACEMENT	: 448cc (84.5×80mm)
VALVE DESIGN	: Side valves
COMPRESSION	: 5:1
POWER OUTPUT	: 11.5BHP
ELECTRICS	: 6 volt
CARBURETTOR	: One – Amal
GEARBOX	: Foot change, 4 speed, unit construction
TRANSMISSION	: Exposed chain final drive
FRAME	: Tubular construction
SUSPENSION	: Rubber damped trailing link front forks
	: Rubber damped trailing rear forks
TIRE SIZE	: 26×3.5″
BRAKES	: Internal expanding front wheel drum
	: Internal expanding rear wheel drum
DRY WEIGHT	: Solo 160kg
DIMENSIONS	: Wheel base 1280mm, Ground clearance 200mm
MAX SPEED:	: Solo 65mph

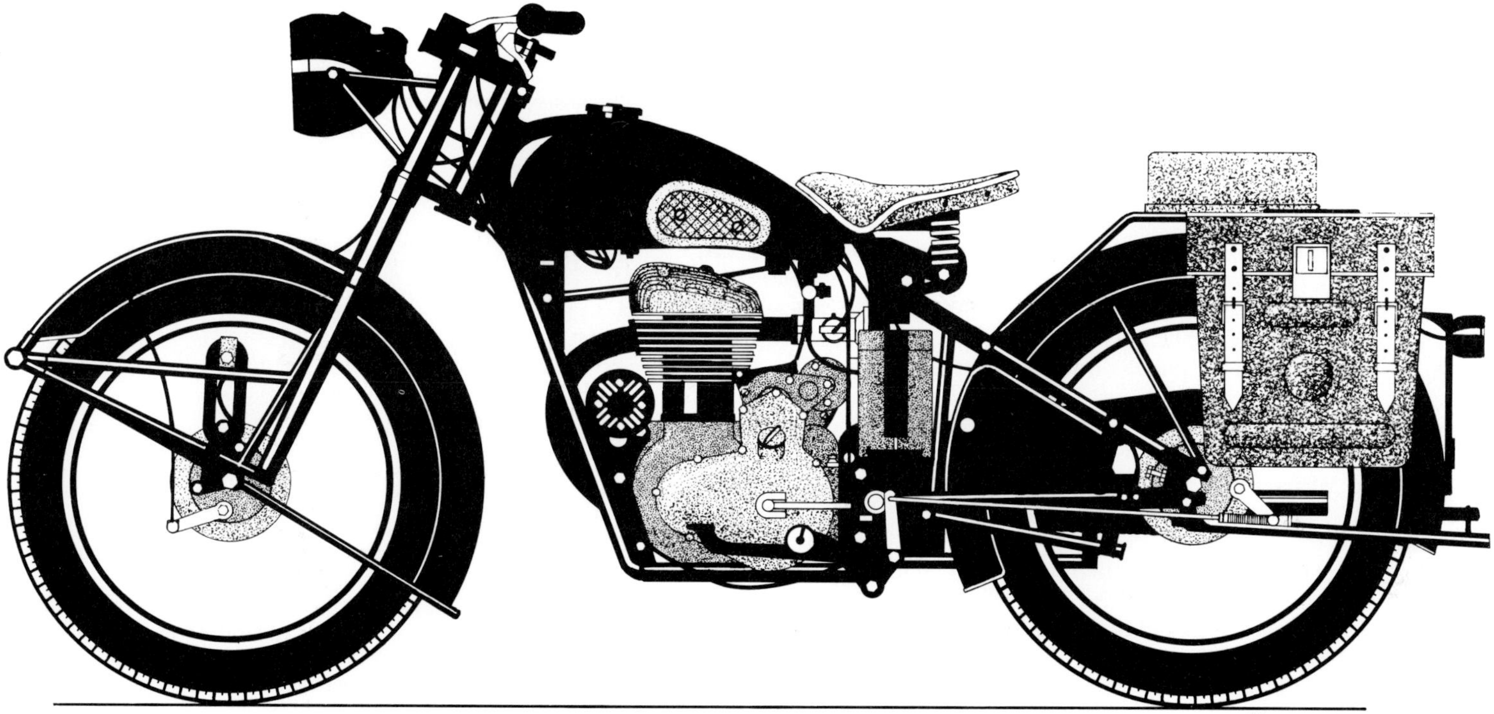

1951 FN MILITARY MODEL 13
BELGIUM

· 1952 ·
MOTO GUZZI AIRONE
(Italy)

The Moto Guzzi Airone model was first introduced in 1939. It had a single cylinder 250cc engine mounted horizontally in a tubular cycle frame, with girder-type front fork and friction damped rear sub-frame suspension. Although experimental work began on a military version the following year it was not until after the Second World War that this machine was adopted by the Italian armed forces. The Military Airone model was used for solo despatch, escort, and general police duties, but apart from the colour, was basically a civilian machine with only minor military modifications. It remained in military service until the early 1950's when superseded by a further development.

An improved Military Airone model was introduced in 1952, with a very similar horizontal engine but higher output, mounted within a redesigned cycle frame with telescopic front fork suspension. This machine was also very similar to the contemporary civilian version. The military equipment included various pillion seats mounted on the rear mudguard, frame mounted front crash bars, leg shields, and an overall coat of the appropriate service livery. This machine was adopted by various police and military departments. The Moto Guzzi Military Airone model remained in production until 1957, when manufacture ceased without any similar replacement.

Brief specification

ENGINE TYPE	: Moto Guzzi – Horizontal single cylinder
DISPLACEMENT	: 246cc (70×64mm)
VALVE DESIGN	: Overhead valves
COMPRESSION	: 6:1
POWER OUTPUT	: 12BHP at 5,200rpm
ELECTRICS	: 6 volt
CARBURETTOR	: One – Dell'Orto 22
GEARBOX	: Foot change, 4 speed, unit construction
TRANSMISSION	: Exposed chain final drive
FRAME	: Tubular construction
SUSPENSION	: Hydraulic damped telescopic front forks
	: Friction damped rear sub-frame
TIRE SIZE	: 19×3.25″
BRAKES	: Internal expanding front wheel drum
	: Internal expanding rear wheel drum
DRY WEIGHT	: Solo 150kg
DIMENSIONS	: Wheel base 1371mm
MAX SPEED:	: Solo 55mph

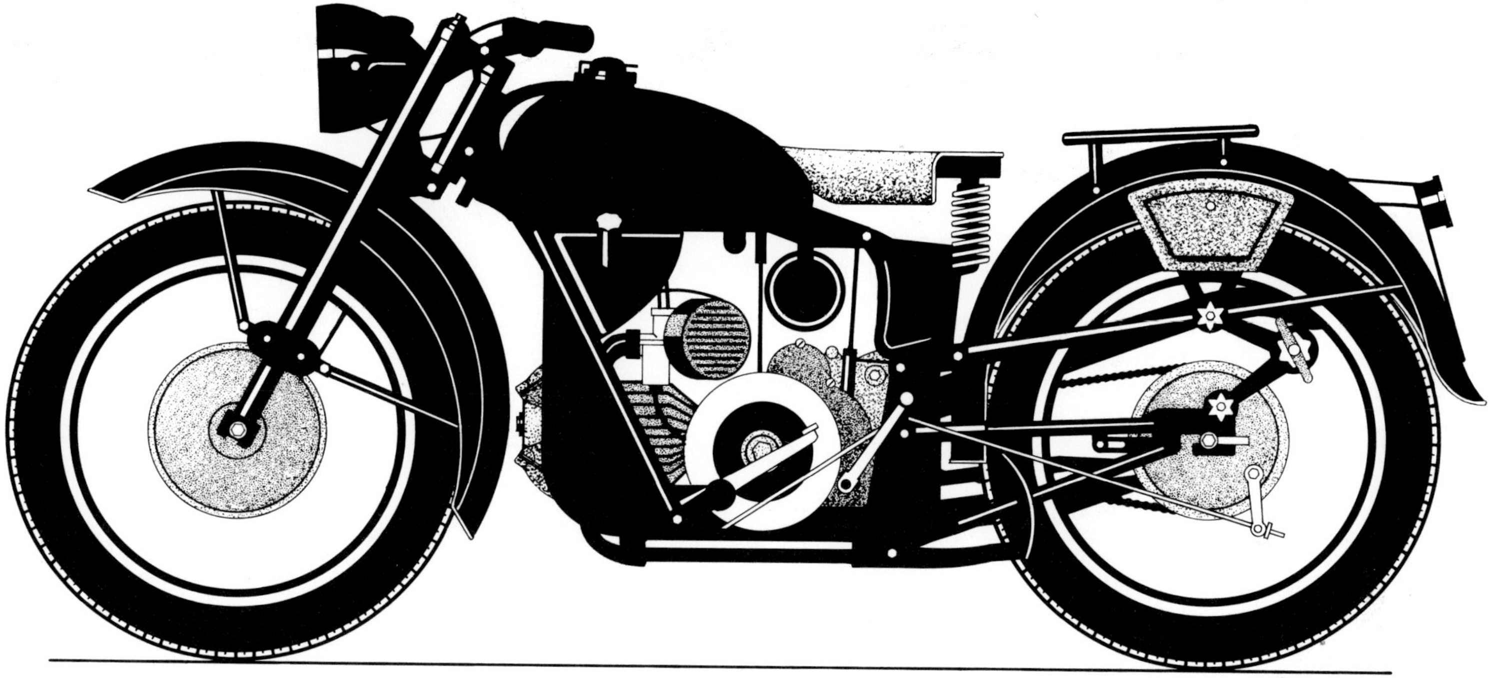

1952 MOTO GUZZI AIRONE
ITALY

· 1955 ·
BMW MODEL R–50
(West Germany)

During the mid 1950's the BMW factory of Munich introduced a new model range, centred upon their established single-cylinder 250cc, opposed twin-cylinder 500cc, and opposed twin-cylinder 600cc engines of the previous five years. These new machines featured Earles-type front forks and damped trailing fork suspension. With this design BMW replaced the previously used telescopic front forks and plunger-type rear wheel suspension. Other major changes included an enclosed shaft final drive, smaller 18" wheels, larger silencers, full width drum brakes, a larger carburettor filter, and the option of a dual seat.

Although originally designed as civilian machines, all of these models were adopted for military service by armed forces throughout the world, e.g. Austria, France, Netherlands, etc. They were used both solo and with various sidecars attached, for despatch, escort, and general police duties. The military-type accessories included a frame mounted fairing, a radio phone, additional lighting and syren mounted on crash bars or fairing, and a pair of leather pannier bags. The BMW model R–50 remained in production until 1969, by which time a total of 32,532 had been assembled. This was the longest and most productive manufacturing period for any of the Earles-type BMW models, and as result the most numerous assembled.

Brief specification

ENGINE TYPE	: BMW – Transverse opposed twin cylinder
DISPLACEMENT	: 494cc (68×68mm)
VALVE DESIGN	: Overhead valves
COMPRESSION	: 6.8:1
POWER OUTPUT	: 26BHP at 5,800rpm
ELECTRICS	: 6 volt, 60/90 watt
CARBURETTOR	: Two – Bing 1/24/45 and 1/24/46
GEARBOX	: Foot change, 4 speed, unit construction
TRANSMISSION	: Enclosed shaft final drive
FRAME	: Tubular construction
SUSPENSION	: Hydraulic damped Earles-type front forks
	: Hydraulic damped trailing rear forks
TIRE SIZE	: 18×3.5, W/SC 18×4.00"
BRAKES	: Internal expanding front wheel drum ⌀ 200mm
	: Internal expanding rear wheel drum ⌀ 200mm
DRY WEIGHT	: Solo 195kg
DIMENSIONS	: Wheel base 1423mm, Ground clearance 165mm
MAX SPEED:	: Solo 85mph

**1955 BMW MODEL R-50
WEST GERMANY**

· 1955 ·

DKW RT–175–VS
(West Germany)

The DKW factory of Zschopau became part of East Germany after the Second World War, and began to produce motor cycles under the name of IFA and later MZ (Motorradwerke Zschopau). The DKW company resumed production at a new factory at Ingolstadt in 1949 and later at Dusseldorf. At first these machines were of virtually pre-war design, but with telescopic front fork suspension, but by the mid 1950's the DKW factory had introduced the new VS model range. These machines had a unit construction single-cylinder engine and four-speed gearbox, mounted within a pressed steel and tubular frame with Earles-type front fork and trailing rear fork suspension. Other major features included the use of pressed steel for an enclosure around the carburettor, a pair of auxiliary side boxes, and a headlamp nacelle.

The DKW RT–175–VS model was supplied to the West German armed forces between 1955 and 1958. This machine was used for solo despatch and general police duties, and remained in service until the early 1960's when superseded by the more powerful Maico M–250–B model. Apart from the colour, this machine remained basically a civilian model with only minor military modification, front and rear crash bars, and a pair of canvas pannier bags.

Brief specification

ENGINE TYPE	: DKW – Vertical single cylinder
DISPLACEMENT	: 175cc (62×58mm)
VALVE DESIGN	: Two stroke
COMPRESSION	: 6.2:1
POWER OUTPUT	: 9.6BHP at 5,000rpm
ELECTRICS	: 6 volt
CARBURETTOR	: Two – Bing 24mm
GEARBOX	: Foot change, 4 speed, unit construction
TRANSMISSION	: Enclosed chain final drive
FRAME	: Pressed steel & Tubular construction
SUSPENSION	: Hydraulic damped Earles-type front forks
	: Hydraulic damped trailing rear forks
TIRE SIZE	: 19×3.25″
BRAKES	: Internal expanding front wheel drum
	: Internal expanding rear wheel drum
DRY WEIGHT	: Solo 135kg
DIMENSIONS	: Wheel base 1278mm, Ground clearance 120mm
MAX SPEED:	: Solo 60mph

**1955 DKW RT-175-VS
WEST GERMANY**

· 1955 ·

MONARK MC–252
(Sweden)

The Monark motor cycle factory re-established its partnership with the German ILO company after the Second World War. As a result the Monark Blue Arrow series featured engines of ILO design and manufacture. A total of five versions of this model were introduced in 1954. The M–550 was assembled in standard road trim with a high-level exhaust system, and was also offered with various accessories to the army as the MC–252 model. The M–551 was produced in a similar trim but with a standard level exhaust system. The M–560 was assembled as a moto-cross machine, and was also offered with various accessories to the army as the MC–253 model. All of these machines had the same twin-cylinder 250cc two-stroke engine and four-speed gearbox with a fully enclosed chain final drive, mounted in a tubular frame with telescopic front and trailing rear fork suspension.

The Monark MC–252 model was adopted by the Swedish armed forces in 1955 for solo despatch and general police duty, and remained in military service until 1963 when superseded by the more powerful Monark MC–356A model. This machine had a JAWA twin-cylinder 350cc two-stroke engine, also with a fully enclosed chain final drive, but mounted within a redesigned frame with Earles-type front and trailing rear fork suspension. The MC–356A model was also designed for multi-terrain use, and had a high ground clearance, high mounted mudguards, and wide handlebars. To enable the use of ski attachments on snow this machine was also equipped with hand operated rear brake and gear change fittings. Further military type accessories included a rear carrier rack and an auxiliary box mounted on the petrol tank.

Brief specification

ENGINE TYPE	: ILO – Vertical twin cylinder
DISPLACEMENT	: 246cc (52×58mm)
VALVE DESIGN	: Two stroke
COMPRESSION	: 6.8:1
POWER OUTPUT	: 15.1BHP at 6,000rpm
ELECTRICS	: 6 volt, 45/60 watt
CARBURETTOR	: Two – Bing 1/24
GEARBOX	: Foot change, 4 speed, unit construction
TRANSMISSION	: Enclosed chain final drive
FRAME	: Tubular construction
SUSPENSION	: Hydraulic damped telescopic front forks
	: Hydraulic damped trailing rear forks
TIRE SIZE	: 19×3.25″
BRAKES	: Internal expanding front wheel drum
	: Internal expanding rear wheel drum
DRY WEIGHT	: Solo 165kg
DIMENSIONS	: Wheel base 1360mm, Ground clearance 160mm
MAX SPEED:	: Solo 70mph

Monark

**1955 MONARK MC-252
SWEDEN**

· 1956 ·
AJS MODEL 18CS
(Great Britain)

As a result of the worldwide depression, the AJS business of Wolverhampton became part of Associated Motor Cycle Ltd, and resumed production within the Matchless factory of South London in 1931. During the Second World War, AMC concentrated military production on Matchless motor cycles and introduced the Matchless model G3L in 1941. This was the first British manufactured motor cycle to feature hydraulic damped telescopic front fork suspension. With the return to civilian production, AJS models became almost identical to those of Matchless and both names adopted the new front fork design. In 1949 AMC also introduced a new cycle frame with hydraulic damped trailing fork suspension.

That year a number of the new AJS model 18S machines were adopted by the Swedish armed forces. Apart from the colour, these machines remained basically civilian models with few military modifications, and were used for escort, despatch, and general police duty. The machines remained in service until 1956 when superseded by the more powerful AJS model 18CS. This version featured a shorter stroke all-alloy engine, full width drum brakes, and was designed for cross-country type use. To enable service on snow both adopted models were also equipped with additional hand operated rear brake and gear change fittings for use with ski attachments.

Brief specification

ENGINE TYPE	: AJS – Vertical single cylinder
DISPLACEMENT	: 497cc (86×85.5mm)
VALVE DESIGN	: Overhead valves
COMPRESSION	: 8.7:1
POWER OUTPUT	: 33BHP at 6,200rpm
ELECTRICS	: 6 volt
CARBURETTOR	: One – Amal Monobloc
GEARBOX	: Foot change, 4 speed, separate unit
TRANSMISSION	: Enclosed chain primary drive
	: Exposed chain final drive
FRAME	: Tubular construction
SUSPENSION	: Hydraulic damped telescopic front forks
	: Hydraulic damped trailing rear forks
TIRE SIZE	: 21×3.00/19×4.00"
BRAKES	: Internal expanding front wheel drum ⌀ 7"
	: Internal expanding rear wheel drum ⌀ 7"
DRY WEIGHT	: Solo 147kg
DIMENSIONS	: Wheel base 1402mm, Ground clearance 165mm
MAX SPEED:	: Solo 85mph

A·J·S

**1956 AJS MODEL 18CS
GREAT BRITAIN**

· 1956 ·
GILERA MILITARY G–175
(Italy)

The Gilera factory of Arcore resumed civilian production immediately after the Second World War. Their machines remained basically pre-war designs until the early 1950's when the majority of models were equipped with telescopic front and trailing rear fork suspension. While the Saturno 500cc model remained the centre of the range until the late 1950's, Gilera also introduced during this period a number of smaller models which proved to be of reliable and lasting design.

One such machine was the Gilera G–175 model. A military version was supplied to the Italian armed forces from 1956, with a number of similar machines from the MV and Morini factories. They were used for solo escort, despatch, and general police duties within urban areas, and remained basically civilian models with few modifications. The military conversion mainly included a rear carrier rack or pair of pannier bags, frame mounted crash bars, and an overall coat of the appropriate service livery. The Gilera Military G–175 model remained in military service throughout the 1960's.

Brief specification

ENGINE TYPE	: Gilera – Vertical single cylinder
DISPLACEMENT	: 172cc (60×61mm)
VALVE DESIGN	: Overhead valves
COMPRESSION	: 6.5:1
POWER OUTPUT	: 7.5BHP at 6,000rpm
ELECTRICS	: 6 volt, 45 watt
CARBURETTOR	: One – Dell'Orto MA 18 B
GEARBOX	: Foot change, 4 speed, unit construction
TRANSMISSION	: Exposed chain final drive
FRAME	: Tubular construction
SUSPENSION	: Hydraulic damped telescopic front forks
	: Hydraulic damped trailing rear forks
TIRE SIZE	: 19×2.5/2.75"
BRAKES	: Internal expanding front wheel drum
	: Internal expanding rear wheel drum
DRY WEIGHT	: Solo 109kg
DIMENSIONS	: Wheel base 1300mm, Ground clearance 160mm
MAX SPEED:	: Solo 60mph

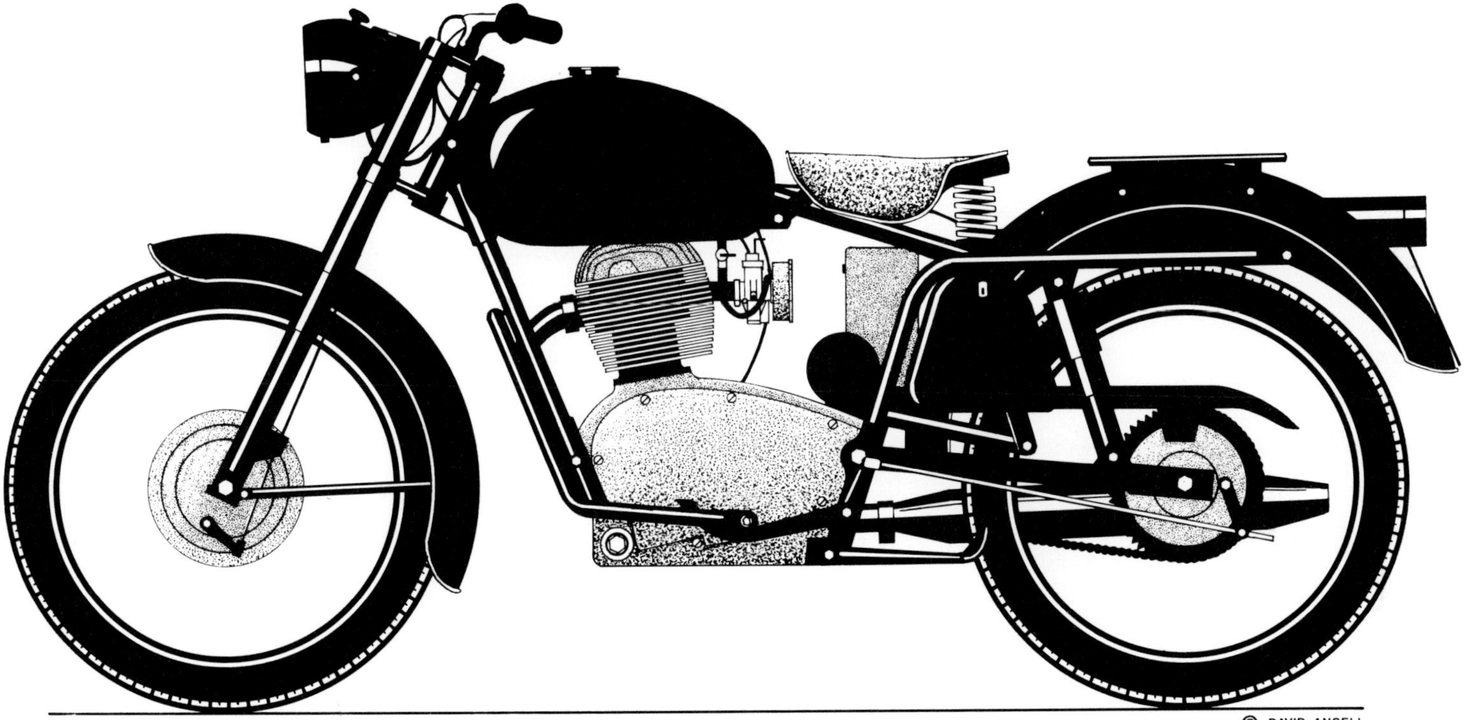

1956 GILERA MILITARY G-175
ITALY

· 1956 ·

HARLEY-DAVIDSON FL
(America)

The Harley-Davidson factory of Milwaukee resumed civilian production immediately after the Second World War. During this period, their established 1200cc engine was reintroduced with an overhead valve design. In 1948 this engine first featured hydraulic valve lifters and the following year was mounted within a redesigned cycle frame with telescopic front fork suspension. While designated the FL model this machine became known as the Hydra Glide, and soon became the basis for the most numerous post-war Harley-Davidson model to be adopted for police or military service.

With the introduction of a trailing rear fork suspension the Hydra Glide became the Duo Glide in 1958, and with the fitting of an electronic ignition the Duo Glide became the Electra Glide in 1965. These machines were all powered by the same ever developed 1200cc engine until 1966 when a redesigned unit was introduced. Designated models FL and FLH, these engines were offered with either standard or a high compression ratio respectively until 1979 when the model FL was discontinued. The previous year, and enlarged 1300cc version was made available, and in 1908 a five-speed gearbox was introduced.

Throughout the production of these models, Harley-Davidson has offered various accessories for police or military service, and these machines have been sold to government agencies throughout the world, e.g. Belgium, Egypt, Greece, Iran, Japan, Kuwait, Mexico, etc. The most common fittings for a standard model have been front and rear crash bars, a rear carrier rack, handlebar mounted windscreen, syren, pursuit lights, and a suppressed electrical system for radio use. The deluxe model is equipped with a pair of pannier bags, handlebar mounted fairing, and during the 1980's the option of cast wheels. These machines were normally finished in black or white, with special colour schemes available with a fleet purchase.

Brief specification

ENGINE TYPE	: Harley-Davidson – V-twin cylinder
DISPLACEMENT	: 1206cc (87.3×100.8mm)
VALVE DESIGN	: Overhead valves
COMPRESSION	: 7.25:1
POWER OUTPUT	: 55BHP at 5,400rpm
ELECTRICS	: 6 volt
CARBURETTOR	: One – Linkert 33mm
GEARBOX	: Hand change, 4 speed, separate unit
TRANSMISSION	: Enclosed chain primary drive
	: Exposed chain final drive
FRAME	: Tubular construction
SUSPENSION	: Hydraulic damped telescopic front forks
	: No rear suspension
TIRE SIZE	: 16×5.00"
BRAKES	: Internal expanding front wheel drum
	: Internal expanding rear wheel drum
DRY WEIGHT	: Solo 299kg
DIMENSIONS	: Wheel base 1524mm, Ground clearance
	: 79mm
MAX SPEED	: Solo 85mph

HARLEY–DAVIDSON

1956 HARLEY-DAVIDSON FL AMERICA

· 1957 ·
JAWA 350 KYVACKA
(Czechoslovakia)

The Janeck factory of Prague introduced the Jawa 350 Kyvacka in 1956. This machine had a twin-cylinder 350cc two-stroke engine, mounted within a pressed steel and tubular cycle frame with telescopic front and trailing rear fork suspension. As previous post war Jawa machines, the Kyvacka model had a unit construction engine and gearbox with a semi-automatic clutch. A major difference with earlier machines was the adoption of smaller 16" wheels, and a fully enclosed chain final drive, both of which became characteristic features of most subsequent Jawa machines.

The Jawa 350 Kyvacka was adopted by the Czechoslovak armed forces in 1957, and was used both solo and with various sidecars attached, for escort, despatch, and general police duty. A number were also equipped with parachute rings for service within airborne troops. Further military specifications included a pair of pannier bags and an overall coat of the appropriate service livery. This model remained in active military service until 1974, when superseded by the more powerful Jawa 350 type 634–4.

After undergoing various trials in 1957 the Jawa 350 Kyvacka was also adopted by the armed forces of Sweden. These machines were fitted with 19" trials type tires, and, to enable service with ski attachments, were equipped with additional hand operated rear brake and gear change fittings. Further military specifications included a heavy-duty rear carrier rack and an overall coat of the appropriate service livery. The same Jawa military model was also adopted by the armed forces of Finland during the 1960's. This machine also became the forerunner of the Monark MC–356–A, a quite different military model designed and manufactured in Sweden, but powered by the same Jawa 350cc engine.

Brief specification

ENGINE TYPE	: JAWA – Vertical twin cylinder
DISPLACEMENT	: 343cc (58×65mm)
VALVE DESIGN	: Two stroke
COMPRESSION	: 8:1
POWER OUTPUT	: 18BHP at 4,700rpm
ELECTRICS	: 6 volt, 55 watt
CARBURETTOR	: One – Jikov
GEARBOX	: Foot change, 4 speed, unit construction
TRANSMISSION	: Enclosed chain final drive
FRAME	: Pressed steel and tubular construction
SUSPENSION	: Hydraulic damped telescopic front forks
	: Hydraulic damped trailing rear forks
TIRE SIZE	: 16×3.25"
BRAKES	: Internal expanding front wheel drum
	: Internal expanding rear wheel drum
DRY WEIGHT	: Solo 136kg
DIMENSIONS	: Wheel base 1295mm
MAX SPEED	: Solo 70mph

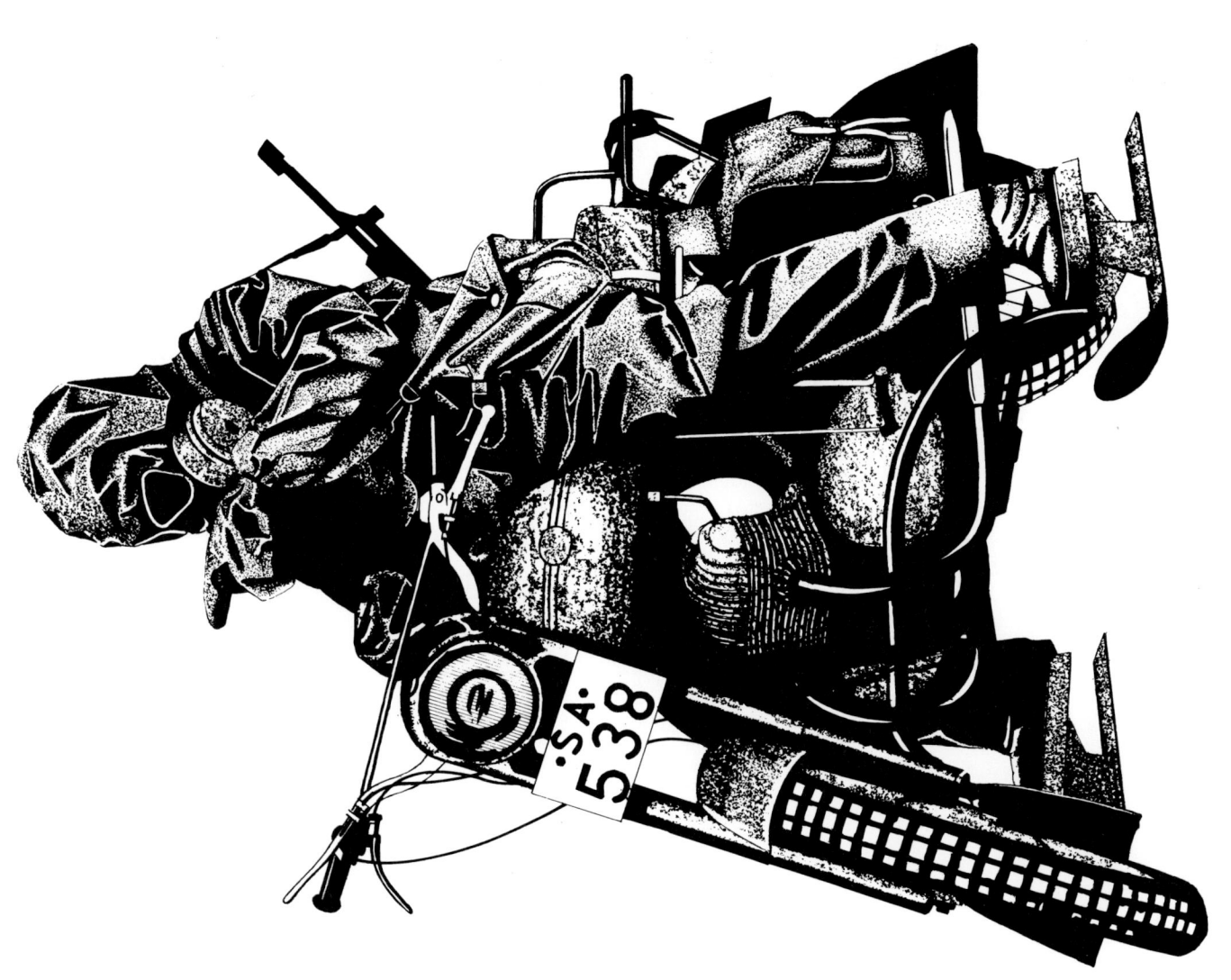

1957 JAWA 350 KYVACKA & FINNISH SOLDIER © DAVID ANSELL

· 1959 ·
PUCH TYPE 175–MCH
(Austria)

With the declaration of the Second World War, the Steyr-Daimler-Puch organization began full-time military production. As result, the Steyr and Puch factories were virtually destroyed by Allied bombing, but by 1949 rebuilt and a new range of Puch motorcycles had been introduced. These machines featured their well-established split-single cylinder two-stroke engine design of Giovanni Marcellino. The Puch factory continued to develop this design and introduced the type 250–SG touring and type 250–SGS sports machines in 1954. A smaller version type 175–MCH was assembled soon after.

The Austrian armed forces adopted the Puch type 250–SG in 1956, and the Puch type 175–MCH in 1959. The machines were used for solo escort, despatch, and general police duties within urban areas. They remained basically civilian models with few modifications. The military conversion included the mounting of a pillion pan-type saddle on the rear mudguard, a pair of canvas pannier bags, and the appropriate service livery. As these machines were adopted during a period without war service, the civilian chromium fittings were accepted as standard, and remained in military service throughout the 1960's, until superseded by the more powerful Puch type 250–MCH.

Brief specification

ENGINE TYPE	: Puch – Vertical split single cylinder
DISPLACEMENT	: 172cc (2×42×62mm)
VALVE DESIGN	: Two stroke
COMPRESSION	: 7:1
POWER OUTPUT	: 10BHP at 5,800rpm
ELECTRICS	: 6 volt, 40/50 watt
CARBURETTOR	: One – Bing type 1/24/113
GEARBOX	: Foot change, 4 speed, unit construction
TRANSMISSION	: Enclosed chain final drive
FRAME	: Tubular and Pressed steel construction
SUSPENSION	: Hydraulic damped telescopic front forks
	: Hydraulic damped trailing rear forks
TIRE SIZE	: 19×3.25″
BRAKES	: Internal expanding front wheel drum ⌀ 160mm
	: Internal expanding rear wheel drum ⌀ 160mm
DRY WEIGHT	: Solo 135kg
DIMENSIONS	: Wheel base 1320mm, Ground clearance 190mm
MAX SPEED	: Solo 50mph

**1959 PUCH TYPE 175-MCH
AUSTRIA**

· 1960 ·
BMW MODEL R–27
(West Germany)

The BMW factory of Munich was virtually demolished by Allied bombing during the Second World War and Hitler ordered the remaining facilities to be destroyed. This command was ignored, however, and a lot of equipment was commandered as Soviet property when the BMW owned Dixi car factory of Eisenach became part of the East Germany. The Eisenach factory later supplied the EMW model R–35 to the East German armed forces. This machine was similar to the BMW model R–35 of 1937, but with a plunger-type rear wheel suspension.

Production resumed at the BMW factory in 1949, with the introduction of the model R–24. This machine was based upon the pre-war BMW model R–23 of 1938, but with an increased engine output and a larger petrol tank. Although the larger BMW twin-cylinder machines were also reintroduced, while the German economy recovered the BMW single-cylinder machines continuted to be developed. In 1950 the model R–25 was introduced with telescopic front fork and plunger-type rear wheel suspension, and variants of this machine remained in production until 1955, when the model R–26 was introduced, with Earles-type front forks and damped trailing rear fork suspension. This, in turn was superseded in 1960 by the similar but more powerful model R–27.

The BMW model R–27 was adopted by various armed forces such as France, Netherlands, West Germany. It remained basically a civilian model and was used for solo despatch rider service with few modifications. The military conversion included a pair of leather pannier bags, a petrol tank carrier rack, a high-level exhaust system, and an overall coat of the appropriate service livery. The BMW model R–27 remained in military service throughout the 1960's and continued in production until 1967, by which date a total of 15,364 had been manufactured.

Brief specification

ENGINE TYPE	: BMW – Vertical single cylinder
DISPLACEMENT	: 247cc (68×68mm)
VALVE DESIGN	: Overhead valves
COMPRESSION	: 8.2:1
POWER OUTPUT	: 18BHP at 7,400rpm
ELECTRICS	: 6 volt, 90 watt
CARBURETTOR	: One – Bing 26/68
GEARBOX	: Foot change, 4 speed, unit construction
TRANSMISSION	: Enclosed shaft final drive
FRAME	: Tubular construction
SUSPENSION	: Hydraulic damped Earles-type front forks
	: Hydraulic damped trailing rear forks
TIRE SIZE	: 18×3.25″
BRAKES	: Internal expanding front wheel drum ⌀ 200mm
	: Internal expanding rear wheel drum ⌀ 200mm
DRY WEIGHT	: Solo 162kg
DIMENSIONS	: Wheel base 1380mm, Ground clearance 115mm
MAX SPEED	: Solo 80mph

1960 BMW MODEL R-27 WEST GERMANY

· 1960 ·
MOTO GUZZI STORNELLO
(Italy)

The Moto Guzzi factory of Mandello del Lario first introduced the Stornello model in 1960. This machine was continually developed until 1975 and assembled in various standard road and trials trim. Its engine output progressively increased and the displacement eventually became 160cc. While these machines proved to be of reliable and lasting design, they were also one of the first Moto Guzzi models to adopt a more conventional appearance. Until this time it had always been characteristic of Moto Guzzi machines to have the engine mounted horizontally.

The Moto Guzzi Stornello Turismo model was manufactured between 1960 and 1968, and during this period a military version was also supplied to the Italian armed forces. Basically a civilian model, it was used for solo despatch rider service with little modification. The military conversion mainly included an overall coat of the appropriate service livery. This machine in service throughout the 1960's until superseded by the more traditional Moto Guzzi design of the Nuovo Falcone Militare.

Brief specification

ENGINE TYPE	: Moto Guzzi – Forward sloping single cylinder
DISPLACEMENT	: 123cc (52×58mm)
VALVE DESIGN	: Overhead valves
COMPRESSION	: 8:1
POWER OUTPUT	: 7BHP at 7,200rpm
ELECTRICS	: 6 volt
CARBURETTOR	: One Dell'Orto ME 18 BS
GEARBOX	: Foot change, 4 speed, unit construction
TRANSMISSION	: Exposed chain final drive
FRAME	: Tubular construction
SUSPENSION	: Hydraulic damped telescopic front forks
	: Hydraulic damped trailing rear forks
TIRE SIZE	: 17×2.5/2.75″
BRAKES	: Internal expanding front wheel drum
	: Internal expanding rear wheel drum
DRY WEIGHT	: Solo 113.5kg
DIMENSIONS	: Wheel base 1250mm
MAX SPEED	: Solo 60mph

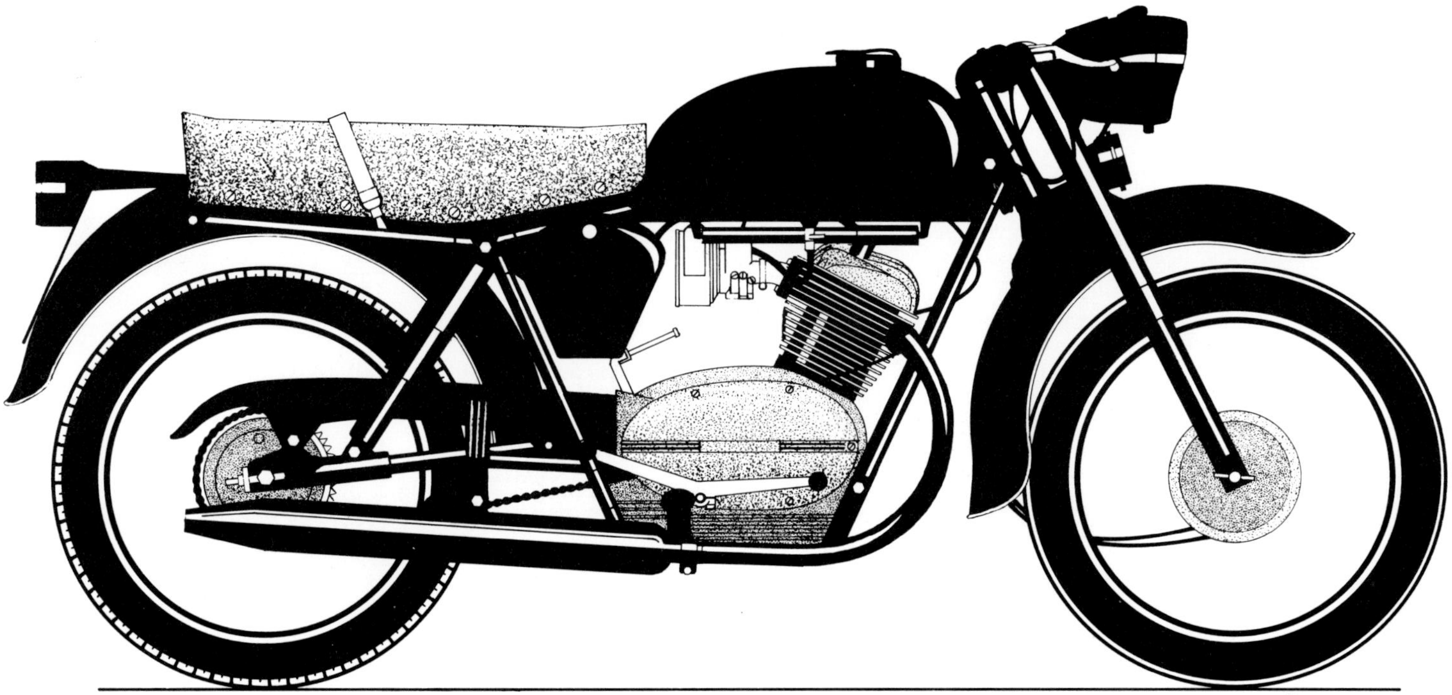

1960 MOTO GUZZI 125
ITALY

· 1965 ·
BSA MODEL B–40
(Great Britain)

The BSA factory of Birmingham supplied approximately one third of all military motor cycles produced by British manufacturers during the Second World War. As a result, the company established a lasting reputation for providing suitable machines for public service, and various armed forces throughout the world remained regular customers. Their model B–40 was adopted for solo despatch and display team use, in particular by the Australian and British forces during the mid 1960's.

The model B–40 had a unit construction single-cylinder 350cc engine, with an iron barrerl and light alloy head featuring coil springs, mounted within a single downtube frame. It was first seen in public at the Earls Court show of 1960, where it replaced the long lived model B–31. While different forces adopted a variety of specifications, the military conversion included a pair of canvas pannier bags, front and rear frames mounted crash bars, and an overall coat of the appropriate service livery. A number of post-war display teams also adopted large areas of chromium plate, although this would quickly be overpainted for battlefield conditions.

As the model B–40 was clearly an enlarged derivative of the earlier 250cc model C–15, to maintain the lightest possible machine the Australian military specified the larger engine within the smaller model frame. Further military specifications included a repositioned electric horn, a fully enclosed chain final drive, and the use of front fork gaiters. The British military model also had an oil filter. These machines remained in service within the Australian and British forces until the late 1970's, when they were replaced by the Suzuki GS–400 and Bombardier 250 respectively.

Brief specification

ENGINE TYPE	: BSA – Vertical single cylinder
DISPLACEMENT	: 343cc (79×70mm)
VALVE DESIGN	: Overhead valves
COMPRESSION	:
POWER OUTPUT	: 18BHP at 6,000rpm
ELECTRICS	: 6 volt
CARBURETTOR	: One – Amal 190
GEARBOX	: Foot change, 4 speed, unit construction
TRANSMISSION	: Enclosed chain final drive
FRAME	: Tubular construction
SUSPENSION	: Hydraulic damped telescopic front forks
	: Hydraulic damped trailing rear forks
TIRE SIZE	: 18×3.25/4.00"
BRAKES	: Internal expanding front wheel drum
	: Internal expanding rear wheel drum
DRY WEIGHT	: Solo 162.3kg
DIMENSIONS	: Wheel base 1359mm
MAX SPEED	: Solo 55mph

1965 BSA MODEL B-40 & AUSTRALIAN SOLDIER © DAVID ANSELL

· 1965 ·
TEMPO MILITARY 175
(Norway)

The Norwegian armed forces did not use many motor cycles before the Second World War and those adopted were imported from various countries. After 1945 a number of war-surplus machines were acquired, the majority of British origin, with few modifications. The main Norwegian conversion was the fitting of ski attachments for service in the snow. Many of these machines remained in active military service for more than twenty years. The Ariel W–NG model continued to be used until 1959, and some BSA M20 and Norton 16H models were used until 1965.

By this date, the Norwegian factory of Jonas Øglaend A.s of Sandnes had supplied a number of their Tempo 175 model to the armed forces. This company had manufactured a number of lightweight motor cycles and mopeds with various proprietary engines for domestic sales since 1949. Although with few modifications, a total of 650 of these machines were delivered between 1961 and 1966 for military service, the largest number being adopted in 1965. The military conversion included a restyled petrol tank and dual seat, a rear carrier rack, and an overall coat of the appropriate service livery. The Tempo military 175 model also remained in service for many years and a small number were still being used during 1981.

Brief specification

ENGINE TYPE	: Sachs – Vertical single cylinder
DISPLACEMENT	: 175cc (62×58mm)
VALVE DESIGN	: Two stroke
COMPRESSION	: 6.5:1
POWER OUTPUT	: 10BHP at 5,250rpm
ELECTRICS	: 6 volt, 45 watt
CARBURETTOR	: One – Bing type 1/24/77
GEARBOX	: Foot change, 4 speed, unit construction
TRANSMISSION	: Enclosed chain final drive
FRAME	: Tubular construction
SUSPENSION	: Hydraulic damped telescopic front forks
	: Hydraulic damped trailing rear forks
TIRE SIZE	: 19×3.25″
BRAKES	: Internal expanding front wheel drum
	: Internal expanding rear wheel drum
DRY WEIGHT	: Solo 104kg
DIMENSIONS	: Wheel base 1270mm
MAX SPEED	: Solo 50mph

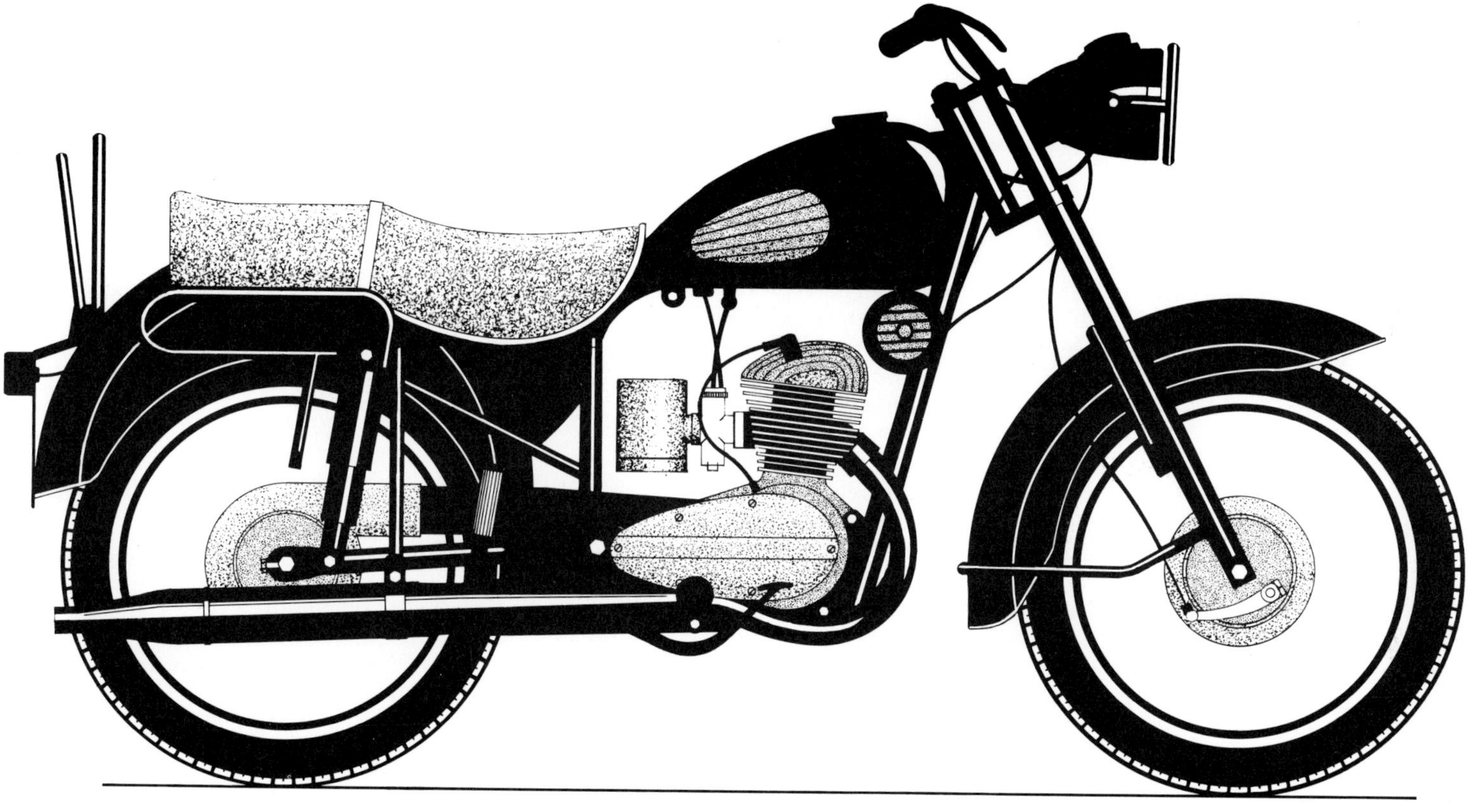

**1965 TEMPO MILITARY 175
NORWAY**

· 1967 ·

HUSQVARNA 256–A
(Sweden)

The Swedish armed forces requested a number of the Husqvarna 112 models in 1940, but the factory was heavily committed to other military production at this time, and these machines were eventually assembled at the Albin-Motor and Monark factories. Although the Husqvarna factory had supplied eight of their Silver Arrow machines for evaluation in 1962, these were not adopted, and the 256–A model became the first Husqvarna motor cycle to be delivered in any quantity to the Swedish military since the 180 model in 1926.

The Husqvarna 256–A model was designed for solo multi-terrain use within military service. For this purpose, the machine featured a high ground clearance, high-level exhaust system, high clearance mudguards, trails type tires, wide handlebars, and a large carburettor filter. Further military specifications included a rear carrier rack, an auxiliary case mounted on the petrol tank, additional masked lighting, and an overall coat of the appropriate service livery. Between 1967 and 1968 a total of 1,100 of these machines were supplied, and remained in service throughout the 1970's, until superseded by the Husqvarna 258–A in 1980.

Brief specification

ENGINE TYPE	: Husqvarna – Vertical single cylinder
DISPLACEMENT	: 245cc (69.5×64.5mm)
VALVE DESIGN	: Two stroke
COMPRESSION	: 8.9:1
POWER OUTPUT	: 15.4BHP
ELECTRICS	: 12 volt, 53 watt
CARBURETTOR	: One – Bing 22.5mm
GEARBOX	: Foot change, 4 speed, unit construction
TRANSMISSION	: Exposed chain final drive
FRAME	: Tubular construction
SUSPENSION	: Hydraulic damped telescopic front forks
	: Hydraulic damped trailing rear forks
TIRE SIZE	: 21×3.00/18×4.00"
BRAKES	: Internal expanding front wheel drum
	: Internal expanding rear wheel drum
DRY WEIGHT	: Solo 130kg
DIMENSIONS	: Wheel base 1380mm, Ground clearance 230mm
MAX SPEED	: Solo 75mph

Husqvarna

**1967 HUSQVARNA 256-A
SWEDEN**

· 1967 ·
MOTO GUZZI V-7
(Italy)

The Moto Guzzi V–7 model was assembled around a further development of the engine that had powered the Moto Guzzi 3×3 model, a unique military designed tricycle manufactured for the Italian armed forces between 1960 and 1963. The V–7 model continued this tradition and was originally designed for police or military use only. It was not until a renewed interest in motor cycles was realised that the Moto Guzzi factory began to introduce this machine for private use as well. The major developments during the following ten years included a continued increase in engine capacity, hydraulic operated disc brakes, an integral front and rear braking system, a five-speed gearbox, and an automatic gear change machine.

The military potential remained, however, and the Moto Guzzi factory offered various equipment with selected models. These accessories included a handlebar mounted windscreen, front and rear mounted crash bars, additional lighting and syren, radio equipment, and a pair of pressed steel panniers. The Moto Guzzi V–7 model was first introduced in 1967, and immediately adopted by Italian police and military departments. This machine proved to be so successful that later versions were adopted by public departments throughout the world. While the majority of these were used for solo escort and general police duties, a number also had various sidecars attached.

Brief specification

ENGINE TYPE	: Moto Guzzi – V-twin cylinder
DISPLACEMENT	: 703cc (80×70mm)
VALVE DESIGN	: Overhead valves
COMPRESSION	: 7.2:1
POWER OUTPUT	: 35BHP at 5,000rpm
ELECTRICS	: 12 volt, 300 watt
CARBURETTOR	: Two – Dell'Orto VHB 29 CD, or 20 CS
GEARBOX	: Foot change, 4 speed, unit construction
TRANSMISSION	: Enclosed shaft final drive
FRAME	: Tubular construction
SUSPENSION	: Hydraulic damped telescopic front forks
	: Hydraulic damped trailing rear forks
TIRE SIZE	: 18×4.00″
BRAKES	: Internal expanding front wheel drum Ø 220mm
	: Internal expanding rear wheel drum Ø 220mm
DRY WEIGHT	: Solo 250kg
DIMENSIONS	: Wheel base 1445mm
MAX SPEED	: Solo 95mph

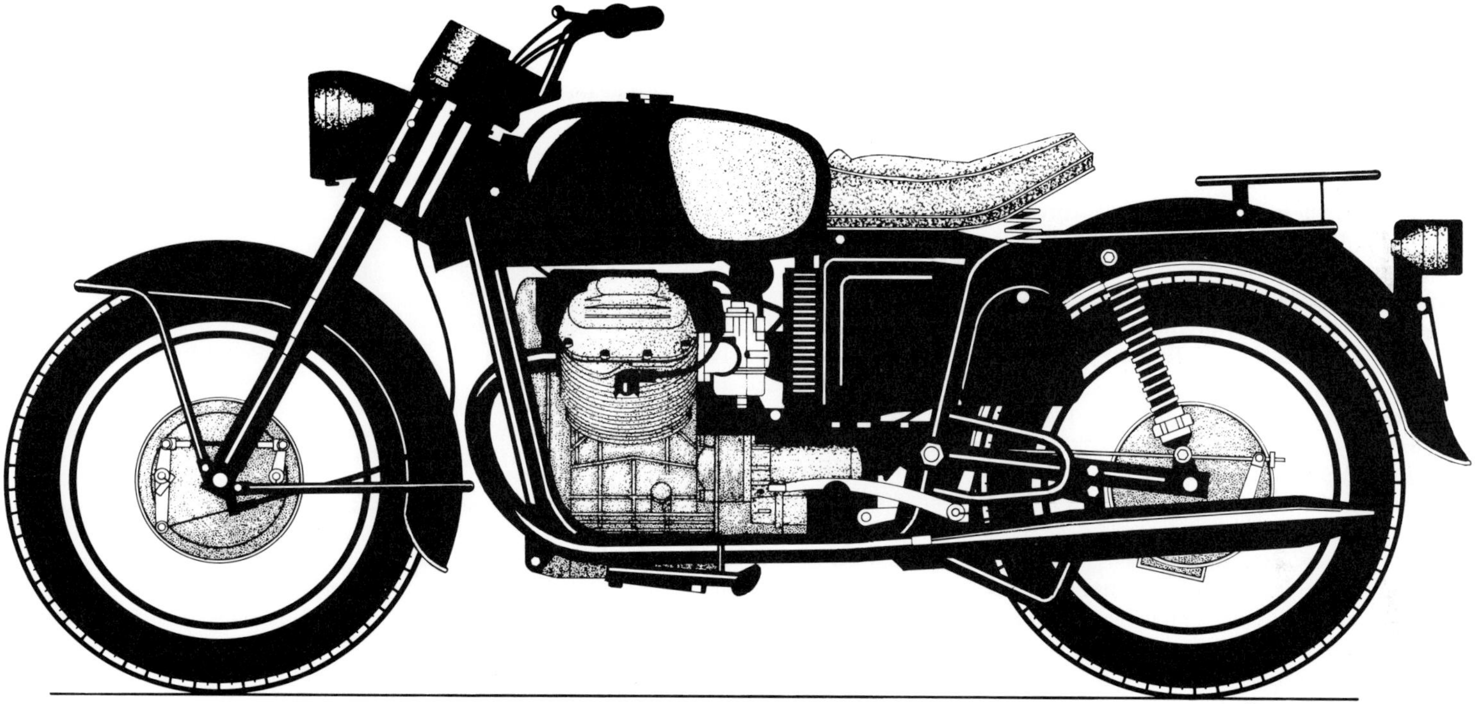

1967 MOTO GUZZI V-7
ITALY

· 1968 ·
CONDOR MODEL A–250–68
(Switzerland)

During the mid 1950's the Swiss military administration prepared specifications for their ideal military motorcycle, and after a three-year trial period the Condor model A–250 was adopted in 1959. With this machine, the Condor factory of Courfaivre replaced their opposed twin-cylinder sidevalve engine design and introduced a vertical single-cylinder engine with an overhead valve lay out. While the model A–250 had a shaft drive there were no other similarities with any earlier Condor military motor cycle. Further major features for military service included high ground clearance and relatively low weight.

The Condor model A–250 was continually developed until the final version introduced in 1968, by which date a total of 573 of these machines had been supplied to the Swiss armed forces. The majority of changes were only minor and the machine remained besically the same throughout its production. These machines were used for solo despatch, escort, and general police duties, and the military specifications included various armament carrying fittings, auxiliary masked lighting, a pair of leather pannier bags, and an overall ocat of the appropriate service livery. A large number of these machines were still in active military servie in 1980.

Brief specification

ENGINE TYPE	: Condor – Vertical single cylinder
DISPLACEMENT	: 247cc (68×68mm)
VALVE DESIGN	: Overhead valves
COMPRESSION	: 7.8:1
POWER OUTPUT	: 13BHP at 6,000rpm
ELECTRICS	: 6 volt, 60/90 watt
CARBURETTOR	: One – Amal Monobloc 376
GEARBOX	: Foot change, 4 speed, unit construction
TRANSMISSION	: Enclosed shaft final drive
FRAME	: Tubular construction
SUSPENSION	: Hydraulic damped telescopic front forks
	: Hydraulic damped trailing rear forks
TIRE SIZE	: 18×3.25″
BRAKES	: Internal expanding front wheel drum Ø 180mm
	: Internal expanding rear wheel drum Ø 180mm
DRY WEIGHT	: Solo 165kg
DIMENSIONS	: Wheel base 1350mm, Ground clearance 180mm
MAX SPEED	: Solo 60mph

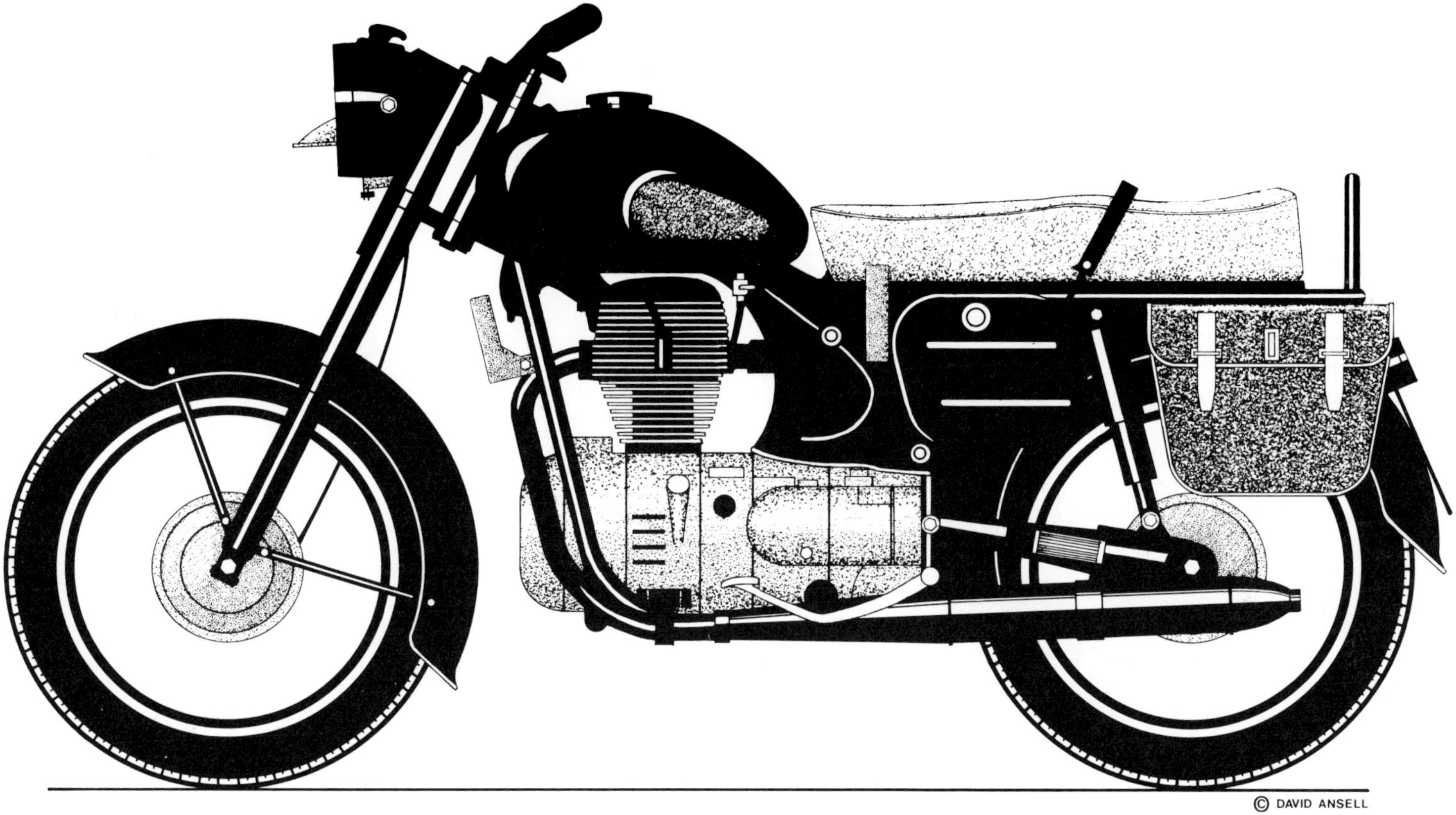

1968 CONDOR MODEL A-250
SWITZERLAND

· 1968 ·

DNIEPER K–650
(Soviet Union)

During the early years of the Second World War the Moska National Works began production on the M–72 for military service within the Soviet armed forces. This machine was a close copy of the BMW model R–71, which had been assembled as the M–71 under license in the Soviet Union since 1939. While a number of the M–72 machines were used solo, they were mainly supplied with a copy of the Steib military sidecar. They were later also produced at the Gorky motor cycle factory, and remained in active military service throughout the 1960's, when superseded by the K–750 from the Kiyev motor cycle factory. While the K–750 retained the same side-valve engine design of 750cc displacement, major new features included a trailing rear fork suspension to replace the plunger type design, and the adoption of full-width drum brakes.

In the late 1960's the K–650 model was also introduced. This used the same cycle parts and transmission as the K–750, but produced a higher output from an engine of 650cc displacement with an overhead valve layout. At the end of the Second World War, a large quantity of BMW equipment had been moved to their factory in Eisenach (which became part of East Germany), and so BMW ingenuity was probably used as the basis of this machine also. The Dnieper K–650 was mainly used as a combination and equipped with three interchangeable wheels with a spare mounted on the sidecar. This machine remained in production until 1970, when superseded by the further developed Dnieper MT–9.

Brief specification

ENGINE TYPE	: Dnieper – Transverse opposed twin cylinder
DISPLACEMENT	: 649cc (78×68mm)
VALVE DESIGN	: Overhead valves
COMPRESSION	: 6:1
POWER OUTPUT	: 32BHP at 5,200rpm
ELECTRICS	: 6 volt, 65 watt
CARBURETTOR	: Two – K–3016
GEARBOX	: Foot change, 4 speed, unit construction
TRANSMISSION	: Exposed shaft final drive
FRAME	: Tubular construction
SUSPENSION	: Hydraulic damped telescopic front forks
	: Hydraulic damped trailing rear forks
TIRE SIZE	: 19×3.75″
BRAKES	: Internal expanding front wheel drum
	: Internal expanding rear wheel drum
DRY WEIGHT	: W/SC 300kg
DIMENSIONS	: Wheel base 1500mm, Ground clearance 120mm
MAX SPEED	: W/SC 60mph

ДНЕПР 1968 DNIEPER K-650 SOVIET UNION

· 1969 ·
BMW MODEL R–60/5
(West Germany)

The BMW factory of Munich introduced the series 5 model range in 1969. These machines had a tranverse mounted opposed twin-cylinder engine of 500cc, 600cc, and 750cc displacement, and the previously used Earles-type front fork suspension was replaced with a more conventional telescopic design. Further major changes included a shorter wheelbase, a return to 19″ wheels, and a slight upward tilt in the engine mounting. The model was superseded in 1973 by the series 6 model range. The 500cc model was discontinued, and two versions of a 900cc machine were included. Three years later the series 7 models were introduced and the 900cc models were replaced by three versions of a 1000cc machine. During this period further developments included the adoption of hydraulic disc brakes, a five-speed gearbox, and a return to a longer wheelbase.

German manufacturers have not been allowed to sell equipment to a military authority since the Second World War, so any post-war BMW motor cycle adopted for service is beyond official knowledge of the factory and has been supplied by a third agent. But they are permitted to sell equipment to the police, and BMW has provided a number of machines to various military police departments. Examples from each of the series 5, 6, and 7 model ranges have been adopted by military police forces throughout the world, the conversion including front and rear crash bars, a pair of pannier bags, additional lights and syren, various radio equipment, and a frame mounted fairing.

Brief specification

ENGINE TYPE	: BMW – Transverse opposed twin cylinder
DISPLACEMENT	: 599cc (73.5×70.6mm)
VALVE DESIGN	: Overhead valves
COMPRESSION	: 9.2:1
POWER OUTPUT	: 40BHP at 6,400rpm
ELECTRICS	: 12 volt, 180 watt
CARBURETTOR	: Two – Bing 26mm
GEARBOX	: Foot change, 4 speed, unit construction
TRANSMISSION	: Enclosed shaft final drive
FRAME	: Tubular construction
SUSPENSION	: Hydraulic damped telescopic front forks
	: Hydraulic damped trailing rear forks
TIRE SIZE	: 19×3.25/18×4.00″
BRAKES	: Internal expanding front wheel drum ⌀ 200mm
	: Internal expanding rear wheel drum ⌀ 200mm
DRY WEIGHT	: Solo 190kg
DIMENSIONS	: Wheel base 1387mm, Ground clearance 165mm
MAX SPEED	: 100mph

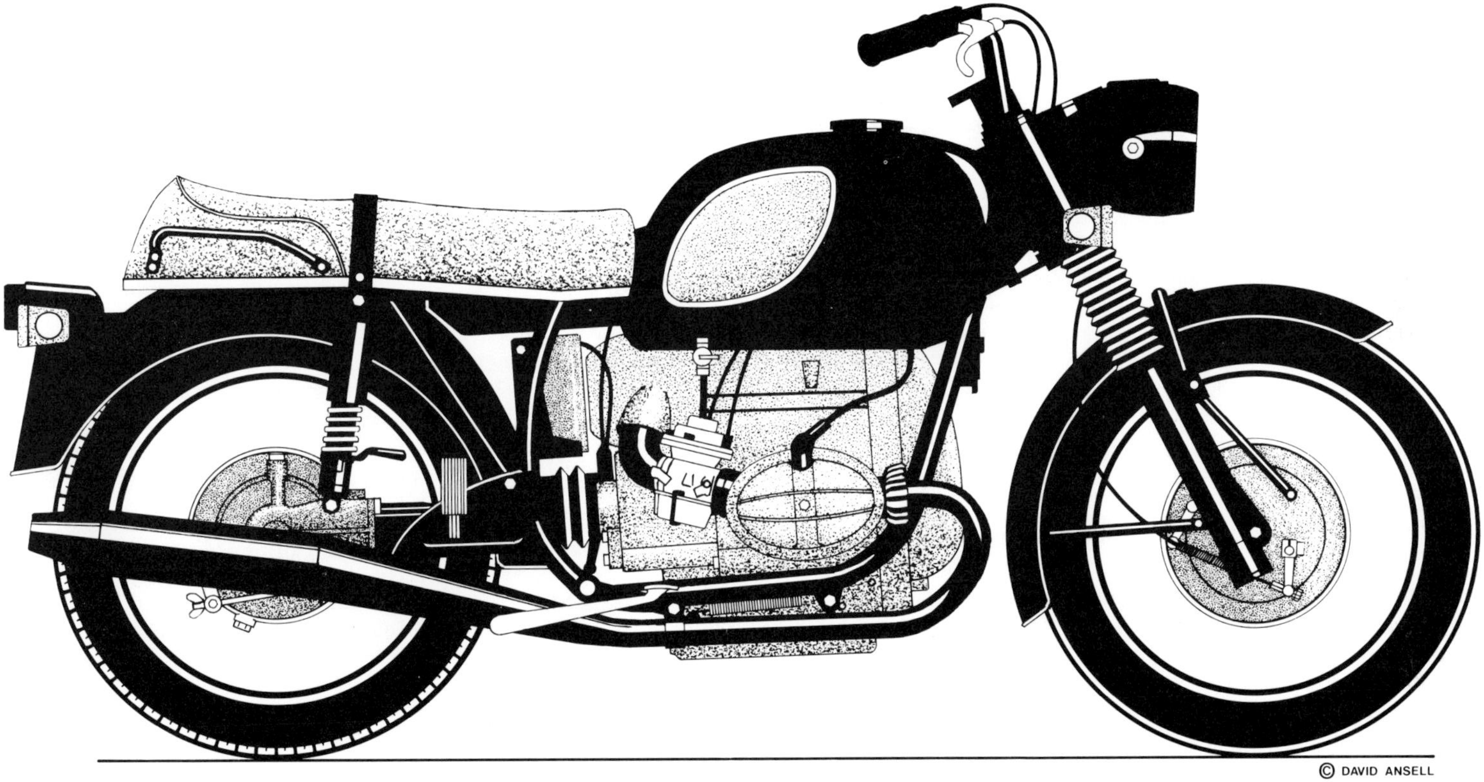

 **1969 BMW MODEL R-60/5 USA WEST GERMANY**

· 1969 ·
MZ MODEL ES–250–2
(East German)

During the Second World War, the motor cycle factory of Zschopau had produced the DKW RT–125 and NZ–350 models for the German armed forces. When peace was declared the Zschopau factory became part of East Germany and the DKW business moved to a new factory at Ingolstadt and later Düsseldorf. From 1946 the Zschopau factory began to produce motor cycles under the name of IFA, and from the late 1950's the initials MZ (Motorradwerke Zschopau) were introduced. The Zschopau factory continued to develop the original DKW design and during the late 1960's the MZ ES range of models was introduced. While the origin of the engine could clearly be seen, it had been mounted within quite a different cycle frame.

The MZ ES range of models had a unit construction single-cylinder two-stroke engine and four-speed gearbox, mounted within a pressed steel and tubular cycle frame with Earles-type front and trailing rear fork suspension. The most noticeable feature of this design being the forward extension of the petrol tank which housed the headlamp. These machines wer offered in standard road and trials trim, with engines of 125cc, 150cc, 175cc, and 250cc displacement. The MZ ES–250 model was adopted by the East German armed forces and remained in military service throughout the 1970's. This machine was used both solo and with various sidecars attached, with few military modifictions.

Brief specification

ENGINE TYPE	: MZ – Vertical single cylinder
DISPLACEMENT	: 243cc (69×65mm)
VALVE DESIGN	: Two stroke
COMPRESSION	: 10:1
POWER OUTPUT	: 21BHP at 5,500rpm
ELECTRICS	: 6 volt
CARBURETTOR	: One – BVF 30mm
GEARBOX	: Foot change, 4 speed, unit construction
TRANSMISSION	: Enclosed shaft final drive
FRAME	: Pressed steel & Tubular construction
SUSPENSION	: Hydraulic damped Earles-type front forks
	: Hydraulic damped trailing rear forks
TIRE SIZE	: 16×3.25/3.5″
BRAKES	: Internal expanding front wheel drum
	: Internal expanding rear wheel drum
DRY WEIGHT	: Solo 138kg
DIMENSIONS	: Wheel base 1270mm
MAX SPEED	: 75mph

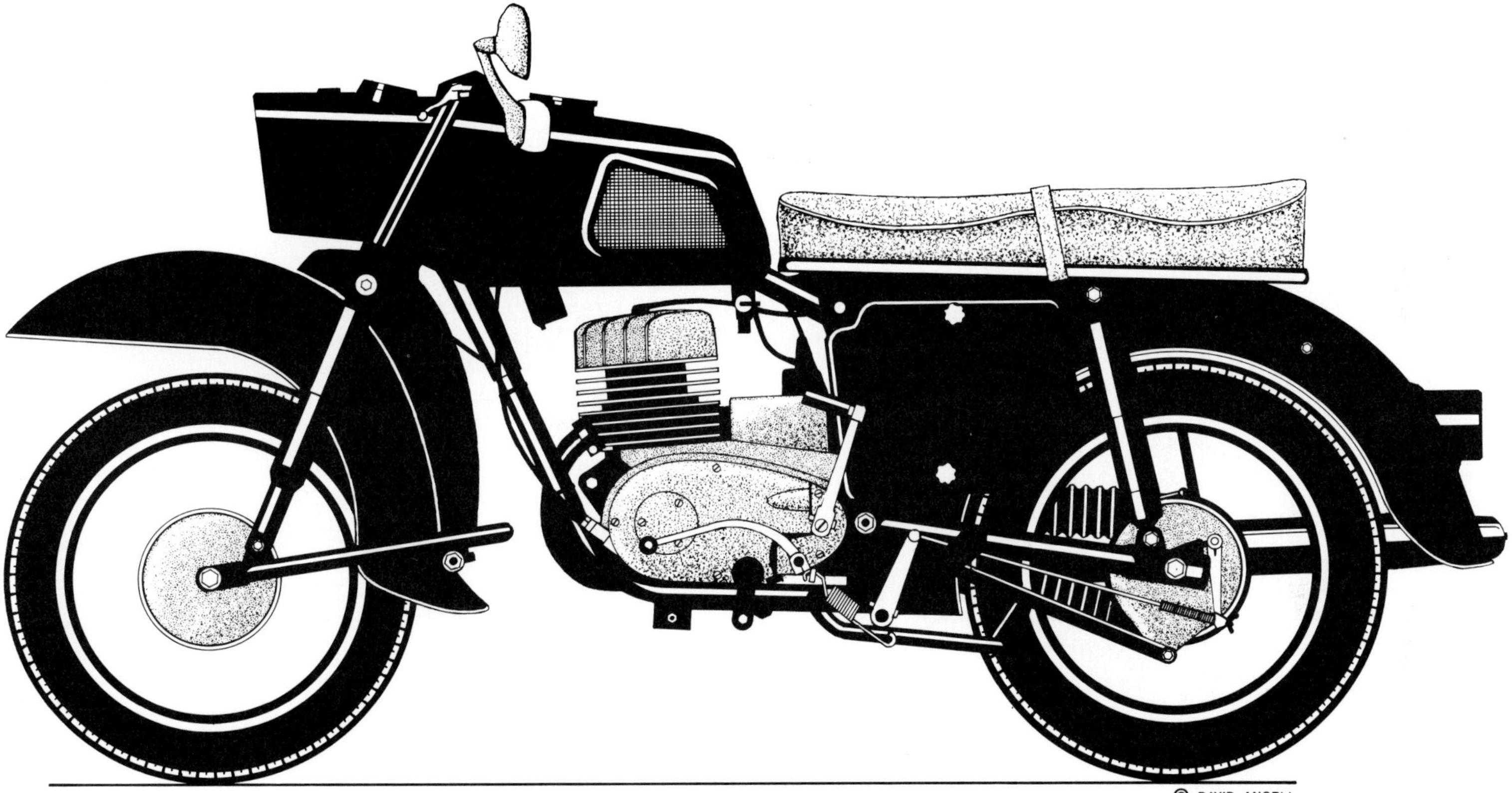

1969 MZ MODEL ES-250-2
EAST GERMANY

· 1969 ·
PUCH TYPE 250–MCH
(Austria)

The Puch factory of Graz continued to develop their split-cylinder engine design throughout the 1960's, and during this period the British Greeves and Polish Promot manufacturers also adopted these engines. The Puch type 250–MCH was first assembled during the late 1960's and, in keeping with contemporary design, was introduced with a redesigned cycle frame with the pressed steel fittings of earlier Puch machines discarded. While the engine provided a very similar performance the cycle frame had a longer wheelbase and gave a higher ground clearance. Further major features included a dual seat and a side stand of 700mm pivoted from beneath this.

The Austrian armed forces adopted the Puch type 250–MCH in 1969 for solo despatch, escort, and general police duties within urban areas. It remained basically a civilian model with few modifications. The military conversion included a pair of canvas pannier bags, and a coat of the appropriate service service livery. As the machine was adopted during a period without war the civilian chromium fittings were accepted as standard. The Puch type 250–MCH remained in service throughout the 1970's until superseded by the more powerful BMW model R–60.

Brief specification

ENGINE TYPE	: Puch – Vertical split single cylinder
DISPLACEMENT	: 248cc (2×45×78mm)
VALVE DESIGN	: Two stroke
COMPRESSION	: 6.2:1
POWER OUTPUT	: 14BHP at 5,500rpm
ELECTRICS	: 6 volt, 45/60 watt
CARBURETTOR	: One – Puch type P 32/1
GEARBOX	: Foot change, 4 speed, unit construction
TRANSMISSION	: Exposed chain final drive
FRAME	: Tubular construction
SUSPENSION	: Hydraulic damped telescopic front forks
	: Hydraulic damped trailing rear forks
TIRE SIZE	: 19×3.5″
BRAKES	: Internal expanding front wheel drum ⌀ 160mm
	: Internal expanding rear wheel drum ⌀ 160mm
DRY WEIGHT	: Solo 155kg
DIMENSIONS	: Wheel base 1350mm, Ground clearance 190mm
MAX SPEED	: Solo 60mph

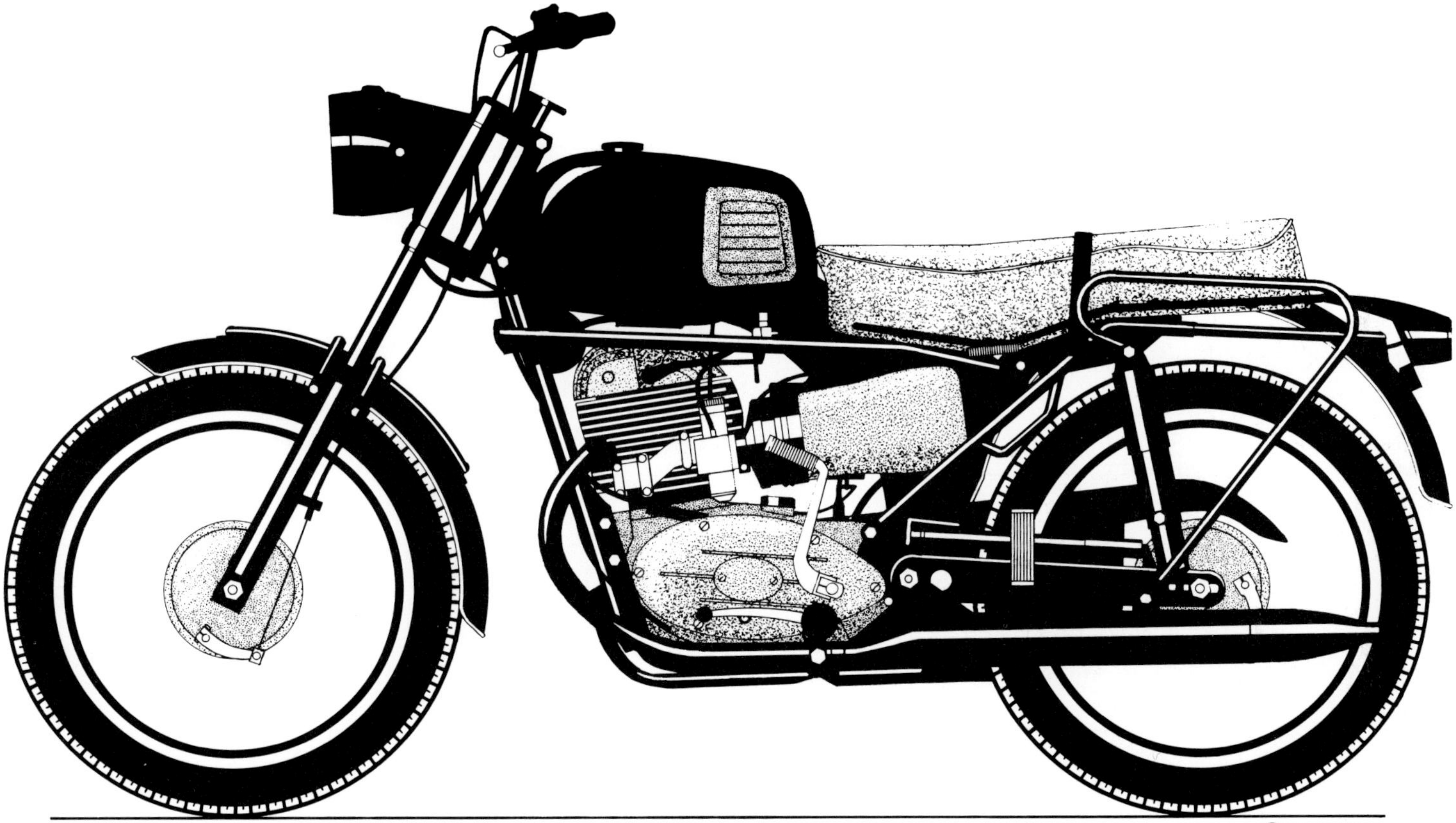

**1969 PUCH TYPE 250-MCH
AUSTRIA**

· 1970 ·
HERCULES K–125–B
(West Germany)

After 18 successful years producing bicycles, the Nürberger Hercules-Werke factory assembled their first motor cycle in 1904. Although the business continued to develop various powered vehicles until 1914, only their bicycle remained in production after the First World War. The Hercules company resumed motor cycle manufacture in 1928, and, with a number of proprietory engines, introduced various machines during the following 10 years. After the Second World War, however, three quarters of the factory had been destroyed, and Hercules production returned to bicycles once again. Concentrating on machines with small capacity two-stroke engines, Hercules introduced their first post-war motor cycle in 1950, and within 10 years had obtained 30 per cent of the German motor cycle market. In 1966 Hercules bought out their rivals in the Zweirad Union, and although the Hercules works team was disbanded at this time the factory began to assist private riders.

During the late 1960's Hercules introduced a range of trials models with Earles-type front fork suspension, and once the military potential of such machines had been realised a suitable model was also prepared. Designated 'B' for Bundeswehr the Hercules K–125 was adopted by the West German armed forces in 1970. This machine was used for solo despatch service with the possibility of on- and off-road use. Basically a civilian model, the military conversion included a rear carrier rack, and an overall coat of the appropriate service livery. The Hercules K–125–B remained in active military service throughout the 1970's, until superseded in 1981 by the further developed Hercules 125 Military, which adopted more conventional telescopic front fork suspension. This machine was also very successful, and by early 1984 the factory had supplied approximately 15,000 units.

Brief specification

ENGINE TYPE	: Sachs – Vertical single cylinder
DISPLACEMENT	: 124cc (54×54mm)
VALVE DESIGN	: Two stroke
COMPRESSION	: 9:1
POWER OUTPUT	: 12.5BHP at 7,000rpm
ELECTRICS	: 6 volt, 35 watt
CARBURETTOR	: One – Bing 24mm
GEARBOX	: Foot change, 5 speed, unit construction
TRANSMISSION	: Exposed chain final drive
FRAME	: Tubular construction
SUSPENSION	: Hydraulic damped Earles-type front forks
	: Hydraulic damped trailing rear forks
TIRE SIZE	: 18×3.25/3.5″
BRAKES	: Internal expanding front wheel drum ⌀ 140mm
	: Internal expanding rear wheel drum ⌀ 140mm
DRY WEIGHT	: Solo 140kg
DIMENSIONS	: Wheel base 1295mm
MAX SPEED	: Solo 60mph

HERCULES

1970 HERCULES K-125-B
WEST GERMANY

· 1970 ·
MOTO GUZZI FALCONE
(Italy)

The Moto Guzzi factory began to design a new military motor cycle in 1967, to replace the ageing military Falcone of the early 1950's. As a result, the Nuovo Falcone Militare model was introduced at the Milan Motor Show in 1969. Although this machine had a completely redesigned engine and cycle frame, it continued the Moto Guzzi Falcone tradition with a horizontally mounted engine of 500cc displacement with 88mm bore and 82mm stroke dimensions. The major new features included an improved hydraulic damped suspension system, a higher compression engine with an increased output, and an improved electrical system with a higher wattage. Although the average performance of this machine was very similar to the earlier model, the extra power of the engine was required as the use of further military equipment had increased the weight by 44kg.

The Moto Guzzi Nuovo Falcone Militare was manufactured and supplied to the Italian armed forces between 1970 and 1976. This machine was used for solo despatch, escort, and general police duties, within urban areas. The military equipment included a handlbar mounted windscreen, front and rear mounted crash bars, pillion seat or rear carrier rack, additional lighting and a syren, various radio equipment, a pair of pannier bags, and an overall coat of the appropriate service livery: the Polizia Stradale (Highway Police) in grey-green, the Carabinieri (Military Police) in blue, and the Esercito (Army) in olive-green. In 1971 a number of these machines were also adopted by the armed forces in Ghana and Yugoslavia.

Brief specification

ENGINE TYPE	: Moto Guzzi – Horizontal single cylinder
DISPLACEMENT	: 498cc (88×82mm)
VALVE DESIGN	: Overhead valves
COMPRESSION	: 6.8:1
POWER OUTPUT	: 26.2BHP at 4,800rpm
ELECTRICS	: 12 volt, 150 watt
CARBURETTOR	: One – Dell'Orto VHB 29 A
GEARBOX	: Foot change, 4 speed, unit construction
TRANSMISSION	: Exposed chain final drive
FRAME	: Tubular construction
SUSPENSION	: Hydraulic damped telescopic front forks
	: Hydraulic damped trailing rear forks
TIRE SIZE	: 18×3.5"
BRAKES	: Internal expanding front wheel drum
	: Internal expanding rear wheel drum
DRY WEIGHT	: Solo 214kg
DIMENSIONS	: Wheel base 1450mm
MAX SPEED	: Solo 80mph

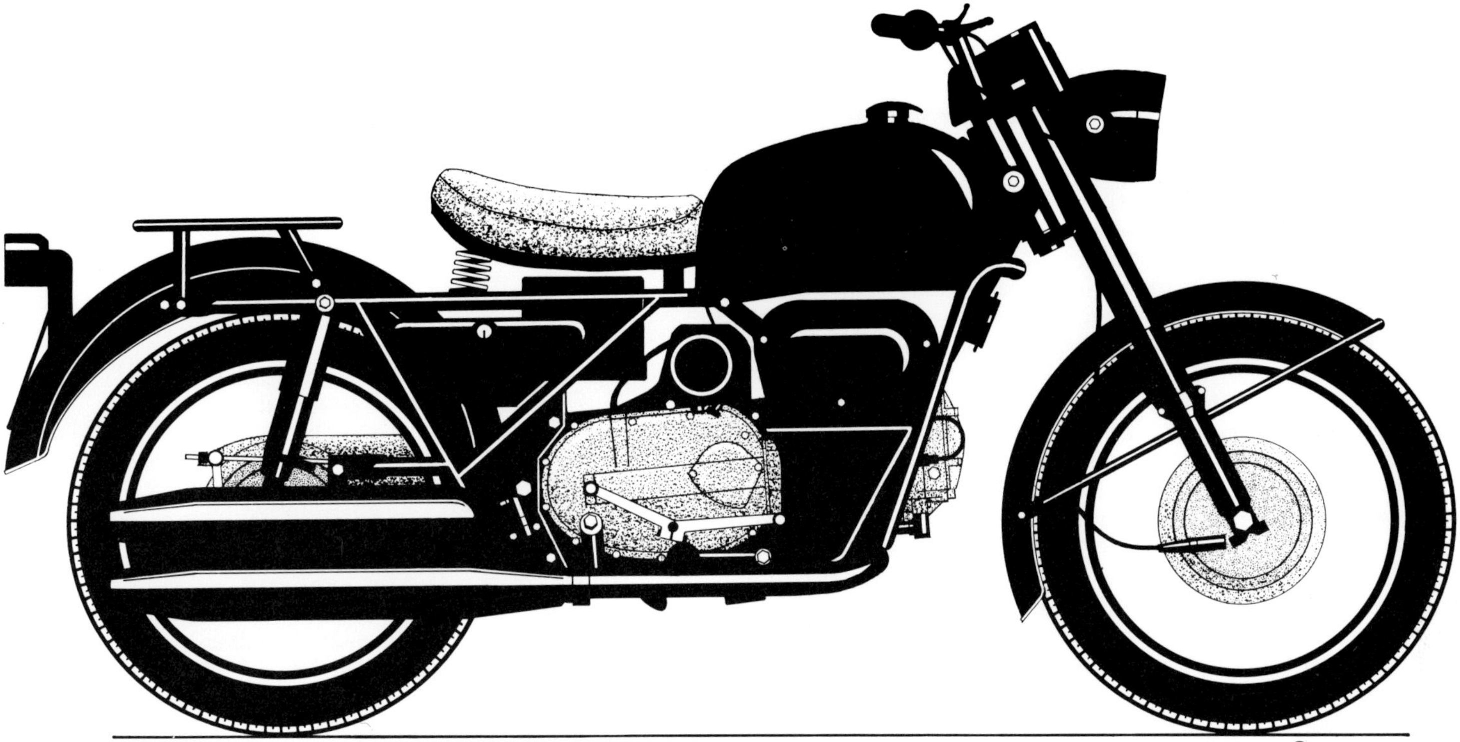

1970 MOTO GUZZI FALCONE ITALY

· 1973 ·
CONDOR MODEL A–350
(Switzerland)

The Condor motor cycle factory of Courfaivre introduced their model A–350 in 1973. With the use of an established engine design from the Italian factory of Ducati, this machine was able to supersede the performance of the Condor model A–250 manufactured throughout the 1960's. The Ducati unit construction engine and gearbox design featured an advanced overhead camshaft and five-speed gearbox. While the Condor model A–350 remained similar in general appearance to the model A–250, a chain final drive was also introduced to replace the previously used shaft drive design. Further new features included an increased wheelbase and a reduced ground clearance.

The Condor model A–350 was first adopted by the Swiss armed forces in 1973, and remained in service throughout the 1970's during which period a total of 3,004 machines were procured. This machine was used for solo despatch, escort, and general police duties. The military specifications included various armament carrying fittings, auxiliary masked lighting, a pair of leather pannier bags, and an overall coat of the appropriate service livery. A large number of these machines were still in active military service during 1980.

Brief specification

ENGINE TYPE	: Ducati/Condor – Vertical single cylinder
DISPLACEMENT	: 340cc (76×75mm)
VALVE DESIGN	: Overhead valves
COMPRESSION	: 8.2:1
POWER OUTPUT	: 16.6BHP at 5,000rpm
ELECTRICS	: 6 volt, 70 watt
CARBURETTOR	: One – Dell'Orto type VHB 27 AD
GEARBOX	: Foot change, 5 speed, unit construction
TRANSMISSION	: Exposed chain final drive
FRAME	: Tubular construction
SUSPENSION	: Hydraulic damped telescopic front forks
	: Hydraulic damped trailing rear forks
TIRE SIZE	: 18×3.5″
BRAKES	: Internal expanding front wheel drum ⌀ 200mm
	: Internal expanding rear wheel drum ⌀ 200mm
DRY WEIGHT	: Solo 177kg
DIMENSIONS	: Wheel base 1400mm, Ground clearance 170mm
MAX SPEED	: Solo 90mph

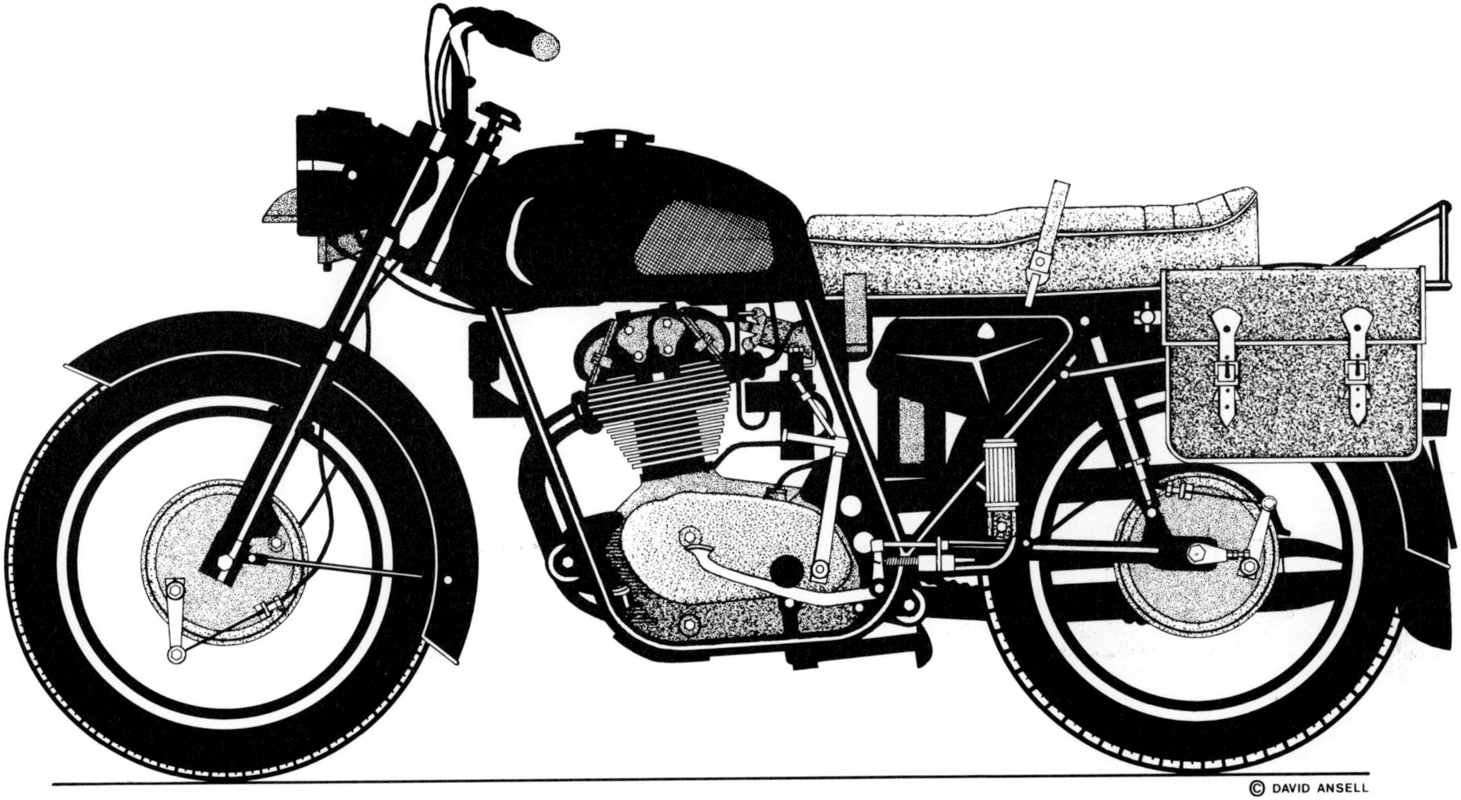

1973 CONDOR MODEL A-350
SWITZERLAND

· 1974 ·

HÄGGLUND XM–74
(Sweden)

In 1971 the Material Administration of the Swedish armed forces requested a military motor cycle prototype from the Hägglund, Husqvarna, and Monark factories. The Hägglund business of Ornskolsvik had not produced motor cycles before but was one of the country's major military vehicle manufactures. The following year, Hägglund presented their XM–72 model with a single-cylinder 293cc two-stroke Sachs engine. Further major features of this machine included an automatic transmission, a pull-cord start, and an enclosed shaft final drive. The cycle frame was a welded steel construction that held the petrol and the carburettor intake, and the suspension consisted of a single Earles-type front fork and a single trailing fork design. The wheels were equipped with hydraulic operated disc brakes. While all three factories presented suitable machines, all were far from completion, but Hägglund was able to gain the contract by quoting the lowest production cost in 1973.

After continued development, the XM-72 model changed considerably and the XM–74 model introduced in 1974 was quite different. It had a single-cylinder 345cc two-stroke Bombardier/Rotax engine. The single front fork suspension was replaced by a more conventional telescopic pair, and the pressed steel wheels with six spokes were replaced with a design of eight. Although disc brakes were intended for this model also, suitable protection could not be designed and drum brakes were fitted. A major feature of the original model had been the automatic transmission, and so after various difficulties with the Hägglund/DAF design the contract was taken over by the Husqvarna factory and the model 258–A was eventually produced. During this period the Hägglund factory had assembled 6 of the XM–72 and 40 of the XM–74 models.

Brief specification

ENGINE TYPE	: Bombardier/Rotax – Vertical single cylinder
DISPLACEMENT	: 345cc (76×76mm)
VALVE DESIGN	: Two strokes
COMPRESSION	: 9:1
POWER OUTPUT	: 24BHP at 5,300rpm
ELECTRICS	: 12 volt, 140 watt
CARBURETTOR	: One – Tillotson HR
GEARBOX	: Hägglund/DAF variomatic, unit construction
TRANSMISSION	: Enclosed shaft final drive
FRAME	: Welded steel construction
SUSPENSION	: Hydraulic damped telescopic front forks
	: Hydraulic damped single rear trailing fork
TIRE SIZE	: 21×3.00/18×4.00"
BRAKES	: Internal expanding front wheel drum
	: Internal expanding rear wheel drum
DRY WEIGHT	: Solo 136kg
DIMENSIONS	: Wheel base 1410mm, Ground clearance 237mm
MAX SPEED	: Solo 80mph

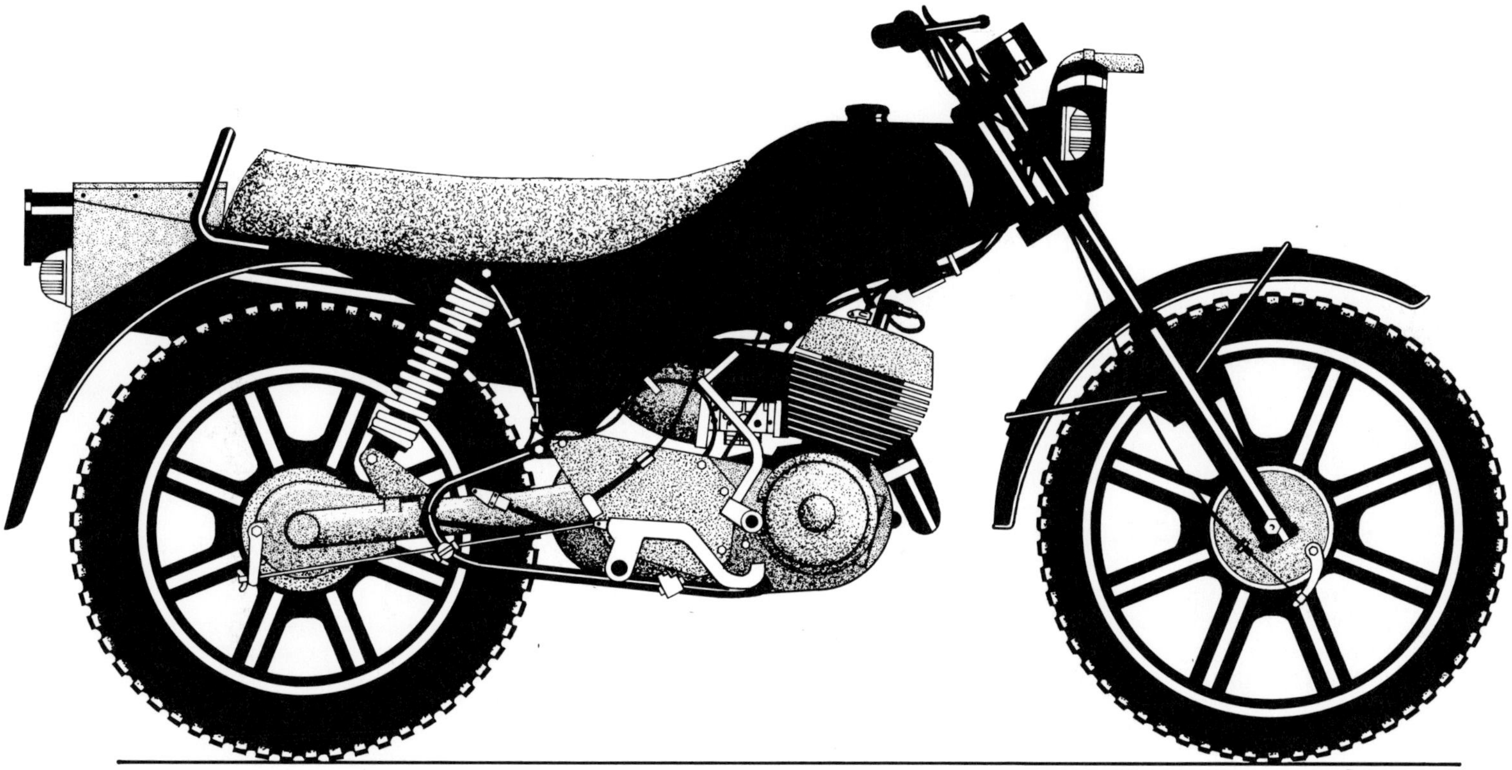

**1974 HÄGGLUNDS XM-74
SWEDEN**

· 1974 ·

JAWA 350 TYPE 634-4
(Czechoslovakia)

The Jawa 350 Kyvacka model of 1957 remained in active military service within the Czechoslovak armed forces until 1974, when it was superseded by the Jawa 350 type 634-4 model. Although this machine was technically similar to its predecessor and also had a twin cylinder 350cc two stroke engine, the new model was produced with a more contemporary appearance. The major new features included a duplex cradle frame with a longer wheelbase and higher ground clearance, a return to 18″ wheels with lightweight mudguards without a deep valance, and an improved electrical system with restyled light fittings and traffic indicators.

While the 634-4 model had an engine with the same bore and stroke dimenstions as the earlier machine, the compression ratio had been increased and produced a greater performance. Further new features included the introduction of an automatic lubrication system, a squarer style without the use of a pressed steel carburettor cover, and a redesigned transmission enclosure. The new machine was adopted for similar military service and was used both solo and with various sidecars attached. This model remained in service throughout the 1970's, and a large number were still in use during 1980.

Brief specification

ENGINE TYPE	: Jawa – Vertical twin cylinder
DISPLACEMENT	: 343cc (58×65mm)
VALVE DESIGN	: Two stroke
COMPRESSION	: 9.2:1
POWER OUTPUT	: 28BHP at 5,250rpm
ELECTRICS	: 6 volt, 75 watt
CARBURETTOR	: One – Jikov
GEARBOX	: Foot change, 4 speed, unit construction
TRANSMISSION	: Enclosed shaft final drive
FRAME	: Tubular construction
SUSPENSION	: Hydraulic damped telescopic front forks
	: Hydraulic damped single rear trailing forks
TIRE SIZE	: 18×3.25/3.5″
BRAKES	: Internal expanding front wheel drum ⌀ 160mm
	: Internal expanding rear wheel drum ⌀ 160mm
DRY WEIGHT	: Solo 157kg
DIMENSIONS	: Wheel base 1350mm, Ground clearance 203mm
MAX SPEED	: Solo 75mph

JAWA

1974 JAWA TYPE 634-4 CZECHOSLOVAKIA

· 1975 ·

MAICO M250–M
(West Germany)

The first Maico motor cycle was produced at a factory at Wurtemburg in 1934. Although successful, the Maico business moved to a larger factory at Pfaffingen and produced military aircraft parts during the Second World War. In 1947 the new factory also began motor cycle production and introduced the model M–150 which had a unit construction single-cylinder 150cc two-stroke engine mounted within a tubular cycle frame, with telescopic front forks and a plunger-type wheel design. By the late 1950's, it had developed into the larger capacity model M–250, with hydraulic damped trailing rear fork suspension. This reliable machine so impressed the West German armed forces that 10,000 were supplied between 1961 and 1965. The military version was designated 'B' for Bundeswehr, and supplied with a pair of leather pannier bags, extra headlamp protection, and an overall coat of the appropriate service livery. A further few thousand were also adopted by other European military forces.

During the 1960's, Maico became more involved with motocross events, and in 1973 a new range of Enduro machines based upon their World Champion motocross machines was introduced, the major difference being the gear ratio, exhaust system, and the fitting of lights. With the possible rough country and normal street use, these machines suited military service well, and the military model M–250–M was introduced, also equipped with a pair of pannier bags, headlamp protection, and an overall coat of appropriate paint.

Brief specification

ENGINE TYPE	: Maico – Vertical single cylinder
DISPLACEMENT	: 247cc (67×70mm)
VALVE DESIGN	: Two stroke
COMPRESSION	: 10:1
POWER OUTPUT	: 17BHP at 6,000rpm
ELECTRICS	: 12 volt
CARBURETTOR	: One – Bing
GEARBOX	: Foot change, 5 speed, unit construction
TRANSMISSION	: Exposed chain final drive
FRAME	: Tubular construction
SUSPENSION	: Hydraulic damped telescopic front forks
	: Hydraulic damped single rear trailing forks
TIRE SIZE	: 18×3.25/4.00″
BRAKES	: Internal expanding front wheel drum ⌀ 136mm
	: Internal expanding rear wheel drum ⌀ 160mm
DRY WEIGHT	: Solo 130kg
DIMENSIONS	: Wheel base 1346mm
MAX SPEED	: Solo 75mph

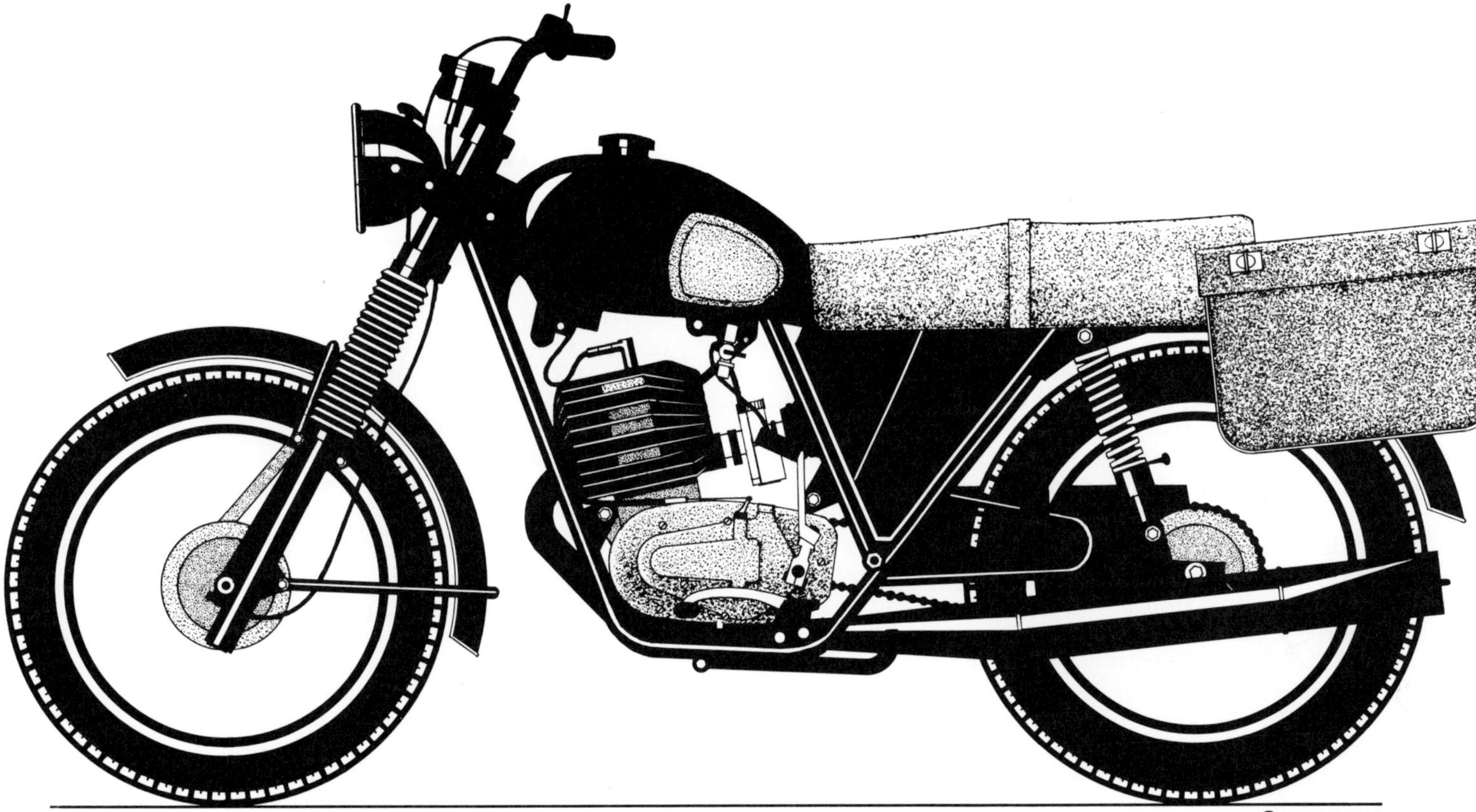

**1975 MAICO M250-M
WEST GERMANY**

· 1976 ·
HONDA CB–250–G5
(Japan)

After several years of assembling simple motorized bicycles, Soichiro Honda founded the Honda Motor Company in 1948, and the first completely Honda engineered motor cycle was introduced the following year. The Honda factory quickly expanded during the early 1950's, and within 5 years its assets had gained more than sixty times in value. Although Honda had been interested in motor cycle racing once the company had established itself, it was a further 10 years before the factory won its first grand prix. By the time an end to this involvement was announced in 1967, the company had established an international reputation for success.

With a return to a concentrated development program for the everyday rider, the Honda factory quickly produced a comprehensive range of machines for all types of use. During the late 1960's and early 1970's, the models with a unit construction 250cc or 350cc engine and five-speed gearbox were introduced. These were superseded by the G models, with a similar overhead camshaft engine, but a six-speed gearbox and hydraulic disc front wheel brake. Examples of the 250cc machines from both model series were adopted by the French armed forces for solo despatch rider service. The military conversion included a pair of leather pannier bags, forward mounted crash bars, and an overall coat of khaki paint. These machines remained in active service until 1979, when replaced by the military Peugeot SX8–AR model.

Brief specification

ENGINE TYPE	: Honda – Vertical twin cylinder
DISPLACEMENT	: 249cc (56×50.6mm)
VALVE DESIGN	: Overhead camshaft
COMPRESSION	: 9.5:1
POWER OUTPUT	: 30BHP at 10,500rpm
ELECTRICS	: 12 volt
CARBURETTOR	: Two – Keihin
GEARBOX	: Foot change, 6 speed, unit construction
TRANSMISSION	: Exposed chain final drive
FRAME	: Tubular construction
SUSPENSION	: Hydraulic damped telescopic front forks
	: Hydraulic damped single rear trailing forks
TIRE SIZE	: 18×3.00/3.25″
BRAKES	: Hydraulic caliper on front wheel disc
	: Internal expanding rear wheel drum
DRY WEIGHT	: Solo 160kg
DIMENSIONS	: Wheel base 1320mm
MAX SPEED	: Solo 90mph

1976 HONDA CB-250-G5 & FRENCH SOLDIER
© DAVID ANSELL

· 1977 ·

WINHA AUTOMATIC 340
(Finland)

During the early 1970's the Polar Metal Plast AG factory of Rovaniemi began limited production of a motor cycle designed for military service. Prototypes of the Winha model were tested in 1974 with a single-cylinder Sachs Sa–340–R two-stroke engine, and a twin-cylinder Kohler K–340–2AX two-stroke engine. For simplicity of use, these engines had a pull-cord start designed to drive through a fully automatic transmission. The machines were equipped for cross-country type use, and featured a high ground clearance, a partly enclosed chain final drive, wide handlebars, high clearance mudguards, and large section tires. Only one example of the Sachs powered machine was assembled, but the second design went into production in 1976.

The following year a small number of Winha snowscooter and motor cycle machines were tested by the Finnish armed forces for border patrol. It was hoped to use these machines together as they were powered by the same Kohler engine, but, after various difficulties, Polar Metal Plast AG was declared bankrupt in 1978 and the Winha motor cycle design was discontinued. The completed Winha machines remained in military service while spares continued, and were replace as necessaru by similar machines produced by the Husqvarna factory of Sweden.

Brief specification

ENGINE TYPE	: Kohler – Vertical twin cylinder
DISPLACEMENT	: 338cc (62×56mm)
VALVE DESIGN	: Two stroke
COMPRESSION	: 7:1
POWER OUTPUT	: 30BHP at 7,000rpm
ELECTRICS	: 12 volt, 100 watt
CARBURETTOR	: One – Walbro WD 33
GEARBOX	: Automatic variable-ratio
TRANSMISSION	: Enclosed belt primary drive
	: Exposed chain final drive
FRAME	: Tubular construction
SUSPENSION	: Hydraulic damped telescopic front forks
	: Hydraulic damped single rear trailing forks
TIRE SIZE	: 21×3.25/18×4.25"
BRAKES	: Internal expanding front wheel drum
	: Internal expanding rear wheel drum
DRY WEIGHT	: Solo 114kg
DIMENSIONS	: Wheel base 1540mm, Ground clearance 300mm
MAX SPEED	: Solo 80mph

WINHA — 1977 WINHA AUTOMATIC 340 FINLAND

· 1978 ·
SUZUKI MILITARY GS400
(Japan)

The Suzuki factory was originally founded by Michio Suzuki to manufacture textile machinery in 1909. As a result of a major recession after the Second World War, the company introduced its first motor cycle in 1952 and the business became the Suzuki Motor Company two years later. While the first machines were little more than powered bicycles, a Suzuki model ridden by Ernst Degner won the 50cc class of the world championships in 1962. This machine had a single-cylinder two-stroke engine, built with the help of Degner who had defected from East Germany and the MZ factory.

Production continued to concentrate on machines with two-stroke engines until the mid 1970's when the Suzuki factory also began to assemble four-stroke engines; eventually they produced models to challenge each engine capacity class established by the other three major Japanese motor cycle factories. The 400cc commuter machine was one such strongly contested category, for which the Suzuki introduced the GS–400 model in 1977.

The Australian armed forces adopted the Suzuki GS–400 model in 1978, to replace the ageing BSA model B–40 that had been used since the mid 1960's, for solo despatch, escort, and general police duties. The GS–400 was given two designations, GP for general purpose, and MP for military police. The GP model was fitted with a pair of leather pannier bags, forward and rear mounted crash bars, and a handlebar mounted windscreen. The MP model was also equipped with a syren, a public address system, auxiliary patrol lights (flashing amber), and a two-way radio mounted on a rear carrier rack. A total of 447 Suzuki GS–400 motor cycles had been purchased by the Australian Army early 1984.

Brief specification

ENGINE TYPE	: Suzuki – Vertical twin cylinder
DISPLACEMENT	: 398cc (65×60mm)
VALVE DESIGN	: Double overhead camshaft
COMPRESSION	: –
POWER OUTPUT	: 36BHP at 8,500rpm
ELECTRICS	: 12 volt, 200 watt
CARBURETTOR	: Two – Mikuni BS 34
GEARBOX	: Foot change, 6 speed, unit construction
TRANSMISSION	: Exposed chain final drive
FRAME	: Tubular construction
SUSPENSION	: Hydraulic damped telescopic front forks
	: Hydraulic damped single rear trailing forks
TIRE SIZE	: 19×3.00/18×3.5″
BRAKES	: Hydraulic caliper on front wheel disc
	: Internal expanding rear wheel drum
DRY WEIGHT	: Solo 172kg
DIMENSIONS	: Wheel base 1358mm, Ground clearance 155mm
MAX SPEED	: Solo 100mph

SUZUKI   1978 SUZUKI MILITARY GS400
JAPAN

· 1979 ·
BOMBARDIER MODEL
(Canada)

In 1973 the Austrian Can-Am division of the Canadian Bombardier Group, the world's largest snowmobil manufacturers, began the first large-scale motor cycle production in Canada. Within a few years' the complete Bombardier range offered engines of 125cc, 175cc, and 370cc displacement, the smaller two designs with six speeds and the larger with five. These machines had a high ground clearance, a high level exhaust system, and high clearance mudguards, for cross country type use, and were equipped with standard lighting, traffic indicators, and mirrors, for standard road use as well. Like a number of similar machines during the late 1970's, the Bombardier models were thought to be suitable for military requirements, and were offered with various modifications for this service.

The Canadian armed forces adopted a small number of the Bombardier 250cc model in 1978. It was used for solo liaison and despatch type use, and during 1981 there were 72 of machines in active service and 5 held in storage. The military conversion mainly included a rear carrier rack, a pair of pannier bags, auxiliary masked lighting, and an overall coat of khaki paint. From 1979 this model was also adopted by the British armed forces, and the BSA factory of Birmingham began to assemble a further version with various British made parts. The major difference in military equipment was the lack of auxiliary masked lighting. The British produced Bombardier 250cc model was also adopted by the Belgian armed forces in 1980.

Brief specification

ENGINE TYPE	: Bombardier-Rotax – Vertical single cylinder
DISPLACEMENT	: 247cc (74×57.5mm)
VALVE DESIGN	: Two stroke
COMPRESSION	: 10:1
POWER OUTPUT	: 26BHP at 7,500rpm
ELECTRICS	: 12 volt, 130 watt
CARBURETTOR	: One – Bing 32mm
GEARBOX	: Foot change, 5 speed, unit construction
TRANSMISSION	: Exposed chain final drive
FRAME	: Tubular construction
SUSPENSION	: Hydraulic damped telescopic front forks
	: Hydraulic damped single rear trailing forks
TIRE SIZE	: 21×3.00/18×4.00″
BRAKES	: Internal expanding front wheel drum
	: Internal expanding rear wheel drum
DRY WEIGHT	: Solo 130kg
DIMENSIONS	: Wheel base 1397mm, Ground clearance 230mm
MAX SPEED	: Solo 70mph

1979 BOMBARDIER MODEL CANADA

· 1979 ·
BULTACO COMMANDER
(Spain)

Following the decision to withdraw from international road racing, the director Francisco Bulto resigned from the Montesa motor cycle factory in May 1958 and founded the Bultaco factory the following month with a number of other former Montesa employees. Within a very short time the Bultaco factory had established an excellent reputation within road and trail events. In 1962 Bultaco machines won the 24 Hour Grand Prix d'Endurance at Barcelona in Spain, and a pair of gold medals in the Six Days Trail at Garmisch in Germany. With the ever faster Japanese road racing models, the Bultaco factory began to concentrate more on their rough country machines from the early 1970's, and as a result, the Bultaco Sherpa trials, Pursang moto cross, and the Alpina trail models were introduced.

Like a number of similar machines during the late 1970's, these models were thought capable of military service; the Bultaco 250cc Alpina model was used as the basis for the Bultaco Commander. The military conversion included a spare petrol container or tool box mounted behind the rider on the left side, provision for a two-way radio mounted on the pillion part of the dual seat, various fittings for a machine gun mounted on the right side, provision for masked lighting, and an overall paint of the appropriate service livery.

Brief specification

ENGINE TYPE	: Bultaco – Vertical single cylinder
DISPLACEMENT	: 237cc (71×60mm)
VALVE DESIGN	: Two stroke
COMPRESSION	: 9:1
POWER OUTPUT	: 14.1BHP at 5,500rpm
ELECTRICS	: 12 volt
CARBURETTOR	: One – Amal 2600
GEARBOX	: Foot change, 5 speed, unit construction
TRANSMISSION	: Exposed chain final drive
FRAME	: Tubular construction
SUSPENSION	: Hydraulic damped telescopic front forks
	: Hydraulic damped trailing forks
TIRE SIZE	: 21×2.75/18×4.00″
BRAKES	: Internal expanding front wheel drum ⌀ 140mm
	: Internal expanding rear wheel drum ⌀ 140mm
DRY WEIGHT	: Solo 232kg
DIMENSIONS	: Wheel base 1310mm, Ground clearance 300mm
MAX SPEED	: Solo 70mph

BULTACO   1979 BULTACO COMMANDER
SPAIN

· 1979 ·
DNIEPER MT–12
(Soviet Union)

The Dnieper MT–12 replaced the military service of the Dnieper K–750 model. Major new features included the adoption of a four-speed and reverse gearbox, and a shaft driven sidecar wheel. A differential was incorporated into the final drive transmission, which supplied the engine torque in the ratio of one third to the sidecar wheel and two thirds to the rear drive wheel. There was a differential lock which gave equal power to each wheel for use on steep hill climbs. The output of the established side-valve engine was also increased from 22 to 26BHP, with a re-profiled camshaft and a higher compression ratio.

Further changes from the K–750 model included a restyled petrol tank, improved lighting equipment with the use of traffic indicators, and redesigned hydraulic suspension units. Although with a quite different performance the MT–12 had a similar appearance to the MT–10, a further development of the K–650 from the same factory. The MT–12 model also had three interchangeable wheels with a spare mounted on the sidecar. As with other state-owned factories of Communist countries, a large range of individual parts was used within a number of Dnieper machines. The Dnieper MT–12 model was first introduced and adopted by the Soviet armed forces during the late 1970's, and, like its predecessors, was supplied within Communist countries throughout the world for military service.

Brief specification

ENGINE TYPE	: Dnieper – Transverse opposed twin cylinder
DISPLACEMENT	: 745cc (78×78mm)
VALVE DESIGN	: Side valves
COMPRESSION	: 6:1
POWER OUTPUT	: 26BHP at 4,900rpm
ELECTRICS	: 6 volt
CARBURETTOR	: Two – K–302
GEARBOX	: Foot change, 4/R speed, unit construction
TRANSMISSION	: Enclosed shaft final drive
FRAME	: Tubular construction
SUSPENSION	: Hydraulic damped telescopic front forks
	: Hydraulic damped trailing rear forks
TIRE SIZE	: 19×3.5"
BRAKES	: Internal expanding front wheel drum
	: Internal expanding rear wheel drum
DRY WEIGHT	: W/SC 350kg
DIMENSIONS	: Wheel base 1510mm, Ground clearance 125mm
MAX SPEED	: W/SC 65mph

ДНЕПР 1979 DNIEPER MT-12
SOVIET UNION

· 1980 ·
HUSQVARNA 258–A
(Sweden)

In 1970 the Material Administration of the Swedish armed forces prepared a list of specifications for their ideal military motor cycle. These included, suitability for on- and off-road use, provision for ski attachments, and reliability with low maintenance. The following year year prototypes were requested from the Hägglund, Husqvarna, and Monark factories. In 1972 Husqvarna presented a machine with a single-cylinder 350cc two-stroke engine, an automatic gear change and exposed chain final drive. The other companies also presented suitable machines that year, but, after quoting the lowest production cost, the Hägglund factory gained the contract in 1973.

Within a few years, however, the Hägglund design had developed trouble within its transmission system, and the Husqvarna factory was approached as a possible source for an alternative engine and gearbox. While this possibility was being discussed a transfer of the entire project was proposed, and the contract was eventually given to Husqvarna in late 1976. Early the following year five prototypes of the 258–A model were supplied for military trials, and Husqvarna received the final production order in mid 1978. The first 1,000 machines were delivered in early 1980, and a further 2,000 the following year.

Brief specification

ENGINE TYPE	: Husqvarna – Vertical single cylinder
DISPLACEMENT	: 245cc (69.5×64.5mm)
VALVE DESIGN	: Two stroke
COMPRESSION	: 11.8:1
POWER OUTPUT	: 20BHP
ELECTRICS	: 12 volt, 140 watt
CARBURETTOR	: One – Mikuni WM
GEARBOX	: Automatic 4 speed, unit construction
TRANSMISSION	: Exposed chain final drive
FRAME	: Tubular construction
SUSPENSION	: Hydraulic damped telescopic front forks
	: Hydraulic damped trailing rear forks
TIRE SIZE	: 21×3.5/17×4.5″
BRAKES	: Internal expanding front wheel drum ⌀ 160mm
	: Internal expanding rear wheel drum ⌀ 160mm
DRY WEIGHT	: Solo 130kg
DIMENSIONS	: Wheel base 1480mm, Ground clearance 280mm
MAX SPEED	: Solo 80mph

Husqvarna

**1980 HUSQVARNA 258-A
SWEDEN**

· 1980 ·

YAMAHA MILITARY 250
(Japan)

The origins of Yamaha motor cycles can be traced to a small reed organ business founded in 1887. Within 10 years this factory had expanded to become the Nippon Gakki (Japan Musical Instruments) Limited Company, and after almost 70 years of diversification Yamaha Motor Co. Ltd was founded in 1955. While motor cycles were only a small part of Yamaha production, their machines quickly established an excellent reputation within competitive events throughout the world. From this experience both standard road and track models were continually developed, and during the 1970's the effective range of engines widened, hydraulic disc brakes replaced the drum design, and monoshock rear suspension was introduced.

The Yamaha motor cycle factory of Shizuoka-Ken introduced the DT–MX model range during the late 1970's. These machines had a high ground clearance, high-level exhaust system, and high clearance mudguards, for cross-country type use, and were equipped with standard lighting, traffic indicators, and mirrors, for standard road use as well. The DT–MX machines featured a unit construction single-cylinder two-stroke engine of 50cc, 125cc, 175cc, and 250cc displacement. The smallest with four speeds, the middle two with six speeds, and the largest with five. This type of machine suited the military strategy of the time well, and in 1980 the Danish armed forces adopted the DT–250–MX model for solo despatch type service. The Danish military conversion included an enlarged petrol tank, a pair of canvas pannier bags, and an overall coat of khaki paint.

Brief specification

ENGINE TYPE	: Yamaha – Vertical single cylinder
DISPLACEMENT	: 246cc (70×64mm)
VALVE DESIGN	: Two stroke
COMPRESSION	: 6.7:1
POWER OUTPUT	: 23BHP at 6,000rpm
ELECTRICS	: 6 volt
CARBURETTOR	: One – VM28SS
GEARBOX	: Foot change 5 speed, unit construction
TRANSMISSION	: Exposed chain final drive
FRAME	: Tubular construction
SUSPENSION	: Hydraulic damped telescopic front forks
	: Hydraulic damped monoshock rear sub-frame
TIRE SIZE	: 21×3.00/18×4.00″
BRAKES	: Internal expanding front wheel drum
	: Internal expanding rear wheel drum
DRY WEIGHT	: Solo 118kg
DIMENSIONS	: Wheel base 1415mm, Ground clearance 245mm
MAX SPEED	: Solo 70mph

YAMAHA   1980 YAMAHA MILITARY 250 JAPAN

SPECIFICATIONS OF MILITARY MACHINES FROM 1904

YEAR	MACHINE	ORIGIN	ENGINE	CYL	BORE & STROKE	CCM	DESIGN	HP	DRIVE	GEARS	ARMED FORCE/S
1904	NSU Model 4HP	D	Own	1-Vt	85×85	482	IOE	4	Belt	2	German
1904	Triumph Model 3.25HP	D	Own	1-Vt	–	425	IOE	3.25	Belt	1	German
1908	FN Model 3.5HP	B	Own	4-Vt	48×57	412	IOE	3.5	Shaft	2	Belgian & Allied
1910	BSA Model 3.5HP	GB	Own	1-Vt	85×88	499	SV	3.5	Belt	1	British
1912	FN Model 2.75HP	B	Own	1-Vt	65×86	285	IOE	2.75	Shaft	2	Belgian & Allied
1912	Indian Model 30	USA	Own	1-RS	82.6×93.3	499	IOE	4	Chain	1	American
1912	Indian Model 61	USA	Own	2-V	82.6×93.3	998	IOE	7	Chain	2	American
1912	Militaire Model 4HP	USA	Own	1-Vt	–	480	SV	4	Chain	3/R	Experimental only
1912	Scott Model 3.75HP	GB	Own	2-FS	69.8×63.5	486	TS	3.75	Chain	2	Experimental only
1914	Ariel Model 3.5HP	GB	Own	1-Vt	85×86.4	490	SV	3.5	Belt	3	British & Allied
1914	Bianchi type A	I	Own	1-Vt	85×88	499	SV	3.5	Belt	1	Italian
1914	BSA Model H	GB	Own	1-Vt	85×98	556	SV	4.25	Chain	3	British & Allied
1914	Douglas Model V	GB	Own	2-HO	60.8×60	348	SV	2.75	Belt	2	British & Allied
1914	Eysink Model 3HP	NL	Own	1-Vt	74×95	408	SV	3	Belt	3	Dutch
1914	Husqvarna Model 75A	S	Moto-Reve	2-V	65×83	550	IOE	4.25	Belt	3	Swedish
1914	James Model 7	GB	Own	2-V	64×77	495	SV	3.5	Chain	3	British & Allied
1914	New Imperial 6HP	GB	JAP	2-V	76×85	771	SV	6	Chain	3	British & Allied
1914	Norton Big Four	GB	Own	1-Vt	82×120	633	SV	4	Belt	1	Russian & Allied
1914	NSU Model 1.5HP	D	Own	1-Vt	58×72	190	IOE	1.5	Belt	2	German
1914	NSU Model 3.5HP	D	Own	2-V	63×80	499	IOE	3.5	Belt	2	German
1914	Peugeot Model 2.5HP	F	Own	2-V	55×80	380	IOE	2.5	Belt	1	French
1914	P & M Model 3.5HP	GB	Own	1-FS	84.1×88.9	495	SV	3.5	Chain	2	British & Allied
1914	Premier Model 3.5HP	GB	Own	1-Vt	85×88	499	SV	3.5	Belt	1	Russian & Allied
1914	Puch type R-I	A	Own	1-Vt	68×70	254	SV	2	Belt	1	Austrian
1914	Puch type R-2	A	Own	1-Vt	68×85	308	SV	2.5	Belt	1	Austrian
1914	Rover Model 3.5HP	GB	Own	1-Vt	85×88	499	SV	3.5	Belt	1	Russian & Allied
1914	Royal Enfield Model 6HP	GB	JAP	2-V	76×85	771	SV	6	Chain	2	Russian & Allied
1914	Rudge 3.5HP Multi	GB	Own	1-Vt	85×88	499	IOE	3.5	Belt	Multi	Russian & Allied

YEAR	MACHINE	ORIGIN	ENGINE	CYL	BORE & STROKE	CCM	DESIGN	HP	DRIVE	GEARS	ARMED FORCE/S
1914	Scott Model 3.75HP	GB	Own	2-FS	69.8×63.5	486	TS	3.75	Chain	2	British
1914	Sunbeam Model 3.5HP	GB	Own	1-Vt	85×88	499	SV	3.5	Chain	3	British & Allied
1914	Sunbeam Model 6HP	GB	JAP	2-V	76×85	771	SV	6	Chain	3	British & Allied
1914	Terrot Military Model	F	MAG	2-V	64×77	495	IOE	3.5	Chain	e	French
1914	Triumph Model 3.5HP	GB	Own	1-V	85×88	499	SV	3.5	Belt	3	British & Allied
1914	Wanderer Model 4HP	D	Own	2-V	65×76	504	SV	4	Belt	3	German
1915	Clyno Model 5–6HP	GB	Own	2-V	76×82	744	SV	5–6	Chain	3	British & Allied
1915	Militaire Model 1300	USA	Own	4-Vt	–	1306	IOE	11	Shaft	3/R	American
1915	NSU Model 7–9HP	D	Own	2-V	80×99	994	IOE	7–9	Chain	3	German
1915	Sunbeam Model 6HP	GB	AKD	2-V	73×95	795	SV	6	Chain	3	British & Allied
1915	Triumph Model H	GB	Own	1-Vt	85×97	550	SV	4	Belt	3	British & Allied
1916	Douglas Model B	GB	Own	2-HO	74.5×68	595	SV	4	Belt	3	British & Allied
1916	Excelsior Model 61	USA	Own	2-V	84.5×88.9	997	IOE	7–10	Chain	3	American
1916	Frera Model 4HP	I	Own	1-Vt	85×88	499	SV	4	Belt	3	Italian
1916	Frera Model 8–10HP	I	Own	2-V	–	1140	IOE	8–10	Chain	3	Italian
1916	Harley-Davidson Model 61	USA	Own	2-V	84.1×88.9	987	IOE	7–9	Chain	3	American & Allied
1916	Husqvarna Model 145–A	S	Moto-Reve	2-V	65×83	550	SV	4.25	Chain	3	Swedish
1916	Indian Model 61	USA	Own	2-V	79.4×100.8	998	IOE	7–9	Chain	3	American & Allied
1916	Sunbeam Model 4HP	GB	Own	1-Vt	85×96	554	SV	4	Belt	3	French
1916	Sunbeam Model 8HP	GB	MAG	2-V	82×94	992	IOE	8	Chain	3	Russian & Allied
1917	Cleveland Model K	USA	Own	1-Vt	63.5×69.8	221	TS	2	Chain	2	American
1917	Clyno Model 8HP	GB	JAP	2-V	85.5×85	986	SV	8	Chain	3	Russian
1917	Excelsior 7–10HP	USA	Own	2-V	84.5×88.9	997	IOE	7–10	Chain	3	American
1917	Harley-Davidson 7–9HP	USA	Own	2-V	84.1×88.9	987	IOE	7–9	Chain	3	American & Allied
1917	Indian Powerplus	USA	Own	2-V	79.4×100.8	998	SV	7–9	Chain	3	American & Allied
1917	Matchless Military Model	GB	MAG	2-V	82×94	992	IOE	8	Chain	3	Experimental only
1921	Itar Model 750	CS	Own	2-HO	–	746	OHV	7	Chain	3	Czechoslovak
1921	Motosacoche Model 500	CH	Own	2-V	64×77	495	IOE	4	Chain	3	Swiss, Dutch, etc.
1921	Motosacoche Model 750	CH	Own	2-V	72×91	741	IOE	6	Chain	3	Swiss, Dutch, etc.
1922	Husqvarna Model 500A	S	Own	2-V	–	992	SV	8	Chain	3	Swedish
1923	Walter Model 750	CS	Own	2-V	–	746	OHV	7	Chain	3	Czechoslovak
1925	Indian Model 61	USA	Own	2-V	79.4×100.8	998	SV	8	Chain	3	Throughout the world
1925	Indian Model 74	USA	Own	2-V	82.6×112.7	1207	SV	9	Chain	3	Throughout the world
1925	P & M Military Model	GB	Own	1-FS	84×90	499	OHV	4.5	Chain	3	British
1925	Victoria Model KR–III	D	Own	2-HO	70×64	492	OHV	12	Belt	3	German
1926	BD Model 500	CS	Own	1-Vt	84×90	499	OHC	15	Chain	3	Czechoslovak
1926	Husqvarna Model 180A	S	Own	2-V	65×83	550	SV	15	Chain	3	Swedish
1926	Husqvarna Model 600A	S	Own	2-V	–	992	SV	–	Chain	3	Swedish
1926	Triumph Model P–II	GB	Own	1-Vt	84×89	493	SV	–	Chain	3	British

YEAR	MACHINE	ORIGIN	ENGINE	CYL	BORE & STROKE	CCM	DESIGN	BHP	DRIVE	GEARS	ARMED FORCE/S
1927	Victoria Model KR–VI	D	Own	2–HO	77×64	596	OHV	18	Chain	3	German
1928	BMW Model R–52	D	Own	2–HO	63×78	487	SV	12	Shaft	3	German
1928	BMW Model R–62	D	Own	2–HO	78×78	745	SV	18	Shaft	3	German
1928	Izhevsk Model Izh–I	SU	Own	2–V	–	1200	SV	–	Shaft	3	Soviet Union
1928	Moto Guzzi GT	I	Own	1–Hz	88×82	499	IOE	13	Chain	3	Italian
1928	Praga Model BD	CS	Own	1–Vt	84×90	449	OHC	15	Chain	3	Czechoslovak
1928	Rene Gillet Model G	F	Own	2–V	70×97.4	749	SV	–	Chain	3	French
1928	Rene Gillet Model H	F	Own	1–Vt	70×90	346	SV	–	Chain	3	French
1929	BMW Model R–11	D	Own	2–HO	78×78	745	SV	18	Shaft	3	German
1929	Douglas Military 350	GB	Own	2–HO	60.8×60	348	SV	–	Chain	3	British
1929	Husqvarna Model 610A	S	Own	2–V	–	992	SV	–	Chain	3	Swedish
1929	Triumph Model CSD	GB	Own	1–Vt	84×99	548	SV	14.5	Chain	3	British
1930	CWS Model M–III	POL	Own	2–V	–	998	SV	14	Chain	3	Polish
1930	Harley-Davidson Model 45	USA	Own	2–V	69.9×96.9	743	SV	20	Chain	3	Throughout the world
1930	Harley-Davidson Model 61	USA	Own	2–V	84.1×88.9	987	SV	22	Chain	3	Throughout the world
1930	Harley-Davidson Model 74	USA	Own	2–V	87×101.6	1207	SV	24	Chain	3	Throughout the world
1930	Krasny–Oktober L–300	SU	Own	1–Vt	74×68	292	TS	–	Chain	3	Soviet Union
1930	Peugeot Model P–107	F	Own	1–Vt	72×85	346	SV	–	Chain	3	French
1931	Motosacoche Model 750	CH	Own	2–V	72×91	741	IOE	18	Chain	3	Swiss
1931	TIZ–AM Model 600	SU	Own	1–FS	85×105	595	SV	15	Chain	3	Soviet Union
1932	BMW Model R–4	D	Own	1–Vt	78×84	398	OHV	12	Shaft	4	German
1932	Husqvarna Model 120A	S	Own	2–V	–	992	SV	–	Chain	3	Swedish
1932	Moto Guzzi GT–17	I	Own	1–Hz	88×82	498	IOE	13	Chain	3	Italian
1933	BSA Military Model	GB	Own	2–V	63×80	498	OHV	22	Chain	3	British
1933	Husqvarna Model 130A	S	Own	2–V	–	992	SV	–	Chain	3	Swedish
1933	PZI Sokol M–III	POL	Own	2–V	–	995	SV	–	Chain	3	Polish
1933	Victoria Model KR–6	D	Own	2–HO	77×64	596	OHV	20	Chain	3	German
1934	Jawa Model 350–SV	CS	Own	1–FS	70×90	346	SV	–	Chain	4	Czechoslovak
1934	Motobecane Model B1V2	F	Own	1–Vt	46×60	99	TS	–	Chain	1	French
1934	Motobecane Model S5C	F	Own	1–Vt	80×98	498	OHV	–	Chain	4	French
1934	Peugeot Model P53	F	Own	1–Vt	46×60	99	TS	–	Chain	1	French
1934	Zündapp K–500–W	D	Own	2–HO	69×66.6	498	SV	16	Shaft	4	German
1934	Zündapp K–800–W	D	Own	4–HO	62×66	797	SV	22	Shaft	4	German
1935	BMW Model R–12	D	Own	2–HO	78×78	745	SV	18	Shaft	4	German
1935	CZ Model 175	CS	Own	1–Vt	60×61	172	TS	5.5	Chain	3	Czechoslovak
1935	Monet Goyon L5A1	F	Own	1–Vt	75×110	486	SV	–	Chain	4	French
1935	Moto Guzzi GTV	I	Own	1–Hz	88×82	498	OHV	19	Chain	4	Italian
1935	PMZ Model A–750	SU	Own	2–V	70×97	746	SV	14	Chain	3	Soviet Union
1936	Bianchi Military Model	I	Own	1–Vt	82×94	496	SV	9	Chain	3	Italian

YEAR	MACHINE	ORIGIN	ENGINE	CYL	BORE & STROKE	CCM	DESIGN	BHP	DRIVE	GEARS	ARMED FORCE/S
1936	Condor Military Model	CH	MAG	1-Vt	82×94	496	IOE	–	Chain	3	Swiss
1936	FN Military Model 86	B	Own	1-Vt	86×86	499	OHV	–	Chain	4	Belgian
1936	Puch type 800	A	Own	4-HO	60×70	791	SV	20	Chain	4	Austrian
1936	Victoria Model KR-9	D	Own	2-HO	60×88	497	SV	15	Chain	4	German
1937	BMW Model R-35	D	Own	1-Vt	72×84	342	OHV	14	Shaft	4	German
1937	FN Military Model 12	B	Own	2-HO	90×78	992	SV	22	Shaft/SC	4×2/R	Belgian (German)
1937	Jawa Model 175	CS	Own	1-Vt	57×67	171	TS	6	Chain	3	Czechoslovak
1937	Nimbus Model 750	DK	Own	4-Vt	60×66	746	OHC	22	Shaft	3	Danish (German)
1937	Ogar Model 4	CS	Own	1-Vt	68×68	257	TS	12	Chain	4	Czechoslovak
1937	Sankyo Model 97	J	Own	2-V	90×94	1195	SV	24	Chain	3	Japanese
1937	Sarolea type 36-M6	B	Own	1-FS	88×97	598	SV	–	Chain	4	Belgian (German)
1937	Suecia Military 500	S	MAG	1-Vt	82×94	496	SV	–	Chain	4	Swedish
1937	Zündapp KS-600-W	D	Own	2-HO	75×67.6	597	OHV	28	Shaft	4	German
1938	BMW Model R-61	D	Own	2-HO	70×78	600	SV	18	Shaft	4	German
1938	BMW Model R-71	D	Own	2-HO	78×78	745	SV	22	Shaft	4	German
1938	BSA Model B-21	GB	Own	1-Vt	63×80	249	OHV	11	Chain	4	British (Training)
1938	BSA Model M-20	GB	Own	1-Vt	82×94	496	SV	13	Chain	4	British & Allied
1938	BSA Model M-21	GB	Own	1-Vt	82×112	591	SV	15	Chain	4	Dutch
1938	BSA Model G14	GB	Own	2-V	80×98	985	SV	24	Chain	4	Dutch
1938	DKW Model RT-125	D	Own	1-Vt	52×58	123	TS	5	Chain	3	German
1938	DKW Model NZ-350	D	Own	1-Vt	72×85	346	TS	12	Chain	3	German
1938	Gillet Herstal Military	B	Own	2-Vt	76×80	725	TS	–	Chain/SC	4/R	Belgian (German)
1938	Gnome et Rhone 750 Armee	F	Own	2-HO	80×72	721	OHV	15	Shaft	4	French (German)
1938	Gnome et Rhone type AX2	F	Own	2-HO	80×80	804	SV	18	Shaft/SC	4/R	French (German)
1938	Moto Guzzi GT-20	I	Own	1-Hz	88×82	499	IOE	13	Chain	4	Italian
1938	Moto Guzzi Condor	I	Own	1-Hz	88×82	499	OHV	27	Chain	4	Italian
1938	NSU Model 251-OSL	D	Own	1-Vt	64×75	241	OHV	10	Chain	4	German
1938	NSU Model 601-OSL	D	Own	1-Vt	85×99	562	OHV	24	Chain	4	German
1938	Phanomen Model AHO	D	Sachs	1-Vt	54×54	123	TS	3.5	Chain	3	German
1938	Puch type GS-350	A	Own	1-FS	2×52×83	347	DP/TS	12	Chain	4	Austrian (German)
1938	TWN Model B-350-W	D	Own	1-Vt	72×85	346	TS	12	Chain	4	German
1938	Victoria Model KR-35	D	Own	1-Vt	69×91.5	342	OHV	18	Chain	4	German
1939	Benelli Model 500	I	Own	1-Vt	–	498	OHV	–	Chain	4	Italian
1939	BSA Model B-30	GB	Own	1-Vt	72×85.5	348	OHV	15	Chain	4	British
1939	BSA Model C-10	GB	Own	1-Vt	63×80	249	SV	–	Chain	3	British
1939	Horex Model S-35	D	Own	1-FS	69×92	344	OHV	13	Chain	4	German
1939	Matchless WD-G3	GB	Own	1-Vt	69×93	347	OHV	16	Chain	4	British
1939	Moto Guzzi Alce	I	Own	1-Hz	88×82	498	IOE	13	Chain	4	Italian
1939	NSU Model ZDB	D	Own	1-FS	50×62	122	TS	5	Chain	3	German

YEAR	MACHINE	ORIGIN	ENGINE	CYL	BORE & STROKE	CCM	DESIGN	BHP	DRIVE	GEARS	ARMED FORCE/S
1939	Puch type 125	A	Own	1–Vt	2×38×55	125	DP/TS	8	Chain	3	German
1939	Royal Enfield WD–S	GB	Own	1–Vt	64×77	248	SV	11	Chain	4	British (Training)
1939	Sarolea Military Model	B	Own	2–HO	88×80	973	SV	20	Shaft/SC	3×2/R	Belgian (German)
1939	Sertum Model 500	I	Own	2–Vt	–	498	SV	–	Chain	4	Italian
1939	Terrot type HDA	F	Own	1–Vt	70×90	346	SV	9	Chain	3	French
1939	Terrot type RDA	F	Own	1–Vt	84×90	498	SV	12	Chain	4	French
1939	Terrot type VAAT	F	Own	2–V	70×79	746	SV	–	Chain	4	French
1939	Triumph Model 3SW	GB	Own	1–Vt	70×89	342	SV	12	Chain	4	British
1939	Triumph Model 3HW	GB	Own	1–Vt	70×89	342	OHV	17	Chain	4	British
1939	Triumph Model 3TW	GB	Own	2–Vt	55×73.4	349	OHV	–	Chain	4	Experimental only
1939	TWN Model BD–250–W	D	Own	1–Vt	2×45×78	248	DP/TS	12	Chain	4	German
1939	1939 Zündapp DB–200–W	D	Own	1–Vt	60×70	198	TS	7	Chain	3	German
1940	Ariel Model W–NG	GB	Own	1–Vt	72×85	346	OHV	13	Chain	4	British
1940	BSA Model C–11	GB	Own	1–Vt	63×80	249	OHV	–	Chain	3	Indian
1940	Izhevsk Model Izh–12	SU	Own	1–Vt	72×85	346	TS	–	Chain	4	Soviet Union
1940	Moto Guzzi Airone	I	Own	1–Hz	70×64	246	OHV	10	Chain	4	Italian
1940	Norton WD–16H	GB	Own	1–Vt	79×100	490	SV	13	Chain	4	British & Allied
1940	Norton Big Four	GB	Own	1–Vt	82×120	633	SV	15	Chain/SC	4	British & Allied
1940	Velocette MDD–WD	GB	Own	1–Vt	68×96	349	OHV	–	Chain	4	French
1940	Zündapp KS–750–W	D	Own	2–HO	75×87	751	OHV	26	Shaft/SC	4×2/R	German
1941	BMW Model R–75	D	Own	2–HO	78×78	745	OHV	26	Shaft/SC	4×2/R	German
1941	Gilera Military Marte	I	Own	1–Vt	84×90	498	SV	12	Shaft/SC	4	Italian
1941	Gilera Military Solo	I	Own	1–Vt	84×90	498	SV	12	Chain	4	Italian
1941	Matchless G3L	GB	Own	1–Vt	69×93	347	OHV	16	Chain	4	British & Allied
1942	Condor A–1000	CH	MAG	2–V	82×94	997	IOE	–	Chain	4	Swiss
1942	Excelsior Welbike	GB	Villiers	1–Hz	50×50	98	TS	2	Chain	1	British (Airborne)
1942	Harley-Davidson	USA	Own	2–V	69.8×96.9	741	SV	23	Chain	3	American & Allied
1942	Harley-Davidson	USA	Own	2–V	86.9×101.6	1205	SV	33	Chain	3	American & Allied
1942	Harley-Davidson ELA	USA	Own	2–V	84.1×88.9	987	SV	29	Chain	3	American & Allied
1942	Harley-Davidson XA	USA	Own	2–HO	77.8×77.8	739	SV	23	Shaft	4	Experimental only
1942	Indian Model 340	USA	Own	2–V	82.5×112.7	1204	SV	30	Chain	3	American & Allied
1942	Indian Model 741–A	USA	Own	2–V	63.5×77.7	492	SV	15	Chain	3	American & Allied
1942	Indian Model 741–B	USA	Own	2–V	73×88.9	744	SV	24	Chain	3	American & Allied
1942	Indian Model 841	USA	Own	2–V	73×88.9	744	SV	24	Shaft	4	Experimental only
1942	James Model ML	GB	Villiers	1–Vt	50×62	125	TS	3	Chain	3	British (Airborne)
1942	Monark MC–42–SV	S	Albin	1–Vt	79×101	495	SV	15	Chain	4	Swedish
1942	Monark MC–42–OHV	S	Albin	1–Vt	79×101	495	OHV	20	Chain	4	Swedish
1942	Moskva Model K–1B	SU	Own	1–Vt	48×54	98	TS	2.5	Chain	2	Soviet Union
1942	Moskva Model M–1A	SU	Own	1–Vt	52×58	123	TS	4.5	Chain	3	Soviet Union

YEAR	MACHINE	ORIGIN	ENGINE	CYL	BORE & STROKE	CCM	DESIGN	BHP	DRIVE	GEARS	ARMED FORCE/S
1942	Moskva Model M–72	SU	Own	2–HO	78×78	745	SV	22	Shaft	4	Soviet Union
1942	Royal Enfield WD–RE	GB	Own	1–Vt	54×55	125	TS	4.5	Chain	3	British (Airborne)
1942	Royal Enfield WD–C	GB	Own	1–Vt	70×90	346	SV	10	Chain	4	British & Allied
1942	Royal Enfield WD–CO	GB	Own	1–Vt	70×90	346	OHV	15	Chain	4	British & Allied
1942	Royal Enfield WD–G	GB	Own	1–Vt	70×90	346	OHV	18	Chain	4	British
1942	Simplex Servi-Cycle	USA	Own	1–Vt	–	125	TS	–	Belt	1	American (Airborne)
1942	Triumph 5TW	GB	Own	2–Vt	63×80	499	SV	–	Chain	4	Experimental only
1942	Universal A–680	CH	Own	2–V	–	676	SV	–	Chain	4	Swiss
1942	Universal A–1000	CH	Own	2–V	–	990	SV	–	Chain	4	Swiss
1942	Velocette MAF–WD	GB	Own	1–Vt	68×96	349	OHV	14	Chain	4	British & Allied
1942	Volugrafo Model 125	I	Own	1–FS	–	125	TS	–	Chain	2	Italian (Airborne)
1943	NV Military Model	S	Own	2–V	79×101	990	OHV	36	Shaft/SC	3×2/R	Swedish
1944	Indian Model 1948	USA	Own	1–Vt	63.5×69.8	221	SV	6.5	Chain	3	American (Airborne)
1945	Douglas Model DV–60	GB	Own	2–HO	74×70	602	SV	–	Chain	3	Experimental only
1945	Royal Enfield WD–350	GB	Own	2–FS	52×82	348	SV	–	Chain	4	Experimental only
1945	Triumph Model TRW	GB	Own	2–Vt	63×80	499	SV	–	Chain	4	Experimental only
1946	Moto Guzzi Superalce	I	Own	1–Hz	88×82	498	OHV	18	Chain	4	Italian
1947	BSA Model B–31	GB	Own	1–Vt	72×85.5	348	OHV	15	Chain	4	Dutch
1947	BSA Model B–33	GB	Own	1–Vt	85×88	499	OHV	23	Chain	4	Swedish
1947	BSA Model M–20	GB	Own	1–Vt	82×94	496	SV	13	Chain	4	Dutch
1947	Harley-Davidson WLA	USA	Own	2–V	69.8×96.9	741	SV	23	Chain	3	Throughout the world
1947	Jawa 250 Perak	CS	Own	1–Vt	65×75	248	TS	9	Chain	4	Czechoslovak
1948	Condor Model A–580	CH	Own	2–HO	70×75.2	578	SV	20	Shaft	4×2	Swiss
1948	Triumph Model TRW	GB	Own	2–Vt	63×80	498	SV	17	Chain	4	Throughout the world
1949	AJS Model 18	GB	Own	1–Vt	82.5×93	498	OHV	23	Chain	4	Swedish
1949	Indian Model 149	USA	Own	1–Vt	69.8×76.2	291	OHV	9	Chain	4	American (Airborne)
1949	James Comet	GB	Villiers	1–Vt	47×57	98	TS	3	Chain	2	British
1949	James Cadet	GB	Villiers	1–Vt	50×62	122	TS	4	Chain	3	British
1949	Matchless G3LS	GB	Own	1–Vt	69×93	347	OHV	16	Chain	4	Throughout the world
1950	Gilera Military 500	I	Own	1–Vt	84×90	499	OHV	22	Chain	4	Italian
1950	Moto Guzzi Falcone	I	Own	1–Hz	88×82	498	OHV	19	Chain	4	Italian
1950	Terrot type HCT	F	Own	1–Vt	70×90	346	SV	–	Chain	4	French
1950	Terrot type RGST	F	Own	1–Vt	84×90	499	OHV	22	Chain	4	French
1951	BMW Model R–25	D	Own	1–Vt	68×68	247	OHV	12	Shaft	4	French
1951	BMW Model R–51/2	D	Own	2–HO	68×68	494	OHV	24	Shaft	4	French
1951	FN Military Model 13	B	Own	1–Vt	84.5×80	448	SV	12	Chain	4	Belgian
1951	Gillet Herstal 400	B	Own	1–Vt	–	400	SV	14	Chain	4	Belgian
1951	Gillet Herstal 500	B	Own	1–Vt	77×105	489	SV	16	Chain	4	Belgian
1951	Matchless G3LS	GB	Own	1–Vt	69×93	347	OHV	16	Chain	4	Throughout the world

YEAR	MACHINE	ORIGIN	ENGINE	CYL	BORE & STROKE	CCM	DESIGN	BHP	DRIVE	GEARS	ARMED FORCE/S
1951	Sarolea type 51–AS	B	Own	1–Vt	75×79	349	SV	10	Chain	4	Belgian
1951	Sarolea type 51–A4	B	Own	1–Vt	75×90	397	SV	10.5	Chain	4	Belgian
1952	EMW Model R–35	DDR	Own	1–Vt	72×84	342	OHV	14	Shaft	4	East German
1952	Derbi Military Model	E	Own	2–Vt	–	250	TS	–	Chain	4	Spanish
1952	Izhevsk Model Izh–350	SU	Own	1–Vt	72×85	346	TS	11.5	Chain	4	Soviet Union
1952	Moskva Model K–125	SU	Own	1–Vt	52×58	123	TS	4.5	Chain	3	Soviet Union
1952	Moto Guzzi Airone	I	Own	1–Hz	70×64	247	OHV	12	Chain	4	Italian
1953	Condor Model A–580–53	CH	Own	2–HO	70×75.2	578	SV	20	Shaft	4×2	Swiss
1953	NV Military Model	S	DKW	1–Vt	52×58	123	TS	9.5	Chain	3	Swedish
1954	Moto Guzzi Zigolo	I	Own	1–Hz	50×50	98	TS	4	Chain	3	Italian
1955	BMW Model R–50	D	Own	2–HO	68×68	494	OHV	26	Shaft	4	Throughout the world
1955	DKW Model RT–175–VS	D	Own	1–Vt	62×58	175	TS	10	Chain	4	West German
1955	Monark MC–252	S	ILO	2–Vt	52×58	246	TS	15	Chain	4	Swedish
1955	TWN Model BDG–250–SL	D	Own	1–Vt	2×45×78	248	DP/TS	12	Chain	4	West German
1956	AJS Model 18CS	GB	Own	1–Vt	86×85.5	497	OHV	33	Chain	4	Swedish
1956	BMW Model R–60	D	Own	2–HO	72×73	590	OHV	28	Shaft	4	Throughout the world
1956	Gileara Military G–175	I	Own	1–Vt	60×61	172	OHV	7.5	Chain	4	Italian
1956	Harley-Davidson KH	USA	Own	2–V	69.8×115.8	886	SV	30	Chain	4	Dutch
1956	Harley-Davidson FL	USA	Own	2–V	87.3×100.8	1206	OHV	55	Chain	4	Throughout the world
1956	Matchless G3LS	GB	Own	1–Vt	69×93	347	OHV	22	Chain	4	Throughout the world
1956	Moto Morini Military 175	I	Own	1–Vt	60×61	172	OHV	7.5	Chain	3	Italian
1956	MV Military 175	I	Own	1–Vt	–	175	OHV	7.5	Chain	4	Italian
1956	Puch type 250–SG	A	Own	1–Vt	2×45×78	248	DP/TS	14	Chain	4	Austrian
1957	Jawa 350 Kyvacka	CS	Own	2–Vt	58×65	343	TS	18	Chain	4	Czechoslovak, Swedish, etc.
1957	Triumph TR5 Trophy	GB	Own	2–Vt	63×80	498	OHV	33	Chain	4	Swedish
1958	Izhevsk Model Izh–350	SU	Own	1–Vt	72×85	346	TS	18	Chain	4	Soviet Union
1958	Moskva Model K–125	SU	Own	1–Vt	52×58	123	TS	6.5	Chain	3	Soviet Union
1959	Condor Model A–250	CH	Own	1–Vt	68×68	247	OHV	13	Shaft	4	Swiss
1959	Puch type 175–MCH	A	Own	1–Vt	2×42×62	172	DP/TS	10	Chain	4	Austrian
1960	BMW Model R–27	D	Own	1–Vt	68×68	247	OHV	18	Shaft	4	Throughout the world
1960	Enfield India 350	IND	Own	1–Vt	70×90	346	OHV	18	Chain	4	Indian
1960	Maico Model M250–M	D	Own	1–Vt	67×70	247	TS	15	Chain	4	West German
1960	Matchless G3LS	GB	Own	1–Vt	69×93	347	OHV	22	Chain	4	Throughout the world
1960	Moto Guzzi 125	I	Own	1–FS	52×58	123	OHV	7	Chain	4	Italian
1960	Sanglas Model 350	E	Own	1–Vt	–	350	OHV	21	Chain	4	S. American, Spanish, etc.
1960	Sanglas Model 500	E	Own	1–Vt	–	500	OHV	25	Chain	4	S. American, Spanish, etc.
1962	AJS Model 18–CS	GB	Own	1–Vt	86×85.5	497	OHV	33	Chain	4	S. African
1963	Harley-Davidson XLA	USA	Own	2–V	76.2×96.8	883	OHV	40	Chain	4	American, etc.
1963	Monark MC–356A	S	Jawa	2–Vt	58×65	343	TS	20	Chain	4	Swedish

YEAR	MACHINE	ORIGIN	ENGINE	CYL	BORE & STROKE	CCM	DESIGN	BHP	DRIVE	GEARS	ARMED FORCE/S
1963	Triumph 3TA Special	GB	Own	2-Vt	55×73.4	349	OHV	19	Chain	4	Dutch
1963	Triumph T20	GB	Own	1-FS	63×64	199	OHV	14	Chain	4	Dutch, French, etc.
1965	BSA Model B-40	GB	Own	1-Vt	79×70	343	OHV	18	Chain	4	Throughout the world
1965	Condor Model A-250-65	CH	Own	1-Vt	68×68	247	OHV	13	Shaft	4	Swiss
1965	Tempo Military 175	N	Sachs	1-FS	62×58	175	TS	6.5	Chain	4	Norwegian
1965	Triumph Tiger 100	GB	Own	2-Vt	69×65.5	490	OHV	34	Chain	4	Throughout the world
1967	Harley-Davidson FL	USA	Own	2-V	87.3×100.8	1206	OHV	66	Chain	4	Throughout the world
1967	Husqvarna Model 256-A	S	Own	1-Vt	69.5×64.5	245	TS	22	Chain	4	Swedish
1967	Moto Guzzi V-7	I	Own	2-V	80×70	703	OHV	35	Shaft	4	Ghana, Italian, etc.
1968	BSA Model A-65	GB	Own	2-Vt	75×74	654	OHV	54	Chain	4	Throughout the world
1968	Condor Model A-250-68	CH	Own	1-Vt	68×68	247	OHV	13	Shaft	4	Swiss
1968	Dnieper K-750	SU	Own	2-HO	78×78	745	SV	22	Shaft	4	Soviet Union
1969	BMW Model R-50/5	D	Own	2-HO	67×70.6	498	OHV	32	Shaft	4	Throughout the world
1969	BMW Model R-60/5	D	Own	2-HO	73.5×70.6	599	OHV	40	Shaft	4	Throughout the world
1969	Honda CB250-K1	J	Own	2-Vt	56×50.6	249	OHC	25	Chain	5	French
1969	MZ Model ES-250	DDR	Own	1-Vt	69×65	243	TS	21	Chain	4	East German
1969	Puch type 250-MCH	A	Own	1-Vt	2×45×78	248	DP/TS	14	Chain	4	Austrian
1970	Hercules Model K-125-B	D	Sachs	1-Vt	54×54	123	TS	13	Chain	5	West German, etc.
1970	Moto Guzzi New Falcone	I	Own	1-Hz	88×82	498	OHV	26	Chain	4	Italian, Jugoslavian
1972	Hägglund XM-72	S	Sachs	1-FS	73×70	293	TS	25	Shaft	Auto	Experimental only
1972	Husqvarna Automatic	S	Own	1-Vt	–	350	TS	26	Chain	Auto	Experimental only
1972	Monark MC-72	S	Sachs	1-Vt	73×70	293	TS	25	Chain	Auto	Experimental only
1972	Moto Guzzi V-850-GT	I	Own	2-V	83×78	844	OHV	51	Shaft	5	Italian
1972	Norton Interpol	GB	Own	2-Vt	77×89	828	OHV	60	Chain	4	Throughout the world
1972	Sanglas Model 400	E	Own	1-Vt	82×79	417	OHV	24	Chain	4	S. American, Spanish, etc.
1972	Sanglas Model 500	E	Own	1-Vt	89.5×79	497	OHV	27	Chain	4	S. American, Spanish, etc.
1973	Condor Model A-350	CH	Ducati	1-Vt	76×75	340	OHV	16.5	Chain	5	Swiss
1973	Triumph Saint	GB	Own	2-Vt	67×70	740	OHV	58	Chain	5	Throughout the world
1974	Hägglund XM-74	S	Rotax	1-Vt	76×76	345	TS	24	Shaft	Auto	Experimental only
1974	Jawa 350 type 634	CS	Own	2-Vt	58×65	344	TS	22	Chain	4	Czechoslovak, etc.
1975	Maico Model M250-M	D	Own	1-Vt	67×70	247	TS	17	Chain	5	West German, etc.
1976	BMW Model R-75/7	D	Own	2-HO	82×70.6	745	OHV	50	Shaft	5	Throughout the world
1976	BMW Model R-100/7	D	Own	2-HO	94×70.6	979	OHV	60	Shaft	5	Throughout the world
1976	Honda CB-250-G5	J	Own	2-Vt	56×50.6	249	OHC	27	Chain	6	French
1976	Honda CB350-F	J	Own	4-Vt	47×50	347	OHC	–	Chain	5	S. African
1977	BMW Model R-80/7	D	Own	2-HO	84.8×70.6	797	OHV	50	Shaft	5	Throughout the world
1977	Winha Automatic	SF	Kohler	2-Vt	62×56	338	TS	30	Chain	Auto	Experimental only
1978	BMW Model R-100 T&RT	D	Own	2-HO	94×70.6	979	OHV	65	Shaft	5	Throughout the world
1978	Bombardier Military 250	CDN	Rotax	1-Vt	74×57.5	247	TS	26	Chain	5	Canadian, British, etc.

YEAR	MACHINE	ORIGIN	ENGINE	CYL	BORE & STROKE	CCM	DESIGN	BHP	DRIVE	GEARS	ARMED FORCE/S
1978	Honda CB400–T	J	Own	2–Vt	70.5×50.6	395	OHC	43	Chain	5	S. African
1978	Triumph T160 Trident	GB	Own	3–Vt	67×70	740	OHV	64	Chain	5	Saudi Arabian
1979	Bultaco Commander	E	Own	1–Vt	71×60	237	TS	14	Chain	5	Spanish
1979	Dnieper MT–12	SU	Own	2–HO	78×78	745	SV	26	Shaft/SC	4/R	Soviet Union
1979	Harley-Davidson FLH	USA	Own	2–V	88.8×107.9	1336	OHV	70	Chain	4	Throughout the world
1979	Moto Guzzi V–35	I	Own	2–V	66×50.6	346	OHV	33	Shaft	5	Jugoslavian
1979	Peugeot Model SX8 AR	F	Own	1–Vt	48×44	79	TS	8	Chain	5	French
1979	Suzuki Model GS400	J	Own	2–Vt	65×60	398	OHC	36	Chain	6	Australian
1980	Husqvarna Model 258–A	S	Own	1–Vt	69.5×64.5	247	TS	20	Chain	4	Swedish
1980	Yamaha Military DT–250–MX	J	Own	1–Vt	70×64	246	TS	23	Chain	5	Danish
1980	Yamaha Model XT–250	J	Own	1–Vt	75×56.5	249	OHC	21	Chain	5	S. African
1981	Hercules Military Model	D	Sachs	1–Vt	54×54	123	TS	13	Chain	5	West German, etc.
1981	MZ Model ETZ 250	DDR	Own	1–Vt	69×65	243	TS	21	Chain	5	East German, etc.
1982	Honda CB400–N	J	Own	2–Vt	70.5×50.6	395	OHC	43	Chain	5	Danish
1984	Norton Interpol 2	GB	Own	Wankel rotary, twin chamber, 588cc,				82	Chain	5	British